Charles Seale-Hayne Library
University of Plymouth
(01752) 588 588
LibraryandITenquiries@plymouth.ac.uk

Dublin

World Cities series

Edited by
Professor R.J. Johnston and Professor P. Knox

Published titles in the series:

Forthcoming titles in the series:

Other titles in preparation

Dublin

The Shaping of a Capital

Andrew MacLaran

Belhaven Press
London and New York

Co-published in the Americas by Halsted Press,
an imprint of John Wiley & Sons, Inc., New York

Belhaven Press
(a division of Pinter Publishers Ltd.)
25 Floral Street, Covent Garden, London WC2E 9DS, United Kingdom

First published in 1993

Co-published in the Americas by Halsted Press, an imprint of John Wiley & Sons, Inc., 605 Third Avenue, New York, NY 10158-0012

Andrew MacLaran is hereby identified as the author of this work as provided under Section 77 of the Copyright, Designs and Patents Act, 1988.

British Library Cataloguing in Publication Data

A CIP catalogue record for this book is available from the British Library

ISBN 1 85293 166 3

Library of Congress Cataloging-in-Publication Data

MacLaran, Andrew.
    Dublin: the shaping of a capital / Andrew MacLaran.
        p. cm. – (World cities series)
    Includes bibliographical references (p.   ) and index.
    ISBN 0–470–22009–0 (U.S.) – ISBN 1–85293–166–3 (U.K.)
    1. Dublin (Ireland) – history. I. Title. II. Series.
DA995.D75M22   1993
941.8′ 35–dc20   92–43255
                                                                              CIP

ISBN 0–470–22009–0 (in the Americas only)

Typeset by Mayhew Typesetting, Rhayader, Powys
Printed and bound in Great Britain by Biddles Ltd., Guildford and King's Lynn

Contents

Contents

List of figures

List of figures

List of tables

Preface

It was in the summer of 1968 that I first visited Ireland and thought how much I would like to live there. That opportunity arose nearly ten years later thanks to a job offer at Trinity College and, in a sense, that is when this book started its lengthy gestation. During that time, many people have helped to shape my ideas and ruin my misconceptions. They include Cecil Beamish, Pauline McGuirk, Paul McNulty, Patrick Malone, John Moore, Laurence Murphy, Declan Redmond and Brendan Williams, postgraduates in the Geography Department who have undertaken research into Irish urban issues. I wish to thank them for their stimulating discussions and for their friendship.

I am particularly indebted to P.J. Drudy of the Department of Economics and fellow Director of The Centre for Urban and Regional Studies at Trinity College for his advice and assistance with the chapter on the economy of Dublin and for allowing me to make use of research material which he has not yet published. I also thank Joe Brady, Christopher Dardis, James Killen, Dympna Kyne and Tony Parker for permission to reproduce various copyright materials. Many others have my gratitude for providing unpublished information, especially Pat Russell, Principal Officer in Dublin Corporation's Development Department, John Bennett of the North Clondalkin Community Development Programme, Pearse Connolly of FAS (Tallaght) and Harry Whittaker, Managing Director of Lisney, for his permission to use unpublished research data. My quest for material relating to Dublin in fiction was greatly assisted by Vivien Igoe and by David and Eileen Drew and my thanks are also extended to Gaye McCarron, Pat McDonnell and Len O'Reilly of the Corporation's Planning Department for their help.

Thanks are also due to the editors of the series, Paul Knox and Ron

Johnston for their comments and suggestions and to Alwyn Scarth and Murray Wilson for their support and guidance over many years. The assistance and encouragement of the staff of the Geography Department at Trinity College have been invaluable, particularly that of Russell King and James Killen. I especially want to thank Terence Dunne and Matthew Stout for their work on the photographs and diagrams, working under considerable time constraints due to my annoying habit of leaving everything to the last minute.

I want to thank family members Donald and Laila, who read chunks of some of the draft chapters and offered valuable criticisms and advice; and most importantly, I am deeply grateful to my wife Morag who has helped at every stage from the initial proposal, through each restructuring and draft, giving constructive criticism and helping to assemble obscure materials. Finally, for keeping me within shouting distance of sanity during the past few months as the deadline loomed and much remained to complete, thanks to our seven dwarfs, four legged and furry. They are even forgiven for spraying the computer!

Andrew MacLaran
Trinity College, Dublin
August 1992

1
Introduction

A world city?

It is a moot point whether Dublin can really be called a 'world city' at all. Although it was the second city of the British Empire in 1800, it lost much of its significance during the subsequent century. With just over a million inhabitants, Dublin hardly ranks alongside cities like Sao Paulo or Mexico City which have 15 times its population. Indeed, although it is capital of the Republic of Ireland, the whole state has a far smaller total population than many cities of the world. In economic terms there is little justification for its inclusion – it is certainly not a power-house of productive industry, neither does it possess the significance in international financial markets of cities like New York, London, Tokyo or Frankfurt. In political terms, apart from embassies, consulates and local offices of the European Parliament and Commission, it has the token presence of only one small European Community institution (the European Foundation for the Improvement of Living and Working Conditions). Nor is the city the ecclesiastical focus of the country, which lies in Armagh in Northern Ireland. At first sight, Dublin's inclusion in this series seems bizarre.

However, in one major respect Dublin truly is a city of world ranking importance. It possesses a cultural significance which is unsurpassed for a city of its size. Its contributors range from eighteenth century essayists, scholars and philosophers, nineteenth century novelists, dramatists and artists, to twentieth century writers and pop musicians. Many eminent individuals of international renown have been associated with the city, though some spent their most productive years abroad. As Desmond Clarke (1977, 142) has observed:

1

. . . much of the literary genius past and present stems from the fact that Dublin has been for many centuries a cultural centre which nurtured genius, though it did not always tolerate and sustain it. In the eighteenth century the social atmosphere and patronage of wealth was conducive to a literary upsurge, and the rise of a new nationalism, particularly from the middle of the last century to the present day, provided the inspiration for a flowering of immense significance.

Writers who had links with the city include Jonathan Swift, William Congreve, Oliver Goldsmith, Richard Brinsley Sheridan, Thomas Moore, Joseph Sheridan Le Fanu, Bram Stoker, George Moore, Oscar Wilde, George Bernard Shaw, William Butler Yeats, John Millington Synge, Sean O'Casey, James Joyce, Elizabeth Bowen, Patrick Kavanagh, Samuel Beckett, Brendan Behan, Hugh Leonard and Christy Brown. Beckett, Yeats and Shaw won Nobel prizes for literature.

The city still retains a thriving cultural life, particularly with respect to its theatrical and musical scenes, and there are also significant collections of works of art. The National Gallery, which receives over one million visitors annually, possesses a widely ranging collection of paintings representing all the major schools of European painting as well as those of Irish artists. In contrast, the Chester Beatty Museum is undeservedly neglected despite housing a collection of international status. It accommodates the bequest of a collector whose interests ranged widely and included Sumerian clay tablets, Biblical papyri, Islamic manuscripts, paintings of Persian, Turkish and Indian Moghul origin, a collection of Chinese paintings, snuff bottles and netsuke-ware as well as many important western manuscripts and books. The Municipal Gallery on Parnell Square houses one half of the Hugh Lane bequest of modern paintings, the other being in London, while the newly created museum of modern art in the Royal Hospital at Kilmainham is worth visiting for the seventeenth century buildings alone.

However, this cultural legacy hardly has the same impact on the built environment as one would find in financial or commercial cities of world significance. In a sense, the literary heritage of the city has become part of its myth, part of a self-image which imbues Irish life with a fondness for language, spoken and written: 'One of the pleasures of Dublin life is that it never allows you the last word; the Dubliner listens to half your sentence, guesses the rest and caps it' (Pritchett, 1967, 30). Pub life is all the richer for the love of talking, and the openness of the population is without contrivance or connivance. In a city reputed once to have possessed 2,000 ale houses, 300 taverns and 1,200 brandy shops, heavy drinking helps one forget the price of an Irish pint.

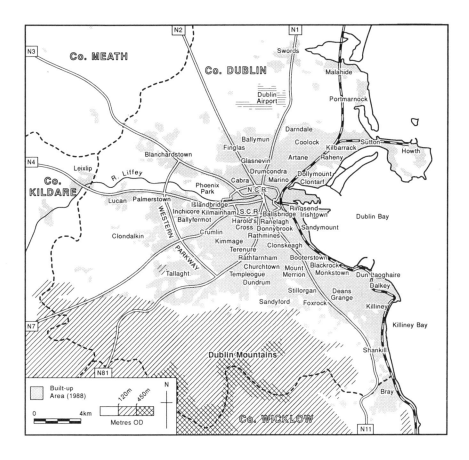

Figure 1.1 Dublin's districts and the western new towns.

First impressions

The most immediately striking feature of Dublin is its situation. Arriving by air, one sees the city bordering a wide bay. To the north and west stretches a lush green landscape of small hedged fields reminiscent of the *bocage* of northern France. Arriving by ferry affirms the proximity of the Dublin Mountains, the northern section of the Wicklow Hills (Figure 1.1), and the quartzite conical outlier of the Great Sugar Loaf (504 metres (1,654 feet)) which looms above Bray to the south of the city (Figure 1.2). Escape is easy if one feels the urge: sea, sandy beaches, extensive mud-flats and rocky foreshores, deserted heather- and peat-covered mountains or pastoral rural Ireland remain close and accessible. All are to be found within less than a hour's drive from O'Connell Street.

3

Figure 1.2 Killiney Bay. The DART line skirts the bay en route southwards to Bray, with the Great Sugar Loaf in the distance.

The Corporation's parks, of which it is justifiably proud, are also welcome places for relaxation (Figure 1.3).

Indeed, ties with rural Ireland remain strong, many of Dublin's residents being first generation urbanites. Coach clubs serving the most far-flung points of the country pack collection points around the central business area on Friday nights to transport youngsters with family ties elsewhere on their weekly pilgrimage home to the 'mammy', safe in rural Ireland. The wealthier leave for second homes in the Wicklows or the west. Indeed, it is difficult to determine whether Dublin is a city of urbane peasants or of rural bourgeois. To a large degree, work is still accorded its rightful place as a necessary evil (after all, was it not created as punishment for humankind after banishment from the Garden of Eden?). It is still possible, without guilt or fear of censure, to admit openly to having done absolutely nothing all day long, though such a carefree approach to life is apt to become infuriating at times.

Although Ireland is one of the poorest states within the European Community (EC) and was ranked twenty first among OECD countries in 1990 in terms of per capita gross domestic product, such figures fail to express the other elements of the quality of life which make Ireland,

Figure 1.3 An open air summer exhibition of art at St Stephen's Green. Similar displays take place the year round on Sundays in Merrion Square.

and Dublin in particular, so attractive. Despite its having all the atmosphere of a capital city and possessing its quota of embassies, the headquarters of business corporations and civil service functions, Dublin must be one of the most intimate of capitals, in many ways being something of an overgrown village. When meeting others for the first time, be it through business or leisure activities, it is common to discover a number of shared acquaintances. Moreover, Dublin's population remains unaffected by that personal distancing which is found in so many other cities, where casual conversations between strangers waiting to cross the road may be greeted with reproachful silence, perhaps in fear of being mugged or conned. Once, while waiting interminably for pedestrian lights to change at College Green, my arm was firmly grasped and I was earnestly advised by an elderly stranger that 'if you're going to the races you'd want to put your artificial hair in your pocket'. I haven't a clue what he meant, but I'm sure it was well intentioned.

In Dublin, people seem still to have time for one another, even in banks and shops, where mercifully the superficial 'have a nice day' syndrome has failed to oust more genuine pleasantness. Friendly advice is freely given. Some years ago my wife was looking for some gloves to send to a young nephew. Knowing little about the appropriate size for a child of seven, she asked the cashier what age of child her chosen gloves would fit. Having no idea, yet not wanting to be unhelpful, she replied inscrutably 'Well, I'd say for a child of about average age'. Somewhat bemused, my wife bought them.

It is also a fairly safe city. Crime statistics are notoriously unreliable, especially when attempting to devise generalised crime indices, yet such statistics do offer a perspective on the prevailing level of public safety. Published crime figures for 1990 show that Dublin has the highest general crime rate in the Republic of Ireland, at 47.6 crimes per 1,000 persons. However, more than 60 per cent of recorded crime in the city is accounted for by larcenies. Inevitably, there are areas which are best not visited by strangers carrying sacks of valuables late at night, but there is a low incidence of crimes of violence. Only 627 of the nearly 50,000 indictable offences which were recorded in Dublin during 1990 were offences against the person. In 1990 there were just 17 murders in the whole of the Republic of Ireland and only two of them remain unsolved (Garda Síochána, 1991).

The city also remains largely untouched by the troubles in Northern Ireland, the activities of the paramilitary Provisional Irish Republican Army in the south being generally hidden from public view. Even the police are normally unarmed. Despite being little more than 165 kilometres (100 miles) from Belfast, and though 'one thing the Northerner shares with the Southerner is a narrowmindedness in matters of sex and religion' (Behan, 1962, 191), the two cities might be on different planets for the degree to which the communities interact. During the 1980s, coach-loads of Dubliners flocked northwards at Christmastime to avail of cheaper retail prices over the border, but even this has declined since the mid-1980s.

Although independent since 1922, visual legacies of British rule remain, from the playing of cricket to the Royal Mail posting boxes now painted green. However, many of the city's renowned statues have been removed. Nelson's pillar in O'Connell Street was blown up by the IRA in 1966 and Queen Victoria's statue suffered the even greater ignominy of transportation to Australia!

As in the days of British rule, unemployment remains an intractable problem. Emigration has long been the remedy sought by many, unsatisfactory as that may have been, which has led to the loss of many of the country's brightest and most highly educated. During the late 1980s, annual net emigration surpassed 30,000 persons. However, when recession gripped the economies of Britain and the USA at the end of the decade, emigration declined and Irish unemployment rates increased. By 1992, the national unemployment rate was around twice the average for the European Community (EC), and the rate of unemployment in Dublin was even higher. The vociferous political lobbies of the west of Ireland, together with a more general anti-urban bias in Irish society in which urbanism is regarded as a foreign imposition on a traditionally rural way of life, have encouraged the misconception that Dublin, additionally tainted for having been the seat of British colonial administration on the island, receives far more than its fair share of resources. In fact, the city has long suffered from discrimination, particularly in terms of industrial development policies.

Religion, of course, has long been a major factor in Irish life, though its role as a dividing force has been changing rapidly as the non-Roman Catholic community has dwindled to fewer than 5 per cent of the population of the Republic. However, those following minority religions do tend to be over-represented among upper socio-economic groups. Primary and secondary education still tend to be segregated, schools remaining largely in church hands, though colleges and universities are now fully integrated. From 1875 until the 1970s, the Roman Catholic hierarchy banned attendance by Roman Catholics at Trinity College Dublin, presumably fearing the danger to students' souls upon entering what was once such a bastion of protestantism. Those who did attend were either able to obtain a special dispensation or had rejected such interference. Today, students there are overwhelmingly of Roman Catholic origin.

Nevertheless, the doctrines of the Roman Catholic church still permeate Irish society. It was only in the late 1970s that politicians summoned sufficient courage to make artificial contraception legal, and even then for a number of years afterwards it was only available for bona fide family planning reasons on the prescription of a doctor (i.e. not for the unmarried). Divorce remains unobtainable as does abortion, despite the fact that some 4,000 Irish women seek terminations of pregancy in Britain each year, allowing Ireland to avoid having to face up to an unpleasant social reality.

The physical environment

The wide and shallow semi-circular bay on which Dublin is situated has never become widely industrialised. For most of its shoreline it presents open vistas. Prestigious residential districts have grown along its length, stretching from Howth through Sutton, Dollymount and Clontarf on the north shore, through Sandymount, Booterstown and Blackrock to Dun Laoghaire and Dalkey in the south. Into the bay at the mouth of the river Liffey stretch the two great walls of Dublin port, while to the south, the massive granite piers of Dun Laoghaire harbour provide 100 hectares (250 acres) of sheltered anchorage.

Introduction

Despite its limited degree of industrial development, the bay is under pressure from competing uses: as a port, for commercial fishing from Howth and Dalkey, for recreation, for discharging waste, and increasingly from marina-related property development. Extensive infilling of the estuary behind the two great walls at Dublin port has taken place to provide land for the expansion of port activities, progressively transforming the outlook southward from Clontarf. Plans to construct an oil refinery, to store liquefied petroleum gas in subterranean rock caverns and the construction of a port relief road running from the docks across the southern part of the bay to Booterstown have all been vigorously opposed.

With the expansion of the city, a significant decline in water quality resulted from the growth in the discharge of industrial wastes and untreated sewage into the Liffey estuary. Although improvement has taken place in recent years, compliance with the EC directive on bathing water quality is still marginal in some areas.

Air quality within the city has also been a cause of some concern. As a result of the oil price rises of the late 1970s, there was a rise in the consumption of alternative sources of energy in Ireland. Increased burning of coal in domestic open fires where combustion is incomplete resulted in a severe deterioration in Dublin's winter air quality during the 1980s after almost a decade of improvement (Sweeney, 1987). Smoke pollution increased to well above European averages, frequently breaching the 1980 European Economic Community (EEC) directive on air quality. Particularly severe incidents of pollution occurred when cold weather coincided with temperature inversions and these covered a wide area because a large proportion of the city lies at an altitude below 15 metres (50 feet). Recordings of smoke pollution levels reached 1,812 micrograms per cubic metre ($\mu g/m^3$) at Cornmarket in January 1981 and exceeded 1,000 $\mu g/m^3$ at some sites over a period of five days in January 1982, while levels greater than the EEC mandatory limit of 250 $\mu g/m^3$ were recorded in the city on a total of 45 days during the winter of 1983–4 (Bailey, 1988). This state of affairs had serious consequences for the population's health (Sweeney, 1987) and led to a ban in 1990 on the sale of bituminous coal in the city which resulted in a marked improvement in winter air quality.

Apart from the views towards the distant Dublin Mountains and the broad expanse of Dublin Bay, physical geography rarely asserts itself. Most of the city lies below an altitude of 60 metres (200 feet), though topography is more accentuated at Howth, Mount Merrion, Dalkey and Killiney. Elsewhere in the city, gradients are gentle, but impart an added ingredient of interest to the character of the built environment. The Liffey is the only river which really imposes its presence, bisecting the city into its northern and southern components. However, following hurricane weather conditions in the Dodder's catchment area of the Dublin Mountains in 1986, the river was transformed into a torrent which flooded cottages at Ballsbridge to a depth of several feet.

Fortunately such extreme conditions are rare. Dublin comes under the influence of the mid-latitudinal westerly atmospheric circulation system. Weather fronts arrive frequently, more than 12 a month on average, associated with westerly, north westerly and south westerly winds. This means that the city is partially situated within the rain shadow of the Wicklows. Whereas central Dublin receives an average of around 710 mm. (28 inches) of rain annually, this amounts to little more than half the level recorded at Glenasmole in the Dublin Mountains (Meteorological Service, 1983). Rainfall is evenly distributed throughout the year, with a tendency to record a slight peak in the month of December. However, the persistent arrival of fronts and their associated cloudy conditions means that bright sunshine is restricted on average to about a third of the maximum possible. Generally, there is less than two hours of bright sunshine daily in December and January, rising to over 6 hours during the sunniest months of May and June.

Temperatures also are rarely extreme. Mean monthly values for central Dublin range from 5.8°C in January to 16.3°C in July. The number of days with ground frost varies from an annual average of 43 at Merrion Square to over 100 at Glasnevin and Phoenix Park, but air frost is far less frequent, being experienced on an average of ten days a year in the central area. Snow rarely stays on the ground for long at low altitudes, lying for fewer than five days a year over most of the city.

The built environment

As with the weather, the built environment is not, on first acquaintance, particularly striking. Dublin does not possess an immediately impressive financial district like New York or London, nor the grandiose monuments of Paris. O'Connell Street, pictured in Figure 1.4, is its one fine boulevard, but the central area is still essentially low-rise and retains an intimacy in its scale of development (Figure 1.5). Indeed, at its very heart lies Trinity College, 17 hectares (42 acres) of educational buildings, students' residences and sports fields; a haven of tranquility amid the hubbub of the city.

Functional differentiation within the core is weakly developed. The city's retailing area is split in two by the river Liffey. The southern element, which focuses on Grafton Street, is the more prestigious and is also the established venue for busking and street theatre. On the north side, Henry Street is the main shopping street, enlivened by the fish, fruit and vegetable stalls lining adjacent Moore Street with their 'brocli' and

Figure 1.4 O'Connell Street, largely rebuilt following the Easter Rising of 1916.

'musharooems' and the cries of the casual traders selling anything from chocolate 'bunny eggs' at Easter, to almost-see-through wrapping-paper at Christmas. Several purpose-built shopping centres have recently been grafted onto these traditional shopping streets. The office core stretches south and eastward from Trinity College, its focus of 50 years ago having migrated from College Green into the eighteenth century subur-ban residential districts around Merrion and Fitzwilliam Squares and beyond into Ballsbridge (Bannon, 1973; MacLaran, 1991a). Recreational functions are scattered throughout the centre and include half a dozen cinemas (mostly multi-screen), nine theatres, over a dozen nightclubs and more than 50 public houses (Figure 1.6).

Although the origins of the city can be traced back over a thousand years, relatively few elements of the contemporary urban landscape pre-date 1650. The eighteenth and nineteenth centuries endowed the city with a legacy of fine public buildings and residential districts, most of which have survived into the modern period. Economic decline during the nineteenth century meant that building maintenance was often neglected, though it also ensured that the city centre was largely spared the onslaught of Victorian developers. Peripheral expansion created prestigious middle-class suburbs and intimate developments of artisans'

Figure 1.5 The view upriver from the roof of Liberty Hall.

homes, but redevelopment within the core was generally confined to a limited number of individual sites, and much work was completed in the neo-classical idiom making it difficult to distinguish from buildings of the previous century. However, some fine clusters of late nineteenth century commercial buildings are to be found in South Great George's Street, Upper Baggot Street, College Green and Dame Street, often executed in neo-Gothic style or incorporating Italian or French Renaissance elements (McDermott, 1988). The scale and heavy Renaissance style of the College of Science and Government buildings in Upper Merrion Street convey an impression of solidity and permanence which belied what was to be almost the parting contribution of the British administration to the city.

The Easter Rising of 1916, which resulted in 1,350 casualties, also occasioned considerable destruction. Some 170 houses were destroyed and O'Connell Street in particular suffered serious damage. The bitterly contested civil war which followed independence in 1922, together with the economic difficulties which Ireland experienced during the Great Depression, extended the reprieve for the Georgian city. Except for the rebuilding of O'Connell Street and the redevelopment of a small number of individual plots, the city centre is remarkably bereft of commercial

11

Figure 1.6 Dublin is renowned for its pub life. James Toner's in Lower Baggot Street has considerable character.

buildings which date from the inter-war period. However, at the fringe of the city centre, larger-scale redevelopment was undertaken by Dublin Corporation under its slum clearance and rehousing programmes.

The preservation of the city's eighteenth century buildings, or, in places, their continued slow deterioration, was ensured during the 1940s by Irish neutrality during World War II and by difficult economic conditions during the subsequent decade. As late as 1960, Dublin retained a virtually intact eighteenth century core. Only then was serious attention devoted to ruining the city's most precious architectural heritage, the widespread domestic architecture of the city's eighteenth century upper and merchant classes. During the next 30 years, no expense seems to have been spared in this project of ill-considered vandalism, making up for lost time with unparalleled enthusiasm. The destruction of a significant proportion of that endowment was effected by the combined efforts of property developers and the Corporation's roads engineers, eager to equip the city with the symbols of the new age: concrete, glass, and tarmac.

The loss of many of Dublin's eighteenth century buildings is compounded by their replacement by edifices of overwhelming mediocrity.

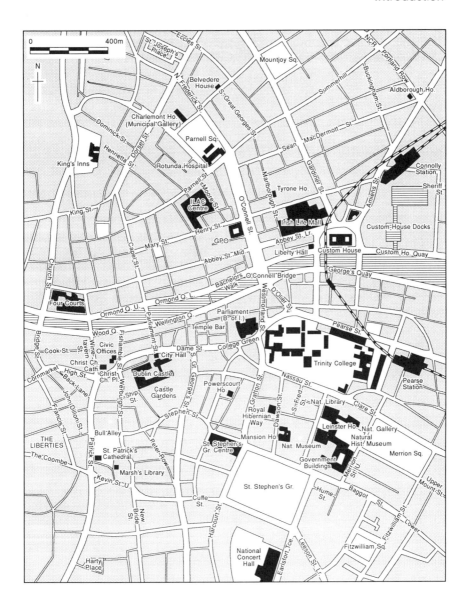

Figure 1.7 Streets and major buildings in central Dublin

Whilst it must be acknowledged that architectural appreciation is largely a matter of taste, the number of distinguished modern buildings in the city is negligible. The author is hard placed to enumerate even a dozen twentieth century buildings which are likely to stand the test of time. It is highly unfortunate that Dublin's greatest surge of redevelopment came during the 1960s and 1970s, decades when architecture plumbed its lowest depths. Most cities possess monuments to the ineptitude of the architectural profession of the twentieth century. Dublin, perhaps, has more than its fair share. A recent competition conducted by the Irish Times inviting readers to list their ten favourite buildings in Ireland and those which they most disliked, elicited a response which suggests that the general public also believes that architects have contributed little of merit to the capital in recent years. Inevitably, the profitability criteria of clients have ensured that architectural solutions were tightly constrained by considerations of cost. However, architects have generally been willing accomplices in the destruction of the eighteenth century townscape. If developers can be regarded as the impresarios of the built environment, perhaps architects should also be seen in a different light, as the American architect Philip Johnson has remarked:

> Since we are the tool of the ruling classes, in this country and indeed in England, why, naturally, we do what we're told. And what we like to do, is to do what we are told the best way we can. Very much like the oldest profession in the world, it has only one aim, which is to please – for a fee. (Johnson, 1985)

Thus, the recent redevelopment of the Custom House Docks as an International Financial Services Centre has created, in the vicinity of the Custom House – James Gandon's eighteenth century architectural master-piece – an assemblage of unattractive modern offices (Figure 1.8), brooding like ugly sisters alongside their bus station and Liberty Hall siblings. The Custom House Docks redevelopment, one of the most valuable pieces of real estate in the country, is all the more striking for its location in close proximity to one of the most deprived public housing schemes in the city, the Sheriff Street flats complex. Indeed, many visitors find remarkable the sharp social contrasts still to be found within the city.

The one collective merit of these neighbouring buildings is that of emphasising the urbane quality of the Custom House itself and demon-strating emphatically that changes in the practice of architecture are not always characterised by progress. Perhaps, though, all cities do require a proportion of ugly-as-you-please modern piles so that one is obliged to appreciate the finer contributions of the architectural profession.

Figure 1.8 Moored opposite the International Financial Services Centre (right), a Guinness tanker awaits loading. The Custom House, James Gandon's architectural masterpiece, features centre left.

Dublin in fiction

The city which will be the subject of the following chapters might be termed its public face. There is, of course, another Dublin – or rather, many other Dublins; the soft city, the private sphere, represented by the city in fiction. Although these are to some degree perceived and imagined worlds, they are not wholly fictitious. It is quite possible that you, like I, became first acquainted with Dublin through reading something by James Joyce, seeing one of Sean O'Casey's plays, or watching the film adaptation of Christy Brown's *My Left Foot* or Roddy Doyle's *The Commitments*. Each Dublin is firmly rooted in the life of the author and therefore grounded in a personal reality of Dublin. Each imparts a singular understanding of Dublin life and what it is to be a Dubliner, though differing in period, class or location. Many authors revel in the singular expressiveness of Dublin language:

Gawn with you, child, an' you only goin' to be marrid; I remember as well as I remember yesterday, – it was on a lovely August evenin', exactly, accordin' to date, fifteen years ago, come the Tuesday folleyin' the nex' that's comin' on, when me own man – *the Lord be good to him* – an' me was sittin' shy together in a doty little nook on a counthry road adjacent to The Stiles . . . (Sean O'Casey, *Juno and the Paycock*, 1925, 42)

Brought up as the last of eight children under hard conditions in one of Dublin's slum tenements, Sean O'Casey (1880–1964) portrays tenement life as it was impinged upon, often inconveniently so, by the politically charged atmosphere and tumultuous events between 1916 and 1922. Christy Brown (1932–81), son of a bricklayer, drew on his upbringing during the 1930s and 1940s in a working-class household of 22 children. He exposes the reality of family life among the labouring class in a patriarchal society, and the perils of sharing a bed with five siblings, one of whom suffered from chronic flatulence.

Dublin provides a rich stage on which the city's even richer variety of eccentric characters enact their dramas. One of the more interesting of modern times was Brendan Behan (1923–64); house-painter, IRA activist, playwright of macabre humour, and coarse tongued, heavy drinker whose alcoholic antics were frequently reported in the press. Behan captures the reaction of the tightly-knit inner-city communities to dispersal through slum clearance. Where this involved the prospect of removal to the other side of the Liffey, it was tinged with a degree of horror, north- and south-side communities traditionally sharing something of a disdain for each other:

Lovely garden estates the Government built when they were clearing the slums but somehow the people hated leaving where they had been reared and where they had reared their children. They had a social status in their way in those slums that was destroyed altogether when they were shifted out to Crumlin or Kimmage and set down in terrace houses mixing with God knows what muck from Irishtown, Ringsend, the Liberties and other parts south of the Liffey. I remember when we got our notice to get moving, hearing one oul' wan moaning to my mother: 'Oh! Mrs. Behing, jewel and darling! don't go out to Kimmage – that's where they ate their young.' Four miles away it was, and no more, where this cannibalism took place. (Brendan Behan, *Brendan Behan's Island*, 1962, 14)

Nowhere is Dublin better brought to life than in the writings of James Joyce (1882–1941), brilliantly evoking city life at the turn of the twentieth century. His work is a homage to the capital and his technique is to recreate the social environment of the city through the lives of its unheroic citizens. Class differences, the terrors and powerlessness of childhood, social relationships, especially family life, pub culture and conversation are keenly observed and perceptively conveyed as the reader becomes submerged within that environment. It is the Dublin with which Joyce is intimately acquainted. In *Ulysses*,

Most of the people belong to the poorer class of Dublin citizen. Hardly any of them are what might be called working people. . . . Nearly all are of the lower middle class, in dire poverty if they have lost their jobs or property, but a shade above the well paid workingman if things are going well with them.The rich bourgeois and the governing patrician, as also the pure and simple wage worker play no great part in the book. (Budgen, 1972, 68)

Discussing *Ulysses*, Joyce once told Frank Budgen that:

I want to give a picture of Dublin so complete that if the city one day suddenly disappeared from the earth it could be reconstructed out of my book. (Budgen, 1972, 69)

However, if this was his intention, the result is somewhat deficient, for there is little visual sensitivity towards the urban landscape. Buildings and streets are present, but it is the people who matter. The setting is unalterably Dublin only thanks to Joyce's keen observation of Dubliners and their conversation:

Ulysses is James Joyce's incantation to, for and of Dublin. It was designed by him as a detailed account of ordinary life on an ordinary Dublin day, and he planned each movement of each character on each street as though he were playing chess. He placed them in houses he knew, drinking in pubs he had frequented, walking on cobblestones he retraced. He made the very air of Dublin, the atmosphere, the feeling, the place, almost indistinguishable, certainly inseparable, from his human characters – Dublin *is* a character in *Ulysses*, the 'womancity' with her skirts lifted. (Delaney, 1981, 10)

Indeed, her skirts seem to be discarded almost altogether. Although Joyce's texts may be peppered with references to districts of the city, to its shops and pubs, we never really get a clear impression of the built environment, its textures and varied colours, nor indeed its smells. There are occasional references to intrusions onto the senses of sight and smell: the multicoloured advertising hoardings, 'the whiffs of ginger, teadust, biscuitmush' or 'the odours that came from baconflitches and ample cools of butter', but for a city which had the highest mortality rate in Britain and Ireland at the time, with appallingly overcrowded and insanitary slum tenements, one might expect evidence of greater visual sensitivity within Joyce's work, despite his (albeit downwardly mobile) middle-class background. Budgen recognises this:

. . . it is not by way of description that Dublin is created in *Ulysses*. There is a wealth of delicate pictorial evocation in *Dubliners*, but there is little or none in *Ulysses*. Streets are named but never described. Houses and interiors are shown to us, but as if we entered them as familiars, not as strangers come to take stock of the occupants and inventory their furniture. Bridges over the Liffey are crossed and recrossed, named and that is all. We go into eating-houses and drinking bars as if the town were our own and these our customary ports of call. (Budgen, 1972, 69–70)

Thus,

. . . it is essential to Joyce that we shall not substitute our own home town for his, and

> yet in *Ulysses* he neither paints nor photographs it for our guidance. It must grow upon us not through our eye and memory, but through the minds of the Dubliners we overhear talking to each other. . . . Dublin exists for us as the essential element in which Dubliners live. It is not a décor to be modified at will, but something as native to them as water to a fish. (Budgen, 1972, 71)

Pierce (1992, 83) maintains that topographical awareness is present in Joyce's work:

> He makes much of the tram routes, the names of the streets, the 'street furniture', the hotels and bars, the realistic texture of turn-of-the-century Dublin. Such devotion might initially appear as obsessive, but it is in this way that the city is recuperated and made familiar.

But what is presented is a two-dimensional map of his native city rather than a three-dimensional model, a weakness of visual imagery which is common to many who have based their fiction in the city. This has created a convenient niche for a number of publications relating to Joyce's Dublin, providing the bones around which Joyce has already constructed the flesh (Bidwell and Heffer, 1981; McCarthy, 1988; Nicholson, 1988; Igoe, 1990).

Joyce's writings have also spawned a small industry of summer schools and Bloomsday tourism, unfortunately reinforcing an impression that Ireland longs to dwell in the past. Joyce was undoubtedly an author of his environment, of his time, of his place and of his class. Much of that social environment has now gone as slum clearance dispersed the communities. But the stage largely remains intact. The places which he mentions are usually still there, often somewhat altered or tattered in places. Sometimes whole sets have been changed, but rarely have they been destroyed entirely. Reading Joyce's writings after visiting the city becomes a completely different experience. So read on, then come, and perhaps you also will stay as I have done.

2
The origins and growth of Dublin

Pre-urban settlement

The precise origins of Dublin are shrouded in obscurity. Even before the arrival of the Vikings in the ninth century, there existed at least two 'proto-urban' settlements, both of which were situated on the southern bank of the river Liffey. The first of these, reference to which is made in a sixth century poem, was probably located on the ridge overlooking the river near Bridge Street. Little is known about this settlement, but it is likely to have comprised a nucleated, irregular cluster of houses which were surrounded by an earthen bank and ditch, housing a farming and fishing community (Clarke, 1977). This controlled the lowest crossing point of what was then a wide and shallow river estuary, effected by a ford comprising bundles of brushwood, giving the settlement its name (*Áth Cliath* – the hurdle ford). The site was of strategic significance, being a border settlement between the kingdoms of Leinster and Meath, and the focus of four long-distance routeways (*slighte*) from Ulster, Munster, Connaught and Leinster. As a border settlement, it may well have had some trading functions and there are indications that people embarked here to cross to Britain (Clarke, 1988). Some writers also speculate that there existed a pre-Viking ring-fort in the vicinity of Dublin castle, though evidence for it is essentially circumstantial and awaits verification by archaeological excavation.

To the south of this possible stronghold, there may have existed an ecclesiastical settlement. A number of the churches in the area possess Irish dedications (to St Patrick, St Brigit, St Cóemgen or Kevin, and St

Mac Táil) though only in the case of St Peter's can foundation be confidently dated as earlier than AD 1000 (Bradley, 1992). The medieval street pattern also suggests the existence of an ecclesiatical enclosure, possibly serving as a sanctuary and cemetery (Clarke, 1977). Its eastern boundary was disturbed following the disestablishment of the monasteries and the development of the Aungier estate between 1660 and 1685 after the land was sold to Francis Aungier, the first Earl of Longford. However, its northern and western extremities remain reflected in the line of Stephen Street and Peter Row. It has been suggested that this settlement derived its name from the 'black pool' (the *Dubh Linn*), a tidal embayment lying on the southern bank of the river Poddle, a tributary of the Liffey, located to the south of the present castle and subsequently reclaimed to form the castle's gardens.

Norse Dublin

Viking raids from the late eighth century led to the first capture of *Áth Cliath* in AD 837 and, four years later, to the construction of a *longphort*, a fortified harbour. The precise location of the original *longphort* remains in dispute. Some favour a site in the vicinity of the present castle, near the black pool, while others believe it was located 2 km. (1.25 miles) upstream at Islandbridge-Kilmainham, where the largest Viking burial site outside Scandinavia was discovered during the nineteenth century (Clarke, 1988). The construction of the ship-enclosure marked a turning point in the development of the settlement and heralded an intensification of Viking activity. As the focus of Norse settlement in Ireland, it became a military base for plundering raids into the surrounding territory and overseas, particularly in search of slaves. Dublin was destined to become an important Viking colony. This early phase was marked in the landscape by the raising of the *thingmount*, an artificial mound 12 m. (40 ft.) high and 70 m. (240 ft.) in circumference, where public business was conducted by the free warriors. This was situated just south of present day College Green at what was then the shoreline, but was demolished in the late seventeenth century to raise the level of the land now forming Nassau Street.

The early Viking encampment had a chequered history; the Norse even being forced to withdraw completely between AD 902 and 917. Upon their return, stronger fortifications were constructed. Raids continued to be launched into Leinster and Meath into the second half of the tenth century, and Dublin became the focus of a small Scandinavian kingdom commanding a strategic coastal strip extending from Swords and Rush in the north, to Leixlip in the west and along the coast as far south as Wicklow. The Irish retaliated by launching attacks on the town.

The settlers turned increasingly away from plunder in favour of trade, so that by the end of the tenth century Dublin was a thriving trading centre minting its own coins. The Norse intermarried with the Irish and formed alliances with their tribal leaders, resulting in the hibernicisation of the settlers. After the Norse defeat at the battle of Clontarf in 1014, until the arrival of the Anglo-Normans most of the rulers of Dublin were imposed by Irish kings. They accepted Christianity in the early part of the eleventh century and founded two churches: Holy Trinity (now Christ Church) which was originally timber-built, and St Olaf's which was in use until 1538.

Although the township was of small size geographically, it was undoubtedly one of the great ports of Western Europe. Its oldest section was centred on the crossroads formed by present day Castle Street, Werburgh Street, Christ Church Place (formerly Skinner Row) and Fishamble Street, incorporating the area now occupied by Dublin Castle, Christchurch Cathedral and the Civic Offices at Fishamble Street. This settlement was probably surrounded by an earthen bank surmounted by a pallisade, remnants of which were discovered during excavations for the Civic Offices.

With prosperity during the eleventh and early twelfth centuries, the township grew, extending in a westerly direction along the ridge to form High Street, with a proper bridge over the Liffey existing by 1013 (Clarke, 1988). A stone wall (c. AD 1100) was constructed to improve the town's defences and to fortify the newly developed areas, enclosing an area of some 12 ha. (30 acres). Remnants of this Old City Wall may still be seen at Ship Street and Cook Street, though much of its former extent at Lamb Alley near Cornmarket was destroyed during road widening. A reconstructed section also exists rather incongruously beneath the new Civic Offices.

Archaeological excavations have yielded valuable information about the Norse township: its crafts, building methods and the diet of the townsfolk (see Wallace, 1984; Ó Ríordáin, 1984). Pottery found during archaeological excavations suggests trading links as far afield as the northern Slavic lands. The excavations at High Street, carried out in the 1960s, revealed houses and workshops of the medieval city, indicating that a number of trades and crafts were being carried out as early as the tenth century, including shoemaking, weaving and comb making from antler and bone.

Even more remarkable was the 2 ha. (4.5 acres) site to the south of Wood Quay where Dublin Corporation developed its Civic Offices. Here, in an excellent state of preservation resulting from damp anaerobic soil conditions, excavations revealed over 5 m. (27 ft.) of habitation layers comprising a whole series of townscapes dating from the tenth century onwards. The late tenth century single-storey houses were of post

21

and wattle construction, varying in dimensions up to 8.5 m. (28 ft.) in length by 4.75 m. (15 ft.) wide, sub-rectangular in shape with a central hearth, though lacking chimneys. The excavations also provided information on the reclamation of the waterfront in nine successive stages from the tenth century to the early fourteenth century, amounting to 80 m. (260 ft.) horizontally (Wallace, 1984). Findings included early Viking embankments dating from around AD 900 to 1000, the latest of which was surmounted by a pallisade and probably surrounded the whole settlement. Beyond this lay a considerable length of the Old City Wall which also encircled the town. This massive structure traversed the Wood Quay site, averaging 1.5 m. (5 ft.) in width and still stood up to 3m. (10 ft.) high.

It was, perhaps, unfortunate that a site of such European significance as Wood Quay should have been located in Dublin. Despite a storm of international and local protest, including a demonstration by 20,000 citizens, the combination of bureaucratic intransigence and an appalling absence of cultural consciousness ensured that much of this site was never properly excavated. Over large areas of the site, upper levels, probably representing fifteenth and sixteenth century habitations, were mechanically removed, stopping to permit archaeological work only when wicker-work levels were reached. Worse still, within two months of its having been declared a National Monument, Dublin Corporation, in its haste to develop the new offices, sought and obtained permission from the Commissioners of Public Works for its destruction. Large areas were mechanically excavated down to bed-rock by earth-moving machines, the unsorted material being taken away by trucks for disposal:

> Archaeologists were seen to be working within feet of heavy bulk excavators, in considerable physical danger, and unofficially the site director was under severe pressure from the developers to get off the site as quickly as possible, and not to raise objections to the demolition of archaeological structures. In spite of this, invaluable evidence of an impressive series of wooden quays was uncovered – in some cases to be seen for a few hours only – extending dry land by stages from the old town wall out to the modern line of the quays. In and around these quays were found the remains of many wooden boats of about the twelfth century, the most extensive group of this period known to survive in Western Europe. (Haworth, 1984, 31).

The Anglo-Norman city

The capture of Dublin by the Anglo-Normans in 1170 signalled a change in the functions of the town, its becoming thereafter the administrative centre for the Pale. It was the seat of the Lord Deputy, the Exchequer and of the Irish Parliament. The Hiberno-Norse were re-settled to the north of the Liffey at Oxmantown, deriving its name from the *Ostmen* settlers. The city was granted a municipal charter in 1172, the first of a series which progressively increased its powers and independence, encouraging economic expansion. The thirteenth century proved to be one of considerable prosperity, which continued into the early fourteenth century. Links with northern Europe were maintained and there was a growth of trade with southern Europe. Wool, hides and grain were exported; imports included foodstuffs (salt, spices, wine), fine cloth and metals.

Apart from its administrative and trading functions, a wide variety of trades was present in the city during the medieval period. Such was the economic vigour of the Anglo-Norman town that by the middle of the thirteenth century over 50 different occupations were represented in the Guild Merchant. Specialised craft guilds were formed soon afterwards and no fewer than 28 guilds were represented at the Corpus Christi pageant of 1498 (Lydon, 1988). An oligarchy of merchant traders rigorously controlled the economic life of the city, strenuously protecting its privileges and rights of property. Guild members possessed a monopoly of the trade or craft which they represented, strictly limiting entry by enforcing the serving of seven year apprenticeships and controlling standards by governing the way in which members carried out their crafts. Although women were accepted into the guilds, the Irish were not. Trades included blacksmiths, bronze smiths, coopers and turners, spinners and weavers, shoemakers, potters, brewers (mostly women), bakers, masons and carpenters (Curriculum Development Unit, 1978). Different areas of the town were often associated with particular trades, and these are sometimes reflected in contemporary street names, such as Fishamble Street, the area in which fishmongers had their stalls (*shambles*), and Winetavern Street which possessed a number of taverns. Bakers were located in Cook Street, beyond the fire-barrier of the Old City Wall. Fire posed a constant threat to timber-built medieval towns and caused damage in 1191 and 1283, with a large area of the city being burnt in 1304 (Lydon, 1988).

Although there are indications that limited extra-mural development took place during the eleventh century, it was during the twelfth century that significant expansion occurred, notably to the west along Thomas Street, down Francis Street and Patrick Street to the south and along Church Street to the north of the river. Land was reclaimed from the Liffey in the area of Cook Street, new gates being created in the City Wall to afford access, with the wall being extended to defend it. There were further port developments at the Wood Quay waterfront during the thirteenth century to accommodate larger ships, culminating in the construction of a stone quay wall c. AD 1300.

The Anglo-Norman period also saw the addition of a number of public buildings, notably a new Tholsel (assembly house) at High Street, which served as a courthouse and headquarters of the city's merchants, a guildhall on Winetavern Street, the founding of St Werburgh's church on Werburgh Street and St Patrick's cathedral (1192). To the north of the Liffey, a Dominican friary was established near the site of the present Four Courts and the Cistercian Abbey of St Mary's was founded a little downstream. Fortifications were improved by the addition of towers to the City Wall, and the construction of Dublin castle (c.1220) took place at the south-eastern extremity of the walled town. It was fortified by towers and a gateway complete with portcullis and drawbridge over a moat.

The medieval town was a densely developed area amounting to about 18 ha. (45 acres). Although substantial timber-framed dwellings of more than one storey were being built from the late fourteenth century, most houses were tiny, dark, damp and smoke-filled. Dublin was 'dirty, over-crowded, unhealthy, and a dangerous place to live' (Lydon, 1988, 35). There is evidence that the population sought solace in drink and the abundance of opium poppy seeds discovered in excavations suggests that something stronger might also have been used. The insanitary, rat-infested and overcrowded conditions provided an ideal environment for the outbreak of plague, and indeed, the arrival of the Black Death in 1348 and its frequent subsequent visitations appear to have been a significant factor in sapping the vitality of the medieval city. The invasion by Edward Bruce's army earlier in the century and the burning by the citizens of the suburb at Thomas Street to deny cover to the Scots should they attack the city, together with spasmodic attacks launched by the Irish against the centre of Anglo-Norman rule, contributed to Dublin's decline.

Late medieval Dublin

English control in Ireland was tenuous during the fourteenth and fifteenth centuries. As in many European cities, plague resulted in considerable population decline and by the late fifteenth century there was a shortage of guild members. During that century, the city also suffered from neglect at the hands of the English monarchy, which was engaged in more pressing matters including wars in Scotland and France. During the Wars of the Roses separate factions also developed in Dublin.

With the Reformation, the dissolution of the monasteries during the late 1530s spelled another blow to a city in which the church had played an important role (Lydon, 1988). Religious foundations had included abbeys of the Cistercian and Augustinian orders; an Augustinian priory and a friary; the priory and hospital of St John the Baptist; the nunnery of St Mary de Hogges; a Carmelite priory; a Dominican priory; and a Franciscan friary. A little further afield, at Kilmainham, lay the priory of the Knights Hospitallers; and there was a priory of the Knights Templar at Clontarf. However, the redistribution of religious lands benefited the merchant patriciate, and Edward VI's charter of incorporation (1548) raised Dublin to the status of a county borough with full powers of local administration. Later charters of 1554, 1569, 1577 and 1582, conferred further advantages on Dublin's merchants and businessmen – particularly during the reign of Elizabeth I – by governments keen to assure civic loyalty at a time when invasion was feared from Spain. Dublin acted as the centre for Tudor conquest of the country and the city slowly expanded despite the Elizabethan wars. Trinity College was founded in 1592 on the site of the twelfth century Augustinian priory of All Hallows.

Leases granted from the middle of the fifteenth century commonly stipulated that houses be built with timber frames and roofed with timber and slates, but during the sixteenth century the growing wealth of the merchant class became reflected in the improved quality of its housing. Many dwellings were built to three storeys and possessed chimneys and glass windows. However, Dublin's vitality continued to be blunted throughout the sixteenth century by seven major outbreaks of plague. That of 1575 was reputed to have killed 3,000 persons when the city probably had a population of only between five and ten thousand persons (Lennon, 1988). Although still the seat of English rule in Ireland and a city which had managed to garner a considerable degree of municipal autonomy, by the end of the sixteenth century the contrast between private wealth and public squalor was sharp. Buildings such as the castle, the Tholsel and the Liffey bridge became neglected and in 1562 the south wall and roof of Christ Church cathedral actually collapsed. This state of decay was aggravated in 1597 by an explosion caused by the ignition of barrels of gunpowder on the quayside. By AD 1600, Dublin had become a small and somewhat dilapidated township.

The early modern period

John Speed's map of 1610 indicates that the city had expanded little between the fourteenth and seventeenth centuries, with a population estimated at between ten and twenty thousand (Cullen, 1992). However, from the early seventeenth century, there followed two centuries of economic growth and physical expansion, punctuated by short periods of regression – as in the politically tumultuous 1640s. This expansion is illustrated in Figure 2.1.

The growing use of brick for building was reflected in the growth of the bricklayers' guild. Evidence suggests that the population may have doubled or even trebled to around 40,000 persons by the 1660s,

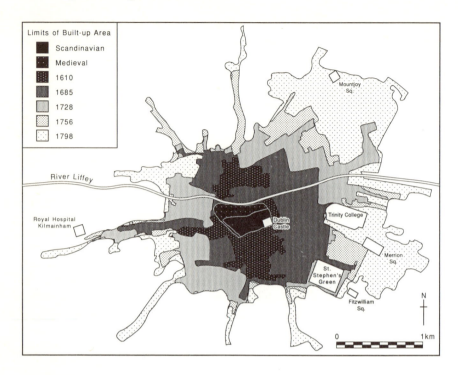

Figure 2.1 The expansion of Dublin up to 1798. The coastline and the course of the river Liffey were much altered by reclamation and channelling.

reaching 60,000 in 1700 (Cullen, 1992). Expansion during the eighteenth century was rapid by European standards. By the middle of the century its population stood at 120,000 and at the end of that century it had reached 182,000 (Daly, 1984). In Britain and Ireland, it was second only to London in terms of size and was probably the sixth largest city in western Europe (Cullen, 1992).

Economic expansion was associated with the growing dominance of the capitalist system and the restrictive practices of the city Corporation and the craft and merchant guilds which had been associated with the Old English catholic patrician class declined in significance. As early as 1640, the city's Old English catholics had become outnumbered by New English protestant incomers, who formed a majority in the city for over a hundred years.

Dublin benefited from its position as capital of a unified Ireland under the rule of British monarchs. It was the political and administrative capital, the centre of civil institutions such as the courts and parliament, it possessed the only university in the country and was also the social capital. From the early seventeenth century it experienced an influx each winter of the rural élite who patronised the city's many theatres and musical venues (Dickson, 1986). Its position as the island's financial centre and leading port was also confirmed. Dublin became the warehouse for the country, though a large proportion of the imports was destined for the city itself. Its ties with Ulster's nascent linen industry were close, bleached linen cloth being the most valuable item exported through the port, and the city's linen factors providing a significant source of capital.

Industrial functions also became increasingly significant in the city's economy during the seventeenth century. The range of craft industries was considerable, growing to serve the expanding Irish market. Some, such as the woollen industry, were based on Irish raw materials, while others, notably sugar refining, silk weaving, the iron and metals trades and the production of glass and porcelain, depended on imported raw materials. The city's woollen and silk trades together accounted for the employment of well over 10,000 persons (Dickson, 1988). Luxury crafts also developed, including coach building, the production of silverware, furniture and glassware, with a number of crafts relating directly to buildings, such as ironwork, wood carving and plasterwork.

From the 1660s, growing market opportunities together with encouragement from the Irish parliament led to the influx of immigrants of English and French Huguenot origin, the latter being responsible for establishing the city's silk industry. They were joined after 1690 by Dutch and Flemish protestants who settled to the south west of Dublin castle in the area known as the Liberties, bringing their own style of brick buildings with gable ends presenting onto the street. Such 'Dutch Billies', were a common feature of the townscape well into the twentieth century, though their construction ceased after 1740 as the parapet-fronted house came into fashion (An Taisce, 1985a). A great many such houses were built in the city, yet like so much of the city's under-valued historic fabric, these gable-fronted buildings were not deemed worthy of preservation and virtually all have now been demolished. One remains in somewhat altered state in solitary isolation on Upper Kevin Street (Figure 2.2).

The dynamism of the seventeenth and eighteenth centuries necessitated the geographical expansion of the city. This was associated with the development of the capitalist land market in which land increasingly became an object of private and personal property right, a commodity like any other to be traded for profit or developed for the purpose of increased revenue.

In the seventeenth century, although some important institutional buildings were built to the west of the medieval core, such as the Royal Hospital at Kilmainham (Figure 2.3) and the King's Hospital (Bluecoat)

Figure 2.2 The gable-fronted 'Dutch Billy' was once common in Dublin. One of the remaining few is located on Kevin Street, near St Patrick's Cathedral. The street was widened to improve traffic flow but is now regularly lined with parked cars.

School, the main thrust of urban expansion was in an easterly direction downstream. This trend was facilitated by the work of the Ballast Office, a sub-committee of Dublin Corporation, which was responsible for channelling the Liffey into its present course.

During the early 1600s, it was still the inner circle of the Corporation which determined where and how development was to occur (Dickson, 1986). Early extensions took place under the authority of the Corporation on reclaimed land at the confluence of the Liffey and the Poddle and development took place later in the century along Dame Street and in the Temple Bar area. The Corporation was also responsible for the development of St Stephen's Green in the 1660s, an area of common pasturage to the south east of the castle where sites were allocated to citizens by ballot on 99-year leases. Another Coporation project to the north of the Liffey at Oxmantown Green (1665) became for a time one of the city's most fashionable suburbs.

After the Restoration of the monarchy, suburban expansion was effected increasingly by private land owners whose family names are often commemorated in the streets' names. Unlike the medieval core

Figure 2.3 The late seventeenth century Royal Hospital, Kilmainham, has been refurbished as a cultural centre and houses the Modern Art Museum.

where the wooden-framed 'cagework' house had been common, Corporation regulations now insisted on the use of brick and stone, a wise precaution in view of the fire which devastated the City of London in 1666.

The Aungier estate, located between Dublin castle and St Stephen's Green, was developed between 1660 and 1685. Its layout was determined by the ground landlord who leased building plots to merchants and builder-developers who subsequently transferred their leasehold interests to the householders. The area nearest to the castle was a prestigious residential location for a generation until its leases terminated in the 1700s, whereupon the buildings were often divided and sub-let.

The construction of new bridges permitted Sir Humphrey Jervis, a wealthy shipowner and merchant, successfully to develop a portion of the lands formerly occupied by St Mary's Abbey on the north bank of the Liffey, to which he had managed to obtain a 500-year lease. Under the influence of the Duke of Ormonde, and in contrast to Blind Quay (now Essex Quay) where rear gardens originally ran down to the river, the Jervis estate was laid out with houses facing southwards towards the river across a spacious and attractive stone quay (Ormond Quay). Thus, from the late 1600s, the social geography of the city underwent a slow transformation as wealthier citizens forsook the cramped and insanitary conditions of the medieval core in favour of the more spacious suburbs.

Dublin's 'golden age'

The eighteenth century in Ireland was a period of peace and economic growth. Port activity expanded fourfold during the century to cater for half the national tonnage by 1800, growing especially rapidly during mid-century. In the second half of the century Dublin became linked to the Shannon via the Royal and Grand canals. Rising rural rents flowed into the city, supporting a class of conspicuous consumers. They provided a market for the manufacture of luxuries and for entertainments of all types. By the end of the century, the city's trade directories enumerated more than 4,000 businesses, only a tenth of which were merchants. Professional functions expanded alongside the growth in the urban economy. By 1763, there were over 700 attorneys and 300 barristers in the city, and half as many again by the end of the century, while the medical profession was also strongly represented (Dickson, 1988).

After 1750, suburban expansion was rapid, endowing the city with a widespread heritage of high-class residential properties downstream from the old city (Figure 2.4). By 1780, the developments to the north and south of the Liffey had each grown to cover an area the size of Edinburgh's new town, though pre-dating it by some twenty years (Cullen, 1992).

Except for the residences of the ruling élite, whose great urban houses were often designed by architects of British origin, most of the construction work was undertaken by Irish speculative builders or craftsmen-contractors who were well able to follow the classical rules of proportion upon which Dublin's Georgian (1714–1830) buildings rely. Unlike in some British cities, there were no cases of 'facadism' where a developer would construct a whole length of facade, then sell off lengths to builders who would construct houses behind the facade, thus imposing complete regularity of design on a streetscape. Only at Harcourt Terrace, developed much later around 1840, was a succession of stuccoed buildings developed with planned symmetry. The grandiosity found in Edinburgh or Bath is thus absent and there is far less uniformity than in London's squares. Houses were commonly built in small groups of two to five, by a consortium of tradesmen, with gaps often being left for in-filling at a later date (Kearns, 1983). Sometimes they were sold as 'shells' ready for interior decoration by the incoming lessee (McCullough, 1989).

The creation of a streetscape which today imparts an aspect of general

Figure 2.4 Upper Mount Street. South-east central Dublin is richly endowed with high quality eighteenth century buildings. Most have been converted from residential to office functions.

regularity was largely the result of lease provisions stipulating the construction materials, building height and street paving. Earlier developments tended to be associated with short leases of 40 years, while those of 60 and 99 years predominated later. Lessees tended to tailor the quality of construction to the length of the lease, resulting in a low survival rate among older and poorer quality buildings (McCullough, 1989).

Characteristically, houses were built in terraces bordering wide streets or squares. There could be considerable variation in plot sizes even within a single terrace, so house sizes also vary, from over 835 sq. m. (9,000 sq.ft.) at Henrietta Street to around 280 sq. m. (3,000 sq.ft.) along parts of Lower Baggot Street and Clare Street. Plots were commonly 7.3–9.1 m. (24–30 ft.) wide, permitting three, four, five or exceptionally seven windows at first floor level, with a depth of 10–12 m. (35–40 ft.) (Figure 2.5). Rear gardens were provided for by sites up to 90 m. (300 ft.) in length. These backlands were served by small lanes giving access to mews buildings used as stables, many of which have subsequently been converted to commercial or residential functions.

Figure 2.5 Variations in plot widths are evident along Fitzwilliam Square East.

Buildings were generally set back only three metres from the public pavement, beneath which was commonly located fuel storage, the coal chutes being capped by circular cast-iron covers set in the pavement. Paving comprised granite slabs varying in colour from quartz-veined greys to buffs flecked with amber and black, now worn smooth by two centuries of Dubliners' feet. Good examples of such paving exist on the east side of Merrion Square, but elsewhere, much has subsequently been replaced by unattractive concrete slabs with only the granite kerbstones remaining. Carriageways were commonly formed of stone setts, though tarmacadam has commonly either replaced them entirely or been applied as a veneer to smooth the path of motorists. When newly developed, the carriageways, pavements and buildings would have presented an attractive mixture of colours and textures.

Although the buildings of this age appear visually somewhat austere and superficially similar, having sometimes even been referred to disparagingly as 'cliffs of brick', considerable individuality is present (Figure 2.6). The colour of brick ranges from russets and pinks to browns and yellows, its varied quality resulting in differing resistance to weathering by Dublin's acidic rain. There are also differences in the manner in which stone is used, in the height of eaves' parapets, in the

Figure 2.6 Buildings on Merrion Square. While presenting an air of general regularity, there is considerable variation in height, building materials and ornamentation.

use of external ornamental iron-work and in the style of entrances. Indeed neighbouring properties are rarely identical. Houses were constructed to a height of three, four or, exceptionally, five storeys, commonly over basements, the light-wells being fronted by cast-iron railings. There exists a general regularity in fenestration with window sizes decreasing on upper floors, though nineteenth century alterations have sometimes enlarged those at first-floor level (An Taisce, 1985a). Roofs were slated, their pitch typically increasing in later developments.

There was a variety of interior room layouts, but the narrow urban plots resulted in compact interior plans. Room sizes were governed by the extent of plot frontage, being typically 4.8–5.5 m. (16–18 ft.) wide and 7.3 m. (24 ft.) deep. The most commonly adopted house plan has two rooms and a staircase on each floor, though the addition of returns (rear extensions) in the nineteenth century often masks this simplicity. Basements accommodated kitchens and storage, a family parlour was located on the ground floor, formal rooms were at first floor level – commonly with lofty ceilings – and bedrooms were above (McCullough, 1989).

Figure 2.7 Ornate plasterwork in Powerscourt House, recently converted into a shopping centre.

Although the exteriors are pleasant and possess a warmth of appearance which is absent in Edinburgh's New Town, the main architectural treasures are normally to be found within the buildings. Interiors of otherwise unremarkable domestic buildings frequently reveal great craftsmanship in fine plasterwork (Figure 2.7) and pedimented interior doorways, wood panelling and carving, and in marble staircases and fireplaces. As Alastair Rowan observes:

> . . . in Dublin the proliferation of elaborate plasterwork in house after house, figurative or abstract, opulently confined or exuberantly free, gives to the City a character that must make it, even for interior work alone, one of the most important urban environments in Europe. (Rowan, 1980, 3)

Numerous developments were initiated during the early years of the eighteenth century, notably the Dawson and Molesworth estates to the south of Trinity College, with the reclamation of the area to the north of the college also taking place. However, the interests of few developers spanned more than a single generation. The Gardiner family in particular differed in this respect in that it dominated urban development in Dublin over a period of more than a hundred years and was responsible for the development of much of north Dublin situated between Henrietta Street and Mountjoy Square.

The property development interests of Luke Gardiner I (d. 1755) began at George's Quay in 1712, but during the 1720s he acquired much of the St Mary's Abbey estate from three separate interests and commenced development at Henrietta Street. This comprised two terraces of massive red brick dwellings and, although the scheme proceeded slowly, he did manage to persuade a number of societal leaders to reside there. By the time of his death, Dorset Street, parts of Great Britain Street (Parnell Street) and the smaller streets between them had been developed. His legacy also includes the impressive mid-eighteenth century development of Gardiner's Mall/Sackville Street (Upper O'Connell Street), 275 m. (300 yards) in length and 46 m. (50 yards) wide, which was later extended southward to the river Liffey to meet Carlisle (O'Connell) bridge. The development of Rutland Square (later Parnell Square) and Marlborough Street were undertaken in mid-century, but the pace of development accelerated significantly when the estate passed from Charles Gardiner to Luke Gardiner II in 1769. Over the next 30 years, an area bounded by Parnell Square, North Frederick Street, Dorset Street, the North Circular Road, Parnell Street and Summerhill had been added to the estate, including impresssive bow-backed houses on the south side of the Summerhill escarpment which were developed in the 1780s. The developments created a series of east-west running terraces through which crossed the north-south line of Gardiner Street, itself comprising a series of terraces running down-slope to the new Custom House. Further to the north, on the fields overlooking Summerhill, the development of Mountjoy Square dates from the 1790s, though it was not completed until 1818, well after Lord Mountjoy's death in 1798.

To the south of the Liffey, the Fitzwilliam (Pembroke) estate comprised an extensive block of land which had been leased from the Corporation. This was developed over a period of almost 100 years under the control of the estate, comprising a wide area of south-east Dublin extending from Merrion Square up Fitzwilliam Street into Fitzwilliam Square and well beyond the Grand Canal. Merrion Square was commenced in the 1760s and created a development which competed successfully with those on the north side for the city's affluent residents. The square's prestige was assured by designing the western side to incorporate the rear garden of Leinster House, developed by the Duke of Leinster as a town house at the eastern periphery of the built up area in the 1740s. By the late 1700s, an address on Merrion Square was considered essential for social success.

In addition to the terraced mansions of the wealthy, the eighteenth century endowed the city with a number of fine individual houses. To the south of the river, these include Joshua Dawson's townhouse (1705), used as the Mansion House since 1715, and Powerscourt House (1771–4). To the north, Charlemont House (1762–5), Tyrone House (1740), Belvedere House (1775) and Aldborough House (1796) are noteworthy. Important public buildings were also constructed, including the Royal Exchange (1769–79), now used as the City Hall, the Parliament House, begun in 1729 and subsequently purchased by the Bank of Ireland, the Four Courts (1786–96) and the King's Inns (1795–1817), as well as a number of churches, army barracks (the Royal, now Collins, barracks dating from 1704) and hospitals, of which the recently restored Dr Steeven's hospital (1719) is one of the finest. Considerable reconstruction had also been taking place at Dublin castle since the late seventeenth century and the west facade of Trinity College (1759) was rebuilt in classical style. The development of a new Custom House (1781–91) heralded the inevitable downstream migration of the port. It was built against considerable opposition from merchants living in the old city or in the vicinity of the former Custom House at what is now Wellington Quay.

The development schemes of the late eighteenth century reflected the growing realisation during the Age of Enlightenment of the role of Dublin as the capital. Individual projects were greater in scale and conceived with a conscious view to their overall effect (McCullough, 1989). Nowhere was this more true than in the operations of the Wide Streets Commissioners, a body which was established by an Act of the Irish parliament in 1757. Originally set up to oversee the development of Parliament Street, the Commission was charged with providing the city with wide and convenient streets. To that end, this early planning body was given powers to acquire property, compulsorily if necessary, for the purpose of demolition and it was permitted to engage in the re-apportionment of property. Furthermore, from 1790, developers were obliged to submit their plans to the commissioners for approval.

Among the Commission's more important schemes were the widening of Dame Street, the alteration of Lower Abbey Street, the creation of thoroughfares along D'Olier Street and Westmoreland Street, and the continuation of Sackville Street (O'Connell Street) southward to the river where a new bridge was constructed. The removal of buildings bordering the Liffey was also completed to create the unbroken length of riverside quays from the Custom House to Phoenix Park.

In a rapidly expanding settlement where centralised influence over developments had been minimal, it was largely through the Commission's work that there developed an effective network of circulation between the new developments and the older core. Through lease arrangements, its work extended to controlling the design of buildings which were to be developed along its own streets. Interestingly, these included designs for residential premises above shops, which well suited the commercial

Table 2.1 The Growth of Dublin's population

	City	Suburbs	Total	Sub-Region	Change (%)
1685	45,000				
1706	62,000				
1725	92,000				
1744	112,000				
1778	154,000				
1800	182,000				
1821	224,000				
1831	232,362	32,954	265,316		
1841	232,726	48,480	281,206		
1851	258,369	59,468	317,837	405,147	
1861	254,808	70,323	325,131	410,252	+ 1.3
1871	246,326	83,410	329,736	405,262	− 1.2
1881	249,602	95,450	345,052	418,910	+ 3.4
1891	245,001	102,911	347,912	419,216	+ 0.7
1901 (old)	260,035				
1901 (new)	290,638	90,854	381,492	448,206	+ 6.9
1911	304,802	99,690	404,492	477,196	+ 6.5
1926				505,654	+ 6.0*
1936				586,925	+ 16.1
1946				636,193	+ 8.4
1951				693,022	+ 8.9*
1961				718,332	+ 3.7
1971				852,219	+ 18.6
1981				1,003,164	+ 17.7
1986				1,021,449	+ 1.8*
1991				1,024,429	+ 0.3*

Notes: the boundaries of the City were changed in 1900; * figures do not relate to a ten year period; Sub-region includes Dublin Co. Borough, County Dublin and Dun Laoghaire Borough.

Source: Daly, 1984; Central Statistics Office, Census of Population, 1851–1991.

districts in which the new streets were located. Recently refurbished examples exist on the west side of D'Olier Street. The Commission's work declined during the nineteenth century until its functions were absorbed by Dublin Corporation during the early 1840s.

Dublin in decline

By the opening years of the nineteenth century, Dublin comprised a compact and almost symmetrical city of 180,000 people (Table 2.1). Almost two centuries of growth had resulted in its becoming the sixth largest city in Europe as well as being second city in Britain and Ireland.

Yet, within a period of merely 60 years, Dublin had been relegated to only the fifth most populous city in the UK, and by the end of the century it had even suffered the ignominy of having been overtaken by Belfast (Daly, 1984). Dublin's growth had been based on its functions as the seat of the national government and of the ruling class, as an entrepôt and financial centre, and the possession of significant subsidiary industrial functions. Within a very short period of time, many of these functions were adversely affected by changing economic and political conditions. Indeed, a major sector of the city's industrial economic base collapsed almost entirely during the early decades of the nineteenth century.

Portents of decline had already been present during the latter part of the eighteenth century. From the end of the eighteenth century, the linen makers and merchants of Ulster increasingly dealt directly with Britain rather than through Dublin, whose financial role and entrepôt function in the linen trade were thus rendered obsolete, as was its once fine Linen Hall near Capel Street.

The growing challenge of the Irish Parliament to British authority during the latter part of the eighteenth century and the rebellion of the United Irishmen in 1798 resulted in the Act of Union (1800), marking the incorporation of Ireland into the world of industrial capitalism (O'Regan, 1980). The loss of the Irish parliament induced an exodus of Irish peers and other wealthy families from the city:

> Property values plummeted to unimaginable levels. Georgian houses which had been purchased for £8,000 in 1791 sold for only £2,500 a mere decade later. And by 1849 the same houses commanded a paltry £500.
>
>   . . . A scant four years after the Union, many of the larger houses around Mountjoy Square and St Stephen's Green were empty and forlorn or had at least been rented out as lodgings. (Kearns, 1983, 41–2)

The significance which the loss of the nobility spelled directly for the fortunes of the city in the nineteenth century should not be over-emphasised; indeed, Merrion Square and Fitzwilliam Square were only completed well into the nineteenth century. Although their loss of spending power was a blow to the city and particularly to the craftsmen working in its luxury trades, of greater importance was the forced abolition by 1824 of protective duties, exposing the Irish market to foreign competition. The application in Britain of factory-based production techniques to the textile industry during the Industrial Revolution was of major significance. This not only facilitated closer control over the production process by disciplining labour to the speed of machines but allowed greater control over the quality of the product. Advantages of increased productivity and declining unit labour costs followed, permitting British mass produced textiles to undercut Irish products. Dublin's textile industries were virtually eliminated. Already by the end of the 1790s some 20,000 persons were unemployed in the woollen trades; the industry which had still employed 4,000 people in 1800 engaged only 57 workers in 1850. With the ending of tariff protection, employment in the silk industry also collapsed, the number of looms declining from 2,100 to 150 during the 1820s, and by 1840 fewer than 400 silk weavers remained (D'Arcy, 1988). By the end of the century, fewer than a thousand people were employed in the textiles industry in the city.

With the decline in manufacturing, employment rose in sectors such as transport, dealing, domestic service and general labouring. Even in 1841, over a third of the workforce had been engaged in manufacturing, but this had fallen to 20 per cent by the opening years of the twentieth century. By 1851, a third of the city's workforce of 120,000 persons was employed either as general labourers or as domestic servants (O'Brien, 1982). Such was the decline in activity in the port that during the 1840s the Custom House had to be adapted to additional public uses. By 1911, general labourers constituted almost a fifth of the workforce: this sizeable proportion of the population drifted through a variety of occupations, concealing significant levels of unemployment or under-employment (Daly, 1984). Some industries, such as the food and drink industry, printing and general manufacturing, recorded increases in employment between 1841 and 1901, but the numbers involved were insufficient to counter the losses in textile production.

The changed economic conditions brought widespread poverty to the city's population at a time when no relief was provided by the state, and the ranks of the city's poor were swelled during the 1840s by an influx of rural migrants fleeing from areas affected by the Famine (see Chapter 3). The poverty of the populace was reflected in the condition of its housing and in its health. The overcrowded and insanitary working-class districts were ideal for the spread of tuberculosis, cholera, typhus, diptheria, smallpox, typhoid and measles among the malnourished poor. A survey carried out in 1845 by a local medical officer estimated that more than a fifth of all infants died before the end of their first year, that fewer than one half lived to the age of five, and that only one third of the working class survived into their twenties (O'Brien, 1982). During the 1840s, annual mortality rates exceeded 30 deaths per 1,000 persons. Although they declined slightly in mid-century to 25 per 1,000, they rose again during the 1860s and 1870s. At a time when death rates in British cities were falling as a result of public health improvements, rates in Dublin remained stubbornly high for the remainder of the century, hovering at around 30 per 1,000 persons, considerably above prevailing rates in such notorious cities as Liverpool, Manchester or Glasgow.

Dublin was, of course, a city of dramatic social contrasts. There was sizeable wealth amid abject poverty, evident even during the city's golden age of the eighteenth century. The Reverend James Whitelaw's house-to-house survey of 1798 reveals the poor living conditions in which a large proportion of the population must have lived, in sharp contrast with the mansions of the bourgeoisie and nobility:

> . . . I have frequently surprised between ten to sixteen persons, of all ages and sexes, in a room not fifteen feet square stretched on a wad of filthy straw, swarming with vermin, and without any covering save the wretched rags that constitute their wearing apparel . . .
>
> Into the backyard of each house . . . is flung from the windows of each apartment the ordure and other filth of its numerous inhabitants; from whence it is so seldom removed that I have seen it nearly on a level with the windows of the first floor. . . . When I attempted in the summer of 1798 to take the population of a ruinous house in Joseph's-lane, near Castle-market, I was interrupted in my progress by an inundation of putrid blood, alive with maggots, which had from an adjacent slaughter-yard burst the back-door and filled the hall to the depth of several inches.

Whitelaw estimated that the city's population of 172,000 dwelt at an average density of 10.5 persons per house. In Plunkett Street, he found residential densities exceeded 28 persons per house and on Braithwaite Street one house contained 108 inhabitants. Meanwhile, about a hundred Irish peers had townhouses in the city, nearly half of them located on Sackville Street alone (O'Brien, 1982).

Table 2.1 shows that Dublin grew slowly during the nineteenth century. However, this growth ran counter to the absolute decline being experienced in many other Irish urban areas. Despite the Act of Union, Dublin remained the commercial, legal and administrative centre of the island and retained a significant class of merchants, business owners, civil servants, army personnel and professional classes. The city's cultural and recreational roles were also affirmed and in the early twentieth century the city possessed seven daily newspapers, three theatres, two concert halls and several music halls (Pierce, 1992).

Increasingly, the wealthier and middle-class residents moved out of the city to take up residence in suburbia, keen to separate themselves from a city which was in decline, being characterised by disrepair, physical dereliction and a distressed and unhealthy population. Throughout the nineteenth century, the businessman's place of work became increasingly separated from that of his residence. After the 1840s, no truly first-class streets were developed in the city centre. Private sector residential development was undertaken instead for clerical and skilled working classes, as in the vicinity of the South Circular Road to the west of Camden Street, where housing was characterised by intimacy of scale and a variety of types including single-storey, two-storey and split-level houses. Meanwhile, in Rathmines and Pembroke, which became self-governing townships in 1847 and 1863 respectively, developers were creating fine residential environments where the 'protestant and unionist

Figure 2.8 Wellington Road, Ballsbridge. The neo-classical style was retained well into the nineteenth century though with the addition of lengthy front gardens.

Dublin middle class could evade the unpleasant reality that they were a minority which was increasingly losing political control in both Ireland and in the city of Dublin' (Daly, 1988, 123).

The layout of developments in the suburbs continued to be based on long individual plots with separate access to the back-lands. During the first half of the century, buildings continued to be designed in the Georgian idiom and differed little from those in the city, though painted façades and stucco were adopted increasingly after 1840, especially in the coastal suburbs of Monkstown, Dun Laoghaire and Dalkey. Front gardens made their first appearance in the 1790s at Marino Crescent, Fairview. They became common from the 1820s and attained considerable length by mid-century, as on Wellington Road (Ballsbridge) shown in Figure 2.8. From the late 1820s, basements began to emerge from their subterranean worlds to become 'garden level' rooms, entry to the main house being gained by a flight of exterior steps leading to a 'ground floor' entrance which was effectively located at first floor level, as at Pembroke Road (Ballsbridge). On the east side of Morehampton Road (Donnybrook), some houses were even built with a garden level over a true basement. As the century progressed, the character of the

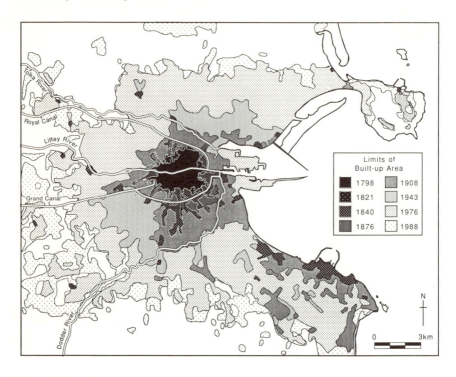

Figure 2.9 The expansion of Dublin. The compact city of the late eighteenth century has been transformed into a sprawling metropolis.

developments underwent a slow transformation which reflected the influence of the romantic movement and changes in architectural taste towards the greater ornamentation of the Irish Gothic revival. Rectilinear layouts slowly gave way to more informal plans, terraces became shorter, and by the 1880s, the semi-detached house and detached villa had become a popular form of development, as on Clyde Road (Ballsbridge).

During the nineteenth century, the symmetrical growth which had characterised previous centuries was broken by marked linear extensions, particularly southwards (Figure 2.9). Rathmines grew rapidly during the late 1800s, from 10,000 in 1841 to 32,000 in 1901. Development here was for the professional and business classes and was controlled by private businessmen with local property interests. Its low rates (property taxes) were an additional incentive, although lower rates often resulted in poor provision of public services with unpaved and muddy lanes being frequently strewn with refuse (Daly, 1984). In 1872, Dublin's first tram service opened linking Rathmines with the city centre. As demand for upper-middle-class housing had been largely satisfied, suburban

Figure 2.10 The Ranelagh district of the Rathmines township attracted residential developments for clerical workers when demand for upper-middle-class housing became fulfilled in the 1870s.

development during the last two decades of the century catered increasingly for clerical workers, particularly in the Harold's Cross and Ranelagh areas of the township, depicted in Figure 2.10. Nevertheless, Rathmines retained a high proportion of professional and business people and high class development was still being undertaken in the Cowper Garden estate and in Terenure.

In contrast to Rathmines, development on the Pembroke estate around Ballsbridge was closely controlled and the estate manager dominated the township Commission after its formation. Development was undertaken with a view to long-term returns from 99- and 150-year leases, whereas 999-year leases and even freeholds were available in Rathmines. The estate itself, rather than individual developers, took responsibility for the provision of roads and sewerage, while building leases detailed the character of construction. This necessitated far higher local rates than characterised Rathmines, even exceeding those of the city itself during the 1890s. Although the township did include a large pre-existing working-class district at Irishtown and Ringsend, the standards of development which were stipulated and the level of rates ensured that little new development took place for the lower middle class. Development therefore slackened after 1880. The district, absorbed by the city as late as 1930, has retained its status into the modern era, being adopted as the heart of Dublin's embassy belt.

The opening of a railway line from Dublin in 1834 was an important stimulus to the expansion of Kingstown (Dun Laoghaire), Monkstown and Blackrock, where development took place for those able to afford the fares, while the seaward slopes of Killiney and Dalkey became dotted with the villas of the wealthy. To the north of the city, the development of Clontarf was hindered by its poorly drained site, its proximity to the declining north-eastern part of the city and by the unhelpful attitude of the major landowner (Daly, 1984). Rapid expansion therefore did not take place here until the twentieth century.

The character of suburban development changed significantly from the 1870s, marked by growing demand for housing from the rising lower middle class of clerks, shopkeepers and public servants. Although there had been horse-drawn omnibuses in the city since the 1830s, it was the commencement of tramway services which permitted growing numbers of the lower middle class to commute to their city centre places of employment. Drumcondra was Dublin's first suburban township (1878) which catered from its inception for the clerical and skilled working classes. The frontal wave of residential development for this growing class of Dubliners expanded outwards from the city centre, infilling the gaps left between previous developments and engulfing the higher class residential areas of the 1840s and 1850s. Grosvenor Square in Rathmines suffered just such a fate and was completed in an inferior style as a result. The response of the upper and upper middle classes was to move even further out.

With their straight streets, terraced or semi-detached houses possessing front and rear gardens, lower-middle-class suburbs were in many ways similar to the prestigious developments, but the elements were all of meaner proportions. From the 1870s, in order to distinguish themselves from the lower status developments, more prestigious residences often incorporated greater levels of ornamentation, including multi-coloured brickwork, while pointed gables became fashionable at the end of the century.

The eighteenth century houses which were vacated by the upper and middle classes frequently underwent conversion to commercial functions. This was especially true in the north-east sector of the city following the division and sale of the Gardiner Estate in the 1840s. Its fate was sealed by its proximity to the port, which attracted the working class in search of employment. The arrival of the railway had further detrimental effects on the area's status, being associated with conversion of properties to hotel use, as also happened in the Harcourt Street area. Elsewhere, homes were turned into tenements and lodging houses. Dwellings built to accommodate a single family and servants were now commonly required to accommodate whole families in single rooms, the poverty of the tenants often obliging them to sublet part of that space to lodgers. Henrietta Street was effectively a slum by the 1870s, but the first tenements did not appear on Mountjoy Square until 1910, by which time almost a fifth of the properties there had become vacant (Cullen, 1992). Their physical structure invariably suffered a heavy toll from having to accommodate 60 or more inhabitants and, as the century progressed, Dublin's housing problems became increasingly associated with the horrors of the tenement house which, unlike those in Scotland, had not been built for multi-family occupancy.

Housing conditions reflected the poverty of the populace. The census of 1841 found that 23,000 families, nearly half of the city's total, lived in single-roomed tenements at an average occupancy rate of 11.6 persons per house. The situation improved little during the remainder of the century. By the 1870s and 1880s, over 40 per cent of the city's 23,830 residential buildings had become tenemented and in 1879, 117,000 people, comprising over 45 per cent of the total, were living in tenements. The Royal Commission on the Housing of the Working Classes in Ireland which reported in 1884 discovered that some 30,000 people lived in 2,300 tenement houses which were deemed unfit for human habitation (Aalen, 1992). In 1913, when there still existed 5,188 tenement houses in the city, they accommodated 25,822 families at an average of 16.4 persons per house. Some 78 per cent of these households occupied a single room. Moreover, 1,100 tenement houses had sanitary provision of only one water closet between 20 to 40 persons (Colivet, 1943). Even as late as 1936, residential densities in Mountjoy Ward in the north-central city area exceeded 440 persons per hectare (about 180 persons per acre), six times that of Rathmines and Ballsbridge (Horner, 1992). Some 75,000 persons then occupied or shared single-roomed dwellings, of whom 23,000 lived in a single room shared with no fewer than five others.

The low levels of rents which could be afforded by tenants were inadequate to ensure adequate levels of building maintenance. Over-occupancy and abuse by tenants, together with exterior attack from acid-laden rain and smoke resulted in the severe deterioration of a large proportion of the city's stock of eighteenth century buildings (Jeffrey, 1988). The collapse of tenements into the street was far from being an unknown phenomenon.

As in Britain, the housing and sanitary reform movements were intimately associated. Understandably, the overcrowded and insanitary tenements became an object of concern on the part of social reformers and Corporation alike, but the slum clearance schemes were responsible for the destruction of numerous once-fine eighteenth century buildings. Apart from the continued operations of the private speculative residential developers who were building in the city to cater for clerical and skilled working classes, several private philanthropic housing ventures were undertaken during the later part of the nineteenth and early twentieth centuries, preceding municipal involvement by several decades (Aalen, 1985). The Guinness Trust (retitled the Iveagh Trust in Dublin after 1903) was established in 1890 as a wholly philanthropic organisation, developing apartment blocks at New Bride Street and at Bull Alley, the former being firmly in the architectural mould of British schemes and rather austere in comparison to the later Bull Alley scheme.

Several philanthropic employers were active in the housing field. Watkin's brewery built 87 roadside terraced dwellings in the Coombe, and Guinness developed over 100 apartments at Rialto in the 1880s and 100 single roomed tenements at Thomas Court. Outside the central area, single-storey cottages and two-storey houses were developed by the textile firm of Pim at Harold's Cross during the 1850s, while the railway companies constructed schemes at Inchicore, to the west of the city, and at Great Western Square, off the North Circular Road.

By far the most influential and enterprising organisation was the Dublin Artisans' Dwellings Company, a semi-philanthropic body established in 1876. It aimed to provide housing for the industrious classes at affordable rents and was a classic example of 'five per cent philanthropy' then current in Britain (see Tarn, 1973). Limiting dividends to 4 per cent per annum, the company catered for artisans and clerical workers, with its early schemes including blocks of apartments at Buckingham Street Upper, Echlin Street and Dominick Street. However, apartments were soon forsaken in favour of the building of self-contained terraced dwellings. Built to a high density of 120 houses per hectare (50 per acre), they generally comprised single-storey two-roomed cottages, as depicted in Figure 2.11, and two-storey houses with parlour, scullery and two bedrooms. It redeveloped an area to the north of The Coombe and at John Dillon Street, but its largest scheme comprised 10 ha. (26 acres) to the north of the Liffey, off Stoneybatter, where 900 houses were built. By 1914, the Company had housed 16,000 people in some 3,300 dwellings scattered at locations around the inner city.

As in London, slum clearance brought unforeseen consequences. The poor experienced a reduced supply of affordable accommodation and were effectively shunted around the city in the wake of slum clearance schemes. One organisation, the Association for Housing the Very Poor Ltd., was established in 1898 to develop housing for Dublin's poorest. It built 118 single-roomed flats to house 600 people at Allingham Street in the Liberties, but found that even these could not be let at rents which were affordable by that class.

Figure 2.11 Harty Place, off Clanbrassil Street, a development of cottages by the Dublin Artisans' Dwellings Company. By the outbreak of World War I, it had built 3,300 dwellings housing 16,000 people.

The activities of the philanthropists clearly demonstrated that there could be no private sector solution to the housing problems of the poor. Inevitably, yet haltingly, Dublin Corporation became involved not only in demolishing slums but in the development of housing for the working classes. Its first scheme at Barrack Street (Benburb Street) dates from the late 1880s and comprised 144 flats in three blocks, with shared sanitary facilities and is reminiscent of British schemes undertaken by Waterlow or the Peabody Trust. The Corporation's early schemes were generally on small sites located in the central area. Most comprised apartments, but in the last decade of the century 80 single-storey cottages were built at St Joseph's Place, though even here the new levels of rent could not be afforded by the original residents (Aalen, 1985).

Twentieth century expansion

By 1914, the Corporation had developed 1,385 houses and apartments, yet there was still an estimated shortage of 14,000 dwellings in the city.

Figure 2.12 Dublin Corporation's cottage housing at Marino was influenced by the Garden City Movement and was an important step in the suburbanisation of Dublin's working class.

Increasingly, and despite considerable opposition from within the Corporation, it was accepted that only through the large-scale sub-urbanisation of the working classes would it prove possible to tackle the city's housing problems. Schemes for 57 houses at Clontarf and for 333 cottages at Inchicore during the first decade of the twentieth century were early signals of this trend, but serious pursuit of this policy had to await the 1920s. It was then given effect in the development of houses for tenant-purchase at Fairbrothers Fields to the south of the Liberties, at Marino (Figure 2.12), Drumcondra, Donnycarney and Cabra. Each comprised over 400 cottages. Large schemes of cottages for renting date from the 1930s and include Crumlin which comprised over 3,200 dwellings (Colivet, 1943). By the outbreak of World War II, the Corporation had developed 7,420 cottages for renting, a further 4,248 for purchase by tenants, and over 3,200 flats.

Despite the scale of local authority housing development during the inter-war years, in 1938 there remained 6,300 tenement houses in the city accommodating 111,950 persons at an average of over 17 persons per house. By the end of the 1940s, there was a housing shortage of

Figure 2.13 Kildonan Avenue, Finglas. After World War II, public housing policy comprised the twin elements of developing inner-city flats and suburban cottage estates built at low densities.

30,000 dwellings. In the 1950s, large-scale public housing development took place at Artane and Ballyfermot, and by 1959, nearly 45 per cent of the 42,360 dwellings built in Dublin since World War II had been developed by the public sector. During the next decade, public housing covered a wide area of countryside to the north of the city stretching from Finglas (Figure 2.13) and Ballymun to Coolock.

Private sector residential construction tended to avoid those areas being developed by public housing. The southern and eastern fringes, with their access to countryside and coast, became particularly popular with middle-class residents. Expansion took place around exisiting settlements at Donnybrook, Blackrock, Dun Laoghaire and Dundrum. The 'garden suburb' of Mount Merrion was also developed from the 1930s to the 1950s, quite separate from the still compact city, although merely 6 km. (4 miles) from the city centre. After World War II, speculative residential developers continued to favour the southern periphery and were the major actors in the development of a broad zone running from Rathfarnham, Churchtown and Dundrum through Stillorgan to Deans Grange and Killiney.

During the 1970s and 1980s, three new towns were developed at the western periphery at Tallaght, Ronanstown (Lucan-Clondalkin) and Blanchardstown. Although they were promoted by the local authorities, it was private sector developers who played the principal role. Elsewhere, infilling and further peripheral expansion of the city continued. Lengthening journey times to work from the increasingly distant suburbs encouraged a spate of apartment construction during the 1970s and developments of small 'townhouses' during the 1980s, often in the gardens of villas originally constructed in the eighteenth or nineteenth centuries or on lands occupied by religious orders or sports clubs. The most favoured locations for such schemes were inner suburbs such as Ballsbridge. Meanwhile, private sector activity had leapt across the northern belt of local authority estates and was taking place in the vicinity of Swords, while in the south, the contiguous built-up area stretched along the coast through Shankill to Bray, which had itself undergone very rapid expansion. Indeed, by the 1990s, most towns within a radius of 48 km. (30 miles) of the city had experienced significant growth as a result of widening commuting fields, with ribbon development of new bungalows stretching along many of the roads in south County Meath. The twentieth century had thus transformed Dublin into a major city region.

3
The economy of Dublin

The transformation of the Irish economy

Until recently, the character of the Irish economy was dominated by its colonial legacy. An over-dependence on agricultural exports, particularly to markets in the United Kingdom, resulted from the country's having been largely by-passed during the nineteenth century by the Industrial Revolution. During the nineteenth and early twentieth centuries, structural changes in the rural economy, resulting from the increasing commercialisation and modernisation of agriculture associated with growing penetration by capitalism, generated a surplus labour force. But, unlike many other European countries, this surplus was not absorbed by the growth of urban-based industrial employment. In the eighteenth century, the Irish Parliament had used tariff barriers, subsidies and grants to encourage the development of industries in Ireland. By the start of the nineteenth century, Ireland had possessed a level of industrialisation which was of a similar order to many European countries, such as Italy, Spain and Portugal. However, the Act of Union (1800) required the removal of all such tariffs by 1824 and exposed Irish industries to the full force of competition from more efficient British industry. This heralded a lengthy period of economic restructuring during the nineteenth century which saw widespread de-industrialisation. The textile sector failed to adapt swiftly enough to the changing conditions of factory production and was particularly badly hit. In 1841 there had been nearly 700,000 people engaged in the textile industry on the island, mostly in domestic production, but by the first decade of the twentieth century this had fallen to 92,000. In the 26 counties which were to become the Irish Free State, only 13 per cent of the labour force was employed in industry

51

in 1911 (Kennedy et al., 1988). The economy had become overwhelmingly dependent upon agricultural production. With the exception of the north-east, Ireland became 'a mere agricultural province of an industrial nation' (O'Regan, 1980, 12). Those manufacturing industries which did survive the century of structural change were concentrated overwhelmingly in the food and drink sectors, and by the 1920s these accounted for nearly 70 per cent of total manufacturing net output.

The Great Famine of the 1840s, when the potato crop, the staple food within the rural diet, successively failed as a result of blight, was a significant turning point in the country's demographic history. During the previous hundred years, the Irish population seems to have increased between three- and four-fold resulting from early marriage and a high birth rate. The rate of population growth had been slowing down since 1821 and around one and a half million people had emigrated during the 30 years prior to the Famine. However, the Famine initiated an era of absolute population decline (Kennedy et al., 1988). Five hundred thousand to more than a million persons are estimated to have died from fever engendered by malnutrition. Far greater losses resulted from emigration, over 1.25 million people leaving for North America alone between 1847 and 1852 and substantial numbers also emigrated to Britain. In the century following the Famine, the size of the Irish population declined continuously, resulting mainly from high levels of out-migration. Over five million people emigrated during the period between the Famine and 1921, at which time the population of Ireland stood at 4,354,000 – barely half of what it had been 80 years previously – of whom 3,096,000 people resided in the 26 counties of the Free State:

> The greatest disaster to happen to any one nation in Europe, until the murder of six million Jews in the last war, was the Irish famine of 1847. Eight million people lived in Ireland at the time, but when the famine ended there were only four million left. I heard an old woman myself, when I was a child of six, tell how she saw a woman on the side of the road at Santry, outside Dublin, with the green juice of the grass running down her lips and a child tugging at her dead breasts. These are things that are not forgotten in a generation. Maybe they say that we Irish have long memories but the Famine is not the kind of thing that can be forgotten in a day or a year. (Behan, 1962, 185–6)

Post Independence

The decade after political independence in 1922 was marked initially by turmoil during the civil war. The economic policies of the newly independent state favoured free trade and agricultural development through attempting to maximise farmers' profits at the expense of the urban working class. This was unsurprising in view of the social origins of those with decision-making power (Lee, 1989). Policies did little to stimulate employment opportunities and between 1911 and 1936 the number of agricultural labourers dropped from 300,000 to 150,000. Emigration accelerated from an average annual level of around 23,000 during the first two decades of the century to over 33,000 during the 1921–31 period, and there was an absolute fall of 89,000 in the size of the population.

The fortunes of the Irish economy during the 1930s were dominated by the impact of the Great Depression, the Economic War with Britain, the protectionist policies pursued by the government and an economic climate which militated against trade. The volume of merchandise exports fell rapidly after 1930 and did not regain that level until 1960. One result of the Great Depression was to reduce the opportunities for overseas employment. In addition, the USA tightened its immigration rules. Emigration was reduced to fewer than 10,000 per annum during the early years of the 1930s, the Irish population actually increasing each year until mid-decade to reach 2,971,000 by 1935, but declining thereafter as emigration returned to its 1920s levels after 1936.

The need to create additional employment was an important factor leading to the re-orientation of government policy away from free trade towards one of protectionism. Anti-dumping legislation marked the start of this process even before the replacement of the Cumann na nGael government in 1932 by Fianna Fail. However, the new government pursued protectionism vigorously as part of its strategy to reduce economic dependence, indigenous industry being assisted to develop by the erection of protective tariff barriers and a range of quotas and import licences. This marked an important step in the slow transformation of the Irish economy away from its overwhelming dependence on agricultural production.

Industrial production grew significantly, albeit from a low starting point, by around 50 per cent between 1931 and 1938, total industrial employment rising by an average of 6 per cent per year from 110,600 to 166,100 by 1938 and doubling between 1932 and 1958 (O'Malley, 1980). However, this industrial policy of self-sufficiency sheltering behind high tariff barriers, resulted in an industrial sector which was weak and inefficient (Hourihan, 1991). Moreover, unemployment remained at a high level throughout the 1930s, and when opportunities overseas again became available later in the decade, emigration rose.

During World War II, the self-sufficiency which had been sought by de Valera was given added emphasis by external events. Although there was a ready outlet for all the agricultural products the country could produce, expansion was difficult due to shortages of imported machinery, fuel and fertilisers. Irish agricultural production was maintained, none the less, and Britain absorbed 99 per cent of its exports. Industrial production was also affected by the hostilities, with Ireland's nascent industries often depending upon imported semi-finished goods for final processing or assembly. Thus, by 1942 the volume of manufacturing production had fallen by 25 per cent since the start of the war. Emigration remained at a high level throughout the war, at over 25,000 per annum, departing emigrants being destined mainly for war-production in British factories.

As the world emerged from war to reconstruction and, subsequently, to rapid economic growth, the Irish economy faced major structural problems. It remained a predominantly agricultural economy whose exports were destined mainly for Britain, whose economy was one of the least dynamic in Europe. The immediate post-war period was characterised by considerable manufacturing growth – averaging over 9 per cent per annum between 1946 and 1951 – but industrial employment growth was insufficient to balance the continued drift out of agriculture, which lost 70,000 jobs between those years. The post-war boom ended rapidly as a policy of fiscal retrenchment was pursued, in response to a balance of payments problem. This policy of fiscal conservatism continued through much of the 1950s, often exacerbating underlying problems rather than improving matters. The terms of trade moved progressively to the detriment of Ireland, particularly with regard to agricultural export prices, with the growing scale of exported manufactured goods being unable to compensate. By 1958, the Gross National Product (GNP) was less than 7 per cent above the level of 1951, a rate of increase which fell well behind the levels attained in most European countries.

The economic miracle

The 1950s are often described as a period of unalloyed economic stagnation. Indeed, it was a decade marked by two major recessions and the continuation of large-scale emigration at levels unseen since the 1890s: the absolute decline in the population between 1951 and 1958 was twice as great as during the whole period since Independence. By 1961, the Republic's population had fallen to 2,818,000 persons, some 400,000 people having emigrated during the decade. Economic restructuring continued, reflected in the inexorable decline in agricultural employment, but industrial employment also registered an overall decline during the decade. Only service sector employment expanded, and, as indicated in Table 3.1, it accounted for a greater proportion of the labour force than did agriculture by 1961.

It was, however, during the 1950s that the seeds were sown for a sustained period of economic expansion over the next two decades: Ireland's 'economic miracle'. It saw the establishment of Córas Tráchtála (the Irish Export Board), the Industrial Credit Company (ICC) as well as

Table 3.1 Irish employment by sector (thousands)

	Agriculture	Industry	Services
1926	653	162	406
1936	614	206	415
1946	568	225	432
1951	496	282	438
1961	360 (380)	252 (259)	405 (414)
1971	272	320	457
1981	196	363	587
1986	168	301	606
1989	163	306	620

Source: After Kennedy, Giblin and McHugh, 1988; 1926–51 figures are based on Census of Population data; 1961–89 figures are based on labour force survey classifications. The figures in parentheses are values for 1961 when computed in the manner adopted for previous years.

the extension of the functions of the Industrial Development Authority (IDA) established in 1949 to include the encouragement of new indigenous industries and the attraction of foreign concerns. An export profits tax relief scheme was also introduced.

Probably of greatest significance was the publication in 1958 of a document entitled *Economic Development*, whose author, T.K. Whitaker, was Secretary at the traditionally conservative Department of Finance. His paper aimed at devising an integrated programme for economic development over a five to ten year period, specifying the goals and the resources which would be required for their fulfillment. It emphasised in particular those areas of the economy with export potential – the first time that economic planning on such a scale had been contemplated for the country.

Many of Whitaker's ideas were embodied in the First Programme for Economic Expansion (1959) covering the period 1959–63 which placed particular emphasis on the creation of non-agricultural employment. Moreover, Whitaker had argued that if domestic capital proved insufficient to meet demand, it would have to be obtained from overseas. This was to be done via taxation relief on exports, capital and re-equipment grants, and loans at favourable rates of interest. The First Programme was fortuitous in terms of its timing, the period being one in which it was relatively easy to attract footloose branch plants of transnational companies. Thus, the economy was to be opened up to foreign capital in a manner which contrasted with the policies which had been pursued since 1932. The Anglo-Irish Free Trade Agreement of 1965 and entry into the EEC in 1973 were important milestones in this process, protection being progressively abandoned in favour of free trade.

55

Economic growth was rapid during the 1960s and early 1970s as the economy continued its transformation. The Gross Domestic Product grew at an average rate of 4 per cent annually between 1961 and 1971. Advances in the manufacturing sector were particularly significant with output expanding by an average of 6.5 per cent per annum and employment growing by 2.3 per cent annually so that during the 1960s it exceeded the numbers employed in agriculture. Between 1961 and 1971, for the first time since the founding of the state, the number of jobs created outside agriculture exceeded the number being lost in that sector (Drudy, 1989). Manufacturing exports rose by an average of 23 per cent annually between 1958 and 1973, almost matching agricultural exports by that year. The dominant role of the British market, which had accounted for 80 per cent of Irish manufactured exports in 1958, declined to 58 per cent by 1972 and 30.3 per cent by 1985 as the EEC became an increasingly important destination for exports (Kennedy et al., 1988).

Although the rate of economic growth subsequently slackened – the Gross Domestic Product (GDP) rising by an average of only 3.8 per cent during the 1970s and by under 2 per cent during the early 1980s – economic restructuring continued. The proportion of national income accounted for by industry rose from 30 per cent in 1965 to 43 per cent in 1984, and the sector's contribution to total exports rose from 37 per cent to 78 per cent. Agricultural employment continued to fall, and by the end of the 1980s, agriculture, forestry and fishing accounted for only 163,200 of the Irish labour force of 1,089,900. Employment in industry increased until the early 1980s but registered a decline thereafter. In contrast, employment in the services sector continued to grow throughout the period, and by 1981 it accounted for a greater proportion of the labour force than the combined totals engaged in agriculture and industry.

Opening up the Irish economy and attracting investment from overseas resulted, however, in a deepening dependency on foreign capital. By 1990, foreign-owned companies employed more than 90,000 people in the state, accounting for half of all industrial output and 75 per cent of industrial exports (Department of Industry and Commerce, 1990). Thirty years of Irish economic policy had transformed Irish industry into a neo-colony specialising in routine, lower status industrial jobs in branch plants which had few local business linkages and which were highly susceptible to closure as a result of the restructuring of production and employment by transnational corporations (Walsh, 1980).

Dublin and the regions

Another development which dates from the 1950s was to prove of long-term significance for Dublin's economic fortunes. The Undeveloped Areas Act of 1952 was the first in a series of measures designed to attract manufacturing industry to the Designated Areas – the 12 counties along the western seaboard with low incomes, a heavy dependence on declining agricultural industry and few alternative employment opportunities. The measures included higher levels of grant aid to manufacturing industry in such areas and these grants remained a permanent feature of Irish industrial policy over the next 40 years. This policy was very successful. Throughout the 1960s and for a greater part of the 1970s, development policy was to discriminate against Dublin. Of the net national gain of manufacturing employment over the period 1973–89, some 98 per cent was located in the western areas of the country (Drudy, 1991a, 1991b). Simultaneously, Dublin recorded very significant losses in manufacturing employment.

Although there was a certain logic behind spreading development more widely geographically, the manner in which this was carried out was wholly inappropriate. While it was recognised that it might be advantageous to focus development at a limited number of 'growth centres' which could promote local business linkages, significant economies of scale and local economic multipliers, this sensible strategy unfortunately proved to be unacceptable to elected representatives from constituencies not including such a centre. A wholly unsatisfactory political compromise was reached, whereby almost any town with a population greater than 1,500 was to be regarded as a growth centre – effectively abandoning any attempt at serious economic spatial planning as every township clamoured for a factory.

The long-term effects of such regional policies on Dublin were dramatic, yet have only slowly been recognised. By 1981, the city accounted for over a quarter of all the unemployed males in the state and over a third of the unemployed females. The absolute number of unemployed males in the Dublin sub-region (Dublin County Borough, County Dublin and Dun Laoghaire Borough) matched the scale of unemployment in Munster, and was more than twice the number out of work in Connaught. Even the rate of male unemployment in the County Borough (13.2 per cent) exceeded the prevailing levels in Munster (10.8 per cent) and in Connaught (11.1 per cent). Indeed, it could be argued that Dublin increasingly represented Ireland's regional problem *par excellence*. Moreover, in continuing to discriminate against the capital, politicians ran the risk of jeopardising the economy of one of the few areas of the country which perhaps possessed sufficient critical mass of economic activity to facilitate the development of a range of economic

Table 3.2 Industrial and service employment in the Dublin sub-region

	1951	1961	1971	1981	1987	1989	1990
Industry	101,715	108,000	122,000	112,900	84,000	82,700	86,300
Services	168,774	162,600	187,800	242,900	242,600	251,800	253,900

Source: Central Statistics Office, Labour Force Survey, various years.

linkages, allowing businesses to function successfully without subsidy on an openly competitive European stage.

Dublin's changing economic base

The past few decades, then, have seen significant changes to Dublin's economic base. Table 3.2 shows that employment in industrial activities expanded slowly throughout the 1950s and 1960s, reaching a total of over 120,000 jobs in the early 1970s. However, since that time the city has been particularly hard hit by losses of industrial employment, which have resulted from the opening up of the Irish economy to international competition, changes in the technologies of production, the re-structuring of local and international capital, and government policies which have concentrated on promoting industrial development outside the Dublin region.

Decline in manufacturing employment in the city has been continuous since 1971. It was particularly severe in long-established activities such as the 'food, drink and tobacco' industries and in the 'textiles, clothing and footwear' sector where employment dropped by nearly 45 per cent between 1971 and 1981. In contrast, employment in more modern sectors, such as 'metals and engineering', grew during the 1970s by over 20 per cent, but even these registered a decline during the subsequent decade (Dublin County Council Planning Department, 1988). The city thus experienced a net decline of around 9,000 jobs in industrial employment during the 1970s at a time when the number of industrial jobs outside Dublin registered a net increase of nearly 48,000. If employment in 'building and construction' is excluded, this reduction is even sharper, exceeding 13,500 jobs.

Between 1973 and 1977 alone, over 12,000 jobs were lost in the manufacturing sector in Dublin, compared to a target of 7,300 additional jobs which the IDA had predicted would be created without grant assistance (Industrial Development Authority, 1978). It was this unforeseen scale of job losses which obliged the IDA in 1976 belatedly to commence promoting Dublin as an industrial centre as well as to become

Table 3.3 Manufacturing employment in Dublin, 1980–90

Numbers employed in:	1980	1990	Net change	%
Non-metallic minerals	3,840	1,977	− 1,863	− 48.5
Chemicals	4,199	3,898	− 301	− 7.2
Metals and engineering	20,676	16,509	− 4,167	− 20.2
Food	15,510	8,243	− 7,267	− 46.9
Drink and tobacco	5,819	3,170	− 2,649	− 45.5
Textiles	2,216	1,228	− 988	− 44.6
Clothing, footwear and leather	9,142	5,124	− 4,018	− 44.0
Timber and furniture	2,399	1,486	− 913	− 38.1
Paper and priniting	10,461	8,835	− 1,626	− 15.5
Miscellaneous industries	3,877	3,634	− 234	− 6.3
Mining, quarrying and turf	473	110	− 363	− 76.7
Total manufacturing	78,612	54,214	− 24,389	− 31.0
Non-manufacturing (grant-aided)	1,289	5,612	+ 4,323	+ 335.4
Total	**79,901**	**59,826**	**− 20,066**	**− 25.1**

Source: Industrial Development Authority.

involved in the development of industrial properties there (MacLaran and Beamish, 1985). The Dublin sub-region lost a further 30,000 industrial jobs during the 1980s, though by this stage, recession was biting into the performance of the rest of Ireland which also experienced a loss of some 29,000 jobs. Table 3.3 indicates that the recession of the 1980s resulted in the loss of nearly a third of all the city's jobs in manufacturing, affecting almost every branch of the manufacturing sector.

In view of the emerging problem of manufacturing decline in Dublin, the Government decided in 1982 to grant Designated Area status for industrial grants purposes to Dublin's inner city for a five year period, though this was not renewed thereafter. As Drudy (1991a) observes, designation of the inner city, with its problems of high land prices, congestion and lack of space, had little prospect of success, and there was no extension of Designated Area status to peripheral areas of the city where prospects might have been better. The IDA did construct a number of enterprise centres in the inner city and accelerated its programme of development and purchase of manufacturing premises in other areas of Dublin during the late 1970s–early 1980s, but it was severely constrained by government policies of financial retrenchment and Dublin lost out heavily to other areas of the country.

By the end of the 1980s, Dublin had suffered a net loss of almost a

Table 3.4 Employment in manufacturing in Dublin, 1973–89

	Irish	Foreign	Total	Foreign %
1973	56,247	27,147	83,394	32.5
1980	52,496	27,377	79,873	34.3
1989	35,646	22,818	58,465	39.0
Net loss (1973–89)	20,601	4,328	24,929	

Source: Drudy, 1991a.

third (32.2 per cent) of the industrial jobs which had existed in the city in 1971 while the rest of Ireland had seen a 9.2 per cent net increase (Drudy, 1991a). Its share of national employment in industry thus declined from 37.3 per cent to 27 per cent between 1971 and 1989. Since 1989 there have been some signs of improvement in manufacturing employment, but considerable progress will be necessary to counter the losses of the previous decade, and it is clear that more attention is required immediately to build up Dublin's manufacturing base.

Over the past two decades, manufacturing employment decline in Dublin has been concentrated overwhelmingly in indigenous companies. Table 3.4 shows that these accounted for 20,601 of the 24,929 jobs which have been lost since 1973. Consequently, by 1989, foreign companies had increased their share of manufacturing employment in the city to nearly 40 per cent. Changes in demand for traditional products, the city's legacy of a high proportion of traditional declining industries and the increasingly competitive environment in which Irish companies were obliged to operate after entry into the EEC, placed indigenous industries in a difficult position and resulted in contraction or closure.

There were also differences in the employment performance of overseas firms according to their country of origin. During the period 1973–89, it was American firms which registered the greatest net increase in jobs, amounting to over 4,900. In contrast, the labour force in British companies suffered a net reduction of over 10,200 jobs (Drudy, 1991a). These British companies were more likely to have been established prior to Ireland's entry into the EC and, like the Irish companies, have suffered subsequently from intensified competition.

The city's contribution to the net output of Irish manufacturing stood at 23 per cent throughout the 1980s. However, although some improvement took place in the late 1980s, both its gross and net output per person is well behind the national average. This is probably because the Dublin area has a higher proportion of under-performing traditional manufacturing. It may also be the case that firms in Dublin have not participated to the same degree as firms elsewhere in employee training,

Table 3.5 Changing employment structure in the Dublin sub-region, 1951–81

Numbers employed in:	1981	1971	1951
Agriculture, forestry, fishing	3,427 (10.1)	4,584	7,445
Mining, quarrying, turf	923 (14.4)	767	530
Food manufacturing	12,785 (33.3)	13,379	13,823
Beverages	4,195 (17.3)	4,799	5,147
Tobacco	1,071 (40.1)	1,233	2,079
Textiles, shoes, clothing	10,433 (66.7)	18,805	17,566
Wood, wood products	3,238 (8.8)	3,661	3,634
Paper, print, publishing	11,743 (28.9)	11,792	9,410
Chemicals, rubber, plastics	6,276 (27.1)	7,625	4,229
Glass, pottery, cement	2,538 (10.6)	3,005	2,207
Metals, machinery	16,470 (22.3)	13,657	7,122
Other manufactures (incl. transport equipt)	7,087 (11.7)	11,320	11,052
Electricity, gas, water	5,613 (13.4)	6,045	5,282
Building, construction	30,963 (4.5)	25,928	24,740
Commerce – wholesale	24,644 (24.3)	19,099	16,387*
– retail	35,884 (39.8)	34,590	33,379
Insurance, finance, business services:			
– insurance	7,032 (42.0)	4,670	3,291
– banking	12,154 (54.7)	4,379	2,164
– other business services	4,963 (40.2)	3,937	1,967
Transport, communic., storage	32,397 (19.0)	28,911	23,861
Public admin., defence	31,904 (35.4)	41,199	19,142
Professional services (health, education)	61,624 (59.0)	41,199	29,907
Personal services	21,582 (61.0)	20,139	29,296
Other	10,702 (33.6)	6,072	9,380

* includes 'trading'; figures in parentheses refer to the female percentage of the labour force.

Source: Central Statistics Office, Census of population, various years.

technological development, rationalisation and marketing which are required to remain competitive. There is also the possibility that firms may have been less able to avail of incentives designed to enable manufacturing to survive and prosper.

In contrast to the fortunes of the industrial sector, Table 3.2 shows that employment in the services sector has increased substantially since the 1950s, the number of jobs growing by nearly 50 per cent between 1961 and 1981. There was substantial expansion among white-collar occupations, the number of office workers in the sub-region (Dublin County Borough, Dun Laoghaire Borough and County Dublin) increasing from fewer than 64,000 to nearly 85,000 between 1961 and 1971. In

The economy of Dublin

Table 3.6 Service sector employment changes, 1981–87

| | Percentage change, 1981–87 | |
	Dublin	Rest of Ireland
Transport, Communications, Storage	− 7.1	− 3.8
Commerce, Insurance, Finance, Business Services	− 9.7	+ 10.9
Public Administration, Defence	− 3.4	+ 5.3
Professional Services	+ 19.6	+ 17.3
Other Services	− 2.2	+ 21.2
Total Services Employment	**− 0.1**	**+ 11.8**

Source: Central Statistics Office, Census of Population 1981, Labour Force Survey, 1987.

central Dublin the rate of growth was even more rapid, from around 42,000 to over 72,000. Table 3.5 reveals that employment growth has been particularly strong in the 'insurance, banking and business services' categories, which grew by 85 per cent during the decade, expansion having been especially swift in the field of banking. Public sector employment in administration also expanded rapidly during the 1980s, from less than 12,000, little above what it had been in 1951, to nearly 20,000 in 1981.

Growth within the services sector faltered during the 1980s for a number of reasons – particularly the serious economic recession of the mid-1980s and cuts in public sector expenditure and recruitment. Employment in services grew by fewer than 9,000 between 1981 and 1989. Indeed, it actually declined slightly during the period 1981–87 at a time when service sector employment in regions outside Dublin experienced a net increase of 11.8 per cent. As a result, the city's share of national employment in the services sector declined slightly from 41.3 per cent in 1971 to 39.8 per cent in 1990.

Table 3.6 shows that the loss of employment in the services sector in Dublin was spread across all categories of employment with the exception of 'professional services', where an increase of almost 20 per cent was sufficient almost to balance the decline in the remainder. Areas outside Dublin fared better, except in the case of professional services. These trends were not assisted by a policy of enforced decentralisation of civil servants towards the regions. In 1991, it was even decided to move the Central Statistics Office to Cork, and by 1992 some 1,100 jobs had departed from Dublin with a further 2,000 projected to leave by 1994.

The consequence of declining employment opportunities in industry and, through much of the 1980s, employment stagnation in the services sector, meant that rising unemployment was the inevitable outcome. This

Table 3.7 Estimated number of persons at work, 1990

Numbers employed in:	Dublin	% of Ireland	East Region	Ireland
Agriculture, forestry, fishing	3,100	1.9	16,000	167,400
Building & construction	20,800	27.4	29,600	76,000
Other production industries	65,600	26.9	89,400	244,200
Commerce, insurance, finance, business services	85,500	38.1	106,300	224,600
Transport, communication, storage	32,200	47.6	37,700	67,700
Professional services	70,300	36.6	85,200	192,200
Public administration, defence	27,600	43.1	34,500	64,000
Other	38,300	42.6	46,200	89,900
Total	**343,400**		**444,900**	**1,126,000**

Source: Central Statistics Office, Labour Force Survey, 1990. 1990 survey based on a sample of 45,400 private households and an unspecified number of non-private households; East Region includes Dublin.

situation was exacerbated by the fact that Dublin's population continued to grow. Between 1981 and 1987, unemployment in the Dublin area more than doubled, from 36,500 to 82,000 (Dublin County Council Planning Department, 1988). By 1990, the rate of unemployment in Dublin was at a higher level than in any other region of the country except the remote north-west. Moreover, the number of unemployed in the city in that year almost matched the combined totals of the unemployed living in the south-west, west, mid-west and north-west regions of the country (Central Statistics Office, 1991).

In a number of districts, unemployment is very high. In the central area, industrial restructuring during the last 20 years has resulted in an unemployment rate of 35 per cent, while unemployment rates of 70 per cent are to be found in some peripheral housing estates and new towns where the growth of employment has fallen behind the expansion of the labour force. In such areas, the existence of chronic unemployment has led to the development of a general malaise and a growing acceptance of worklessness as a normal state. In turn, unemployment has often been displaced on the social agenda by more immediately pressing issues such as criminality, the poor provision of public services and inadequate housing maintenance.

Nevertheless, Table 3.7 shows that Dublin remains the hub of economic activity within the country: it is the administrative centre for national Government and most state-sponsored bodies; it is the largest industrial and commercial centre in the country; it accommodates the

Table 3.8 Measures of concentration in the East Region

Headquarters offices of:	Total number in the state	Percentage in East Region
Central Government Departments	17	100
Embassies accredited to Ireland	22	100
State-sponsored bodies	87	86
Commercial state bodies	20	90
Trade, professional and other organisations	503	93
Trade unions	65	93
Largest publicly quoted companies	50	90
Banking institutions	41	95
Hire purchase firms	41	71
Insurance companies	31	100
Publishing companies	47	89
Advertising agencies	36	97

Source: Bannon, 1984, 251.

headquarters of most Irish industrial companies and trade union organisations; and it is the location of Ireland's Central Bank, stock exchange and the head offices of most of the country's financial and insurance companies. Table 3.8 provides some indication of the dominance of the East Region planning zone in terms of decision making within the Irish economy.

In Dublin port and Dun Laoghaire harbour, the city possesses the most important port in the state, handling around 7 million tons of freight annually and accounting for 43 per cent of the Republic's entire trade (Kelleghan, 1991). There has been little change in the volume of goods handled since 1971: with growth apparent up until 1979, followed by decline during the 1980s and renewed growth thereafter (Steer Davies Gleave, 1992). There has been some change in the types of goods being handled, with a reduction in bulk cargoes and an expansion of load on/load off (LO-LO) and roll-on/roll-off (RO-RO) items. However, labour difficulties in the deep-sea section of the port have militated against expansion.

Dublin's airport possesses direct links with most major European destinations, though its links with North America currently exist only via Shannon airport, a compulsory and tedious interruption which remains a costly sop to the business and political lobby of the Limerick area. The airport's business has grown rapidly since 1986, when it catered for fewer than 3 million passengers. It handled over 5.5 million passengers in 1990 and numbers are projected to exceed 7 million by the end of the century.

Unsurprisingly, the city is a significant tourist destination, catering for over a million visitors annually of whom approximately 490,000 are holiday makers (Casey and O'Rourke, 1992). However, its attraction of North American tourists has undoubtedly been affected adversely by the absence of direct trans-Atlantic flights.

Economic outlook

International trends have a critical significance for Ireland, which is a small open economy. Although the recent recession in the UK has affected Ireland, trade diversification has reduced the impact of these negative trends. Of more serious import has been the recession in the United States, upon which Ireland relies heavily for multinational investment. Deepening integration within the EC has also limited the scope for governmental intervention. In particular, entry into the European Monetary System and the policy of making the Irish Punt track the international exchange movements of the Deutsche Mark have reduced the level of real control over Irish interest rates.

Between 1980–86, the performance of the Irish economy was poor. Recovery occurred during the late 1980s, and its recent performance has been impressive, with the GNP expanding by 7.5 per cent in 1990, spurred by export growth of 9 per cent. However, most of that growth took place in the early part of the year, and 1990 actually witnessed a deceleration of industrial expansion from 11.2 per cent to 5.4 per cent in volume terms compared to the previous year. In mid-1992, the Central Bank was predicting a growth of 2.5 per cent in the GNP for the year, up from 1.5 per cent in 1991.

Despite significant profit repatriation by multinationals and interest repayments on debt, Ireland's balance of payments was in surplus for the fifth year in succession, whereas during the early 1980s there had been major deficits. Inflation has remained at under 4 per cent since 1986, a rate which has compared very favourably with that of the UK. Furthermore, the level of government debt is now under much stricter control, though it still currently almost matches the GDP.

The main negative feature is the continuing high level of unemployment. At the end of a decade in which the total number of jobs nationally contracted by 25,000, unemployment stood at 291,000 in mid-1992, representing an unemployment rate of over 20 per cent excluding those engaged on social employment schemes and training projects. Unemployment rates among females and young workers are considerably higher. Net emigration of 30,000 to 40,000 persons annually during the late 1980s declined to barely 1,000 people during the year ending April 1991 and was followed by net immigration as Irish migrants were unable to find satisfactory employment overseas. In view of the age structure of the Irish population and the need annually to create 20–25,000 jobs just to maintain the current level of unemployment, the problem appears to be intractable. An additional concern for the future is that the construction of the Channel Tunnel will mean that Ireland will be the only state within the EC which lacks direct road and rail access to its markets.

Historically, Irish regional development initiatives have generally represented a reaction to the presence of depressed conditions in rural areas. Such policies were founded on the criterion of spatial equity and were pursued in the absence of strategic regional planning established within the context of coherent national economic development. Now, in an international economic environment of seemingly inexorable trends in capitalist organisation towards increasing centralisation and concentration, the challenges presented by the development of an integrated European market and its possible future enlargement appear formidable. As states, regions and municipalities world-wide embark on the increasingly competitive course of trying to induce international capital to invest in their jurisdictions, continued failure to construct a strategic regional development policy, grounded on an efficiency-based criterion involving a limited number of growth-poles, will mean that the Irish economy will be poorly placed to meet those demands in the future.

4
Politics and government

The Irish state

As in many countries which have achieved political independence during the twentieth century, the Irish State has played an important role in shaping the manner in which the economic system and the class structure of society have developed. The struggle for political independence from Britain brought about the replacement of a colonial capitalist state organisation by a state which was dedicated to principles of conservatism favouring the propertied, farming and business classes. Despite the civil war between the Free State government and those who rejected the political partition of Ireland, the decade which followed political independence in 1922 was characterised by stability and ideological continuity. Most civil servants working for the Free State had been inherited from the British administration and political power was consolidated within the hands of the representatives of the propertied classes, substantial proprietors in agriculture and commerce dominating the government. O'Higgins, Minister of Home Affairs in the first Independence government, boasted that 'we were probably the most conservative-minded revolutionaries that ever put through a successful revolution' (Laffan, 1985, 219). This ensured that the prevailing ideology of capitalist legitimacy was never challenged seriously. The 1920s, therefore, brought little amelioration to the poor social and physical conditions in which Dublin found itself.

Within Cosgrave's government, 'O'Higgins . . . Patrick Hogan (Minister for Agriculture) . . . and Ernest Blyth (Minister of Finance) . . . represented vigorous social reaction. All three came from comfortable rural backgrounds' (Lee, 1989, 97). This conservatism was also present among the senior ranks of the civil service. Brennan (Secretary to the Department of Finance) and McElligott, his Secretary, clung to existing economic orthodoxy and nurtured 'an aversion to the working class in general, and to organised labour in particular' (Lee, 1989, 108). Consequently, the policies of the new state concentrated on rigorous retrenchment.

Economic policy amounted to devotion to a policy of fiscal rectitude and favoured agricultural development through the maximising of farmers' profits. It was believed that rising rural incomes would generate demand for products and services, so stimulating economic growth. This required a policy of free trade to minimise the cost of farmers' purchases. However, the 1920s were years of stagnation in Irish agriculture. Naturally, there was little concern for the situation of agricultural labourers, whose wages fell by 10 per cent between 1922 and 1926, and by a further 10 per cent by 1931. To Hogan, the welfare of the 'agricultural community' was synonymous with the welfare of farmers with large land holdings:

> Attempts by agricultural labourers to acquire a stake in the country were brusquely rebuffed by both farmers and government. There were inevitable tensions between bigger and smaller farmers, but they shared an overriding interest in the security of property against the men of no property. (Lee, 1989, 72)

Despite rapidly rising emigration, unemployment increased during the early 1920s. The Department of Industry, which might have recognised the difficult situation in which the capital found itself, made little impression against entrenched economic and political interests. The British legacy of poverty and bad housing conditions was exacerbated by the class rule of the Irish middle class. The fleeting appearance of Irish Soviets in the early 1920s and the labour unrest of 1923 confirmed the business and rentier classes' fears of the lower orders. The propertied classes' bitter hatred of organised labour and of the lower classes in general became translated into the government's 'coherent campaign against the weaker elements in the community' (Lee, 1989, 124).

With the displacement in 1924 of McGrath as Minister in the Department of Industry, the Government lost the only economic minister with any serious level of sympathy for labour. The blame for unemployment was increasingly placed upon laziness and the restrictive practices of trade unions. McGrath's successor, Patrick McGilligan, the son of an Ulster businessman, claimed that it was no function of the government to provide work, a belief he held to the extent that people might even have to die of starvation. The poor were considered to be responsible for their own poverty and were therefore to be made to pay for their lack of moral fibre. They, together with the blind and the aged, were made to feel the lash from their native class oppressors, intent upon retrenchment in public expenditure. With so much vested economic and ideological interest at risk from any growth of radicalism, the Roman Catholic church threw its weight behind the new state.

In spite of the chronic housing shortage, only 14,000 dwellings were built in Ireland under public subsidy between 1922 and 1929 (Lee, 1989). By 1926, the Irish infant mortality rate was a staggering 120 per 1,000 live births, bearing witness to the poor state of the economy and the lack of government concern for the situation of its citizens. But by the late 1920s, working-class resistance had been crushed by growing unemployment.

However, following an appeal to the sectors of Irish society which had fared poorly during the Cumann na nGaedheal government, including small farmers, farm labourers, small businessmen and the urban working class, the election of 1932 brought de Valera to power with the support of Labour party representatives. Economic policy switched to one of autarky, national self-sufficiency through protectionism. According to de Valera, Ireland should become a place for those who were 'satisfied with frugal comfort and devoted their leisure to things of the spirit' (quoted in Breen et al., 1990, 31), the goal being the construction of an Irish identity based on native resources.

De Valera's constitution of 1937 represents the legal triumph of the Irish propertied classes, in which the socialist aspirations of 1916 were thoroughly to be swept aside. It was an 'amalgam of Catholic moral principles, nationalist aspirations, and American precedents' (Breen et al., 1990, 29). The rights of private property became enshrined in Articles 40.3.2. and 43, which are worthy of quotation in full as they expose the document's underlying ideology, demonstrating that law is a servant of economic power, protecting and legitimising the interests of those possessing power. Article 40.3.2. states that:

> The State shall, in particular, by its laws protect as best it may from unjust attack and, in the case of injustice done, vindicate the life, good name, and property rights of every citizen.

Article 43 further affirms the legitimacy of private property:

> 1.1. The State acknowledges that man, in virtue of his rational being, has the natural right, antecedent to positive law, to the private ownership of external goods.
> 1.2. The State accordingly guarantees to pass no law attempting to abolish the right of private property ownership or the general right to transfer, bequeath, and inherit property.
> 2.1. The State recognises, however, that the exercise of the rights mentioned in the foregoing provisions of this Article ought, in civil society, to be regulated by the principles of social justice.
> 2.2. The State, accordingly, may as occasion requires delimit by law the exercise of the said rights with a view to reconciling their exercise with the exigencies of the common good.

It was the Irish state which was responsible for generating the economic growth and industrialisation of the 1960s. It was inspired by a new generation of intellectuals, civil servants and politicians, who found de Valera's concept of an Ireland based on impoverished self-sufficiency seriously deficient. But the policy was also viewed as essential for national survival at a time when the economic situation was creating a political crisis and the IRA was renewing its activities (Wickham, 1980). The ensuing economic expansion brought about a growth in the Irish state machine, the establishment of a plethora of semi-state organisations and a burgeoning of public sector employment. Between 1960 and 1980, the central civil service doubled in size and by 1980 the total number employed in the public sector had grown to one-third of the workforce. Total public expenditure also doubled as a proportion of the GNP from 32 per cent to 64 per cent.

Such state-induced economic development resulted in the industrialisation of the Irish economy, but it also possessed significant ramifications for the class structure of Irish society. It resulted in the 'emergence of a class structure in which advantage was allocated increasingly on the basis of educational credentials and less through family property' (Breen et al., 1990, 5). However, 'the families that enjoyed privileged positions in the old class structure secured comparable positions in the new one while those families at the bottom of the old class hierarchy have, if anything, drifted downward into a new underclass dependent on state income maintenance for their livelihood' (Breen et al., 1990, 17).

Local government

The role of local government in Ireland is 'to provide various services and to regulate certain matters at local level and to represent and promote the interests of the local community' (Department of the Environment, 1991a, 9). The basis of the existing local authority framework is the Local Government Act of 1898, the last comprehensive reform of local government.

The system of local government in the Dublin metropolitan area is currently in a state of flux. It is still administered by three separate local authorities: Dublin County Borough, comprising the core of the metropolis, is administered by Dublin Corporation; Dublin County Council controls County Dublin; while Dun Laoghaire Corporation runs Dun Laoghaire Borough. However, because of the increasing amount of urban development in County Dublin and the limited degree of mutual interest between the northern, western and southern elements of that authority, this administrative structure has become increasingly inappropriate. Changes have been discussed spasmodically for decades, proposals

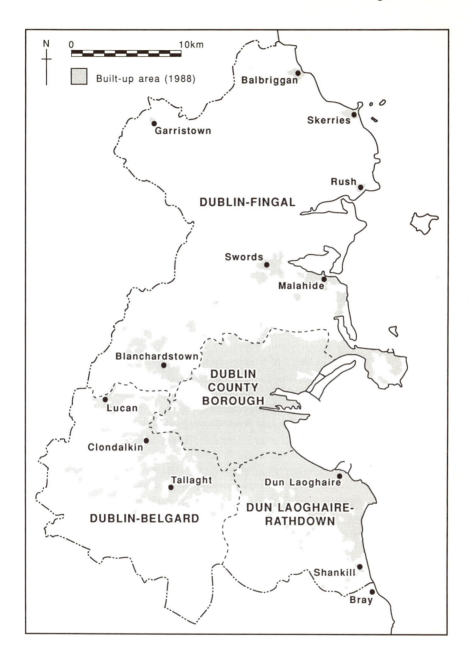

Figure 4.1 The future local authority administrative units in the Dublin sub-region.

including the establishment of a Greater Dublin Council and the creation of a metropolitan authority plus local district councils. The system which was eventually adopted in the Local Government Reorganisation Act of 1985, however, merely involved slightly extending the boundaries of the County Borough and re-constituting County Dublin and Dun Laoghaire Borough to create three new counties. The new areas are mapped in Figure 4.1. Dun Laoghaire-Rathdown comprises a geographical enlargement of Dun Laoghaire Borough. Dublin-Belgard, which lies to the south and west of the County Borough, includes the new towns of Tallaght and Lucan-Clondalkin. The final area, Dublin Fingal, comprises the new town of Blanchardstown to the north-west of the County Borough and stretches north-eastwards to Malahide and Balbriggan to take in a large area of rural County Dublin. It is the intention also to establish a Metropolitan Council, comprising nominees of the four new local authorities, which will have a co-ordinating role for the entire area, and District Councils are to be formed at the scale of the local community.

One might well wonder upon what criteria the reorganisation has been based. While it might be desirable for the purposes of co-ordination that a metropolitan authority be constituted and that local councils be established as a means of enhancing local participation, it is regrettable that the operative administrative arrangements will be based on middle-level authorities which are probably the least desirable or justifiable. However, it is these which have become firmly entrenched. The local government elections of 1991 were fought on the basis of the new areas and three area-committees have been constituted in County Dublin. In addition, the three new area managers have been appointed and charged with establishing an agenda for progress towards administrative reconstruction. However, to date, the local authority departments of Dun Laoghaire and Dublin County Council continue to function as before.

The system of local government which is currently in existence and even that which is in process of being established fail to recognise Dublin's new towns as separate entities. Tallaght, with a population of over 70,000 is the third largest urban area in the Republic, yet it lacks any separate urban administration. It also leads to some absurd situations. The fact that County Dublin is still classified as a rural district means that no new public houses can be created within a mile of an existing licensee. Clearly, this has benefited existing licensees, and public houses with a seating capacity for as many as 2,000 people are described by McDonald (1989, 75) as possessing 'all the ambience of an alcoholic hypermarket'.

Ireland remains a country in which the decentralisation of policy-making is poorly developed. Municipal government amounts to little more than local management. Indeed, central government disaffection with local government in Dublin is such that recent major state initiatives affecting the city are being carried out by independent agencies in order to avoid bureaucratic inertia. The main functions of local government in Ireland are limited in comparison with other European countries. They are narrowly prescribed and relate to: the fields of planning; the acquisition and development of land; the provision of housing, roads, water supply and sewerage; environmental protection; recreation and amenity; and certain aspects of education and welfare (Department of the Environment, 1991a). The more significant of these will now be examined briefly, in so far as they are pertinent to the work of the authorities in Dublin.

Housing and building

Local authorities have the power to provide, manage, maintain and improve local authority housing. They are also charged with the obligation to provide halting sites for travelling people, and to assess housing need. They can provide sites, grants, loans and subsidies to people who are housing themselves or improving their housing, give assistance to the voluntary and co-operative housing sectors, and help to secure accommodation for the homeless. Local authorities also operate mortgage schemes for tenant-purchasers and are responsible for the enforcement of standards in privately rented accommodation. Although these appear to be widely ranging housing functions, the extent to which local authorities are actually able to operate is determined through the Departments of the Environment and Finance which control available funding.

Roads, transportation and safety

The maintenance and improvement of the road network is the responsibility of local authorities, as is the task of traffic management, the employment of parking wardens, the registration of vehicles, the licensing of drivers and road safety education.

Development incentives and controls

Potentially the most significant power vested in the local authority is its planning function. This includes the requirement to devise a Development Plan, to engage in planning control through the granting of planning permissions and to ensure compliance with by-laws. They are also empowered to acquire land and develop it. In addition, the authorities may provide and manage industrial sites, and promote urban renewal by facilitating private sector development and by infrastructural and environmental improvements.

Water supply, sewerage and environmental protection

The provision, operation and maintenance of public water supplies and sewerage schemes is a function of local government, while the control of litter, air and water pollution also lies with local authorities, as do fire protection and fire-fighting, the promotion of civil defence and ensuring the safety of buildings.

Recreation and amenity

Irish local authorities are permitted to develop and run a number of recreational resources, including public libraries, galleries, museums and theatres, swimming pools, recreation centres and parks. Following recent legislation, they are also charged with the prevention and elimination of derelict sites.

Education and welfare

Local authorities play a limited role in the field of education. They make financial contributions to the local Vocational Education Committees, administer grants schemes for higher education, and contribute to residential homes and special schools.

Significant functions which are absent from the above list but which are found typically in many European cities include tourism development, security and the police services, education, health and welfare services. In Ireland, these functions are the responsibilities of a number of other agencies, including semi-state organisations like Bord Failte (the Tourist Board), local Vocational Education Committees, the Higher Education Authority, Regional Health Boards or Government Departments such as the Departments of Justice and Education.

Financing local government

The current arrangements for financing local authorities have been described as owing a great deal to expediency but little to reason (Foster et al., 1985). Until 1978, local authorities in Ireland were largely financed by income from rates. In that year, domestic dwellings were de-rated, and the loss of income to local authorities was made good by direct subvention from the central exchequer. This resulted in local authorities' becoming securely controlled by central government, especially as the Minister is empowered to limit the scale of rates increases on non-residential properties and permitted increases have commonly fallen short of the rate of general price inflation. Almost inevitably during a decade of severe pressure on the public finances, financial stringency resulted in central exchequer subventions also falling behind the rate of inflation. Local authorities have therefore seen their spending powers severely squeezed and have been obliged to raise an increasing proportion of their income from property rents, tolls and service charges. Many councils, such as Dublin Corporation, have baulked at imposing service charges for the provision of water or refuse collection, asserting that these services have been paid for through direct taxation by central government and that additional charges would repre-sent double taxation. Nevertheless, by 1988, such charges comprised 37 per cent of the total income of Irish local government, whereas in 1977 they had accounted for 20 per cent of receipts.

Irish local authorities are empowered to borrow money from the state Housing Finance Agency, from its bankers or from other lending institu-tions. However, this requires the sanction of the Minister for the Environment. Larger capital projects which need long-term funding tend to be financed from grants from central Government, whereas smaller projects are often funded by short-term borrowing from financial institu-tions.

It can be argued that the Irish system of funding local authorities has resulted in their being transformed from local governments into mere local administrations, functioning as central government agencies. It is a system which stands in sharp contrast to numerous European cities, where the delivery of as many services as possible is placed within the remit of local communities and funded locally.

The administrative structure

The administrative arrangements for local government in Ireland are based on the twin elements of the elected members and a chief executive – known as the manager – who is a professional administrator. In Dublin, these arrangements date from the Local Government (Dublin) Act, 1930. The county manager is an officer of the county council, appointed by the members on the recommendation of the Local Appoint-ments Commissioners and, in addition to these duties, is also manager for each of the boroughs and urban district councils within the county area. In Dublin, there is a single city and county manager who delegates functions to five assistant city and county managers (County Management Act, 1940; City and County Management (Amendment) Act, 1955).

The administrative arrangements which existed prior to 1955 accorded considerable power to the manager to make decisions without reference to the council, but the City and County Managers (Amendment) Act, 1955, attempted to achieve greater balance between the elected members and the executive, the intention being that the manager should provide a vehicle for the efficient discharge of normal functions, within a policy framework established by the elected representatives. Certain functions of the local authority became reserved functions of the elected members. Members are elected by proportional representation (single transferable vote) in multi-seat constituencies by secret ballot of adult residents aged over 18 years. From among the elected members, the councillors then elect a chairperson or, in the case of Dublin Corporation, a lord mayor. The reserved functions of the elected members include those matters which relate to the adoption of annual estimates of expenditure, determining the level of rates, borrowing money, adopting and varying development plans, adopting priority schemes for letting local authority dwellings, demanding expenses from other local authorities, making, amending and revoking by-laws, bringing enactments into force in the functional area of the local authority, and nominating persons to act on committees or other public bodies (Department of the Environment, 1991a). They are also empowered to revoke or modify a permission to develop land, and can require the manager to grant planning permission which would result in a material contravention of the development plan.

Executive functions include the discharge of all functions which are not reserved for the elected members. These relate to staffing, the control of tenders and contracts, determining and collecting rents, the collection of rates, the management of local authority property, the letting of local authority dwellings, the allocation of housing loans and grants and decisions on planning applications. The manager may also attend meetings of the Council or Corporation and can take part in discussions, but lacks voting rights.

This arrangement for the division of authority between the elected members and the executive is rendered even more complex by the fact that in conducting these functions, the manager is assisted by professional staff within the relevant departments (planning, housing, finance, roads etc.). In the case of planning, planners formulate policies, councillors are responsible for their adoption, and the manager administers them. Development applications are therefore set before the manager with a recommendation from the professional planning staff. However, it is the manager who is charged with the responsibility of granting or refusing planning permission.

When viewed from the standpoint of individual functions, the separation of local authority roles into independent departments may be justifiable in so far as it may improve the cost efficiency of service delivery. However, when the operation of the local authority system is viewed as a totality, the relative autonomy of departmental empires is likely to render co-operation difficult. Nowhere is this more apparent than in the case of land-use and transportation planning (see Chapter 6) and in the fact that planning and development exist within Dublin Corporation as two separate local authority departments. It is an administrative arrangement which has been justifiably described as a 'tangled maze of bureaucratic undergrowth' (Roche, 1982, 213).

Political parties and local politics

Politics in the Republic of Ireland is dominated by three conservative parties. Some would say four conservative parties, to include the Labour Party, because its policies neither promote nor foresee the transcendence of the capitalist system. Fianna Fail and Fine Gael grew respectively out of the anti-Treaty and pro-Treaty forces of 1922. Fine Gael generally adopts a more liberal stance on social issues than does Fianna Fail, but its economic policies differ only in detail from those of its larger rival. During the 1980s, a small group broke from Fianna Fail over the Northern Ireland issue (specifically the Anglo-Irish agreement) to form the Progressive Democrats (PDs). While its economic policies are further to the 'right' than those of either Fianna Fail or Fine Gael, its stance on social issues tends to be more 'liberal' and its policy towards the Northern Ireland Unionists is one of rapprochement. It subsequently joined Fianna Fail in a somewhat uneasy coalition Government in 1988.

The Labour Party in Ireland is the third largest in terms of seats in the Dail (the directly elected chamber); like its cousin in the UK, it is a trades' union party by origin. In the past two decades it has joined with Fine Gael in national government on one occasion in the 1970s and twice during the 1980s. The Workers' Party had a larger representation in the Dail than the PDs. In origin, it was the political expression of the paramilitary Official Irish Republican Army and possessed a Marxist orientation, but internal division between the Marxists and those with social-democratic leanings led, in 1992, to its Dail members' leaving the organisation and establishing a new party, Democratic Left. A single member registers a Dail presence for the Green Party, in some ways the most radical party in the state. Sinn Fein, a nationalist republican party usually regarded as the political wing of the paramilitary Provisional Irish Republican Army (IRA), has no Dail representation, but does have local government presence. At elections for local government, these political

Politics and government

Table 4.1 Political composition of local government in Dublin, 1991

	FF	FG	Lab	PD	WP	Green	SF	Other	Total
Dublin County Borough	20	6	10	1	5	4	1	5	52
Dublin Fingal	8	6	5	1	–	2	–	2	24
South Dublin	7	6	4	4	3	1	–	1	26
Dun Laoghaire-Rathdown	8	7	5	2	3	3	–	–	28

parties are joined by a number of independent candidates.

Table 4.1 presents the results of the 1991 local elections in Dublin, which resulted in the breaking of Fianna Fail's control over Dublin County Council, attributed in major part to the role which Fianna Fail councillors had played in the re-zoning of green-belt areas of County Dublin. The major beneficiary was the Labour Party, but the election of a significant core of Green Party councillors signalled an important change in the mood of the Dublin electorate.

In the County Borough, the election was immediately followed by the informal establishment of a 'rainbow coalition' forged around a Civic Charter comprising a 15-point programme setting out a conservation-minded agenda to be followed during the five-year term of office. In particular, the election brought about a City Council whose composition no longer had a majority in favour of the destructive road improvements plans being pursued in the city. However, there remains some doubt as to whether the implementation of the Charter will take place given the lack of Fianna Fail contribution to its formulation and the dependency of local authorities on the Fianna Fail-controlled central exchequer and Department of the Environment. The possibility that local authority officers might manage to thwart the intentions of elected members is also a cause for some concern. It is often said that people get the politicians they deserve. If that is so, then perhaps Dublin has at last elected councillors who will try to do them justice. Perhaps it is too much to hope that a similar sea-change will overcome the municipal bureaucracy.

5
Planning the city

In formal terms, urban planning in Dublin is amongst the most democratic of systems to be found anywhere. Indeed, it would be difficult to envisage a more worthy legislative attempt to secure democratic participation. In practice, however, the goal of public access has not been achieved. The urban planning system generally lacks any positive powers to promote required developments, it is almost wholly divorced from regional and economic planning, and has tended to deal with transport planning as an altogether separate issue. Moreover, its scope is limited by the structural role of planning in capitalist society and, in particular, by the rights of private property which are enshrined in the Irish constitution. It is also a system which is open to major abuse and has been characterised historically by a singular lack of public participation in decision making and plan formulation.

From its origins, bursting with high ideals and enthusiasm, the planning system has been turned into a mere bureaucratic procedure which is held in disregard by developers and community groups alike. To the former it represents a costly and unnecessary bureaucratic obstacle which has to be overcome, while community groups regard it as difficult to penetrate and unresponsive to local needs (McGuirk, 1991). Moreover, its inability to tackle the city's major problems in a serious way has been recognised by the national government in its imposition of a special authority to deal with the regeneration of the Custom House Docks, an area of Dublin's docklands neighbouring the central business area.

In order to understand the manner in which urban planning has evolved in Ireland, it is necessary to recognise the inherent favouring by the state of private property rights. The close association between one of the major political parties and the construction/property development sector has further ensured the absence of any serious attempt to socialise the returns from development. Moreover, the passage of amending legislation to close loopholes in the system has been mysteriously low on the political agenda. Yet simultaneously, for the sake of legitimacy, the state has tried to ensure that planning possesses at least an appearance of being open to public participation. In reality, this tends to be a very superficial veneer.

Conceptions of the state and of the role of planning

The role of the state in capitalist societies is subject to a number of interpretations: pluralist, managerialist, reformist and Marxist. The pluralist thesis maintains that society comprises a number of interest groups which vie with one another for influence over government policy, but because power is distributed in a diffused manner, no single group is able to dominate. The prime function of the state is to achieve consensus. Thus, the state is conceived of as operating to effect social stability, maintaining a rough balance of power by accommodating its actions to the variety of competing interests, acting as an arbiter and supervising and regulating these interests to ensure that none maintains mastery. Influence is unidirectional, state policy being wholly determined by the relative strengths of competing groups. While the pluralist thesis acknowledges that conflicts exist within society, it holds that these can be accommodated within the contemporary societal structure. It emphasises the ability of people to organise around issues which concern them – that interest groups each have adequate power and access to enable their demands to be voiced – and it assumes that bureaucrats are receptive to such appeals. It is an inherently conservative conception which views state policy as the 'fair' and 'balanced' outcome of competition between different groups, verging on a market theory of political activity (Broadbent, 1977). It has been subjected to serious criticism, citing the evident inequalities in resources between interest groups in terms of their economic power and available organisational skills. It also fails to take account of the 'second face of power', the ability to limit the scope of the political process to the consideration of things which are generally innocuous and which offer no threat to the bases of economic power.

It is the power of public bureaucracy, however, which is stressed under the managerialist interpretation of the state. Here, the complex structure of the state is cited as making it difficult to penetrate and largely impervious to influence by citizens, while elected members become dominated by bureaucratic rules and are rendered insensitive to community needs by coming to rely on the expertise of the managers. The bureaucracy, including the planners, operates in a managerial capacity, controlling resource allocation, thereby acting as social 'gatekeepers'. While central and local state bureaucracies may indeed be impenetrable, the approach is theoretically weak in that it fails to recognise the limitations on state activity, both centrally and locally, which are imposed by capital itself. Thus, like pluralism, it conceptualises the political realm in isolation from economic structures.

Reformist conceptions of the state emphasise the inevitability of inequality in capitalist society, viewing the state as a fundamentally benign institution which maintains the viability of the economic system but which also ameliorates some of its most undesirable effects through its welfare policies. Planning becomes a means of securing community benefit from development in return for favourable planning permissions.

In contrast, the Marxist conceptualisation of the state regards it as an institution which emerged historically to assuage inflammatory conflicting elements which were inherent in society. Like all social phenomena, its specific form and social role is rooted in the mode of production. The constant conflict between the interests of capital and labour over the division of social product threatens the basic social (including property) relations of the capitalist mode of production. Capitalist society is thus unable spontaneously to ensure the successful reproduction of conditions for its own existence. The state therefore acts primarily to assuage the conflict between capital and labour, to mediate class conflict, to legitimate capitalist society and property relations and guarantee the relations of production. This is effected through ideological or educational programmes, through the legal system and through the state's monopoly of legitimate violence. The role of the state is conceptualised as supporting the continued dominance of capital, which itself is ultimately a social relationship grounded in the concept of private ownership, engaging in policies to encourage assent to the continuation of this dominance. Thus, not only do people believe that capitalism is the best system possible, but it is conceived of as being the *only* viable system.

To perform this role, the state appears to act as an interest which is detached from any specific interest, as being neutral between the partisan groups. When the survival of the system itself becomes threatened, the state adopts policies to ensure its continuation. It employs integrationist ideologies such as the 'nation state' or 'national interest', and may even act directly against the interests of some fractions of capital in order to ensure the survival of the system. Thus, the relationship between the individual and the state seems wholly different to, and separate from, that between the individual and capital (see Holloway and Picciotto, 1978).

The state has also taken on other functions of mediating in the process of capital accumulation, a process which is ridden with crises (see

Harvey, 1982). It therefore attempts to regulate aspects of the economy: it provides cheap utilities which are necessary to the operation of the whole system but are beyond the logic of individual capitalists to produce; and it acts as a major purchaser of products from the private sector. It also engages in social reproduction, helping to ensure the continuity of the system by contributing to the creation of appropriate labour which is healthy, stands in an appropriate relationship of dependency with regard to capital, and possesses the necessary skills for capitalist exploitation. Thus, it engages in housing programmes and provides health services, education and skills training.

Clearly, to Marxists, the state is far from being a benign institution. While it recognises that marginal redistributions are possible, fundamental qualitative change in the relations of production are beyond potential state action because of the structural constraints which are placed upon the state's role *within* capitalism. Indeed, 'demands on the state reformism' has inherent dangers of co-option of protest, reducing it to a clientist position and redirecting conflict towards the state rather than against capital.

The inherent contradictions and dislocations which are present within the capitalist economic system become reflected in the built environment. In order to minimise the consequences, planning becomes a means by which the local state attempts to regulate urban land-use, development and redevelopment, and planners thereby take on the role of state agents, ultimately serving capitalist interests. Thus, urban planning facilitates capitalism in general through attempting to create a landscape of enhanced economic efficiency.

Knox and Cullen (1981, 184) have suggested that 'planning . . . was born a hybrid creature, dedicated on the one hand to humanistic reform, but charged on the other with the management of urban land and services according to the imperatives of a particular mode of production', interpreting it as an 'internal survival mechanism' of the capitalist economy, now institutionalised and directed by the logic of the capitalist system. This is reiterated by McGuirk (1991, 95) who states that 'as a result of the imperatives to which they must accord, planners are prisoners of capitalism', lending support to Scott and Roweis (1977, 1106) who affirm that as the structural causes of problems cannot be addressed, planning is a 'never-ending round of palliative and piecemeal measures'.

The results of planners' actions are implicitly political, inherently favouring particular interests, notably property and business interests, over others. Zoning provides a useful framework within which the development industry can operate, reducing the risk to property investments of undesirable spillover effects (negative externalities) caused by neighbouring incompatible land uses (e.g., a slaughterhouse opening next to a luxury hotel). Moreover, the very practice of planning is diversionary and mystifies the causes of urban problems by pretending that solutions are to be found in the remedies which the planners propose (Castells, 1976). It is a structural position which belies Irish planners' naïve pluralistic interpretation of their role as guardians of the environment and defenders of a non-existent 'public interest' (McGuirk, 1991).

The elements of planning

As an important aspect of local state activity, representing an intervention in the manner in which land is used and developed, planning therefore has numerous interpretations. These interpretations depend fundamentally upon the view which one takes of the role of the state in capitalism; whether it be viewed as fundamentally neutral with regard to sectional or class interests, or consistently biased in favour of some rather than others. The conception of the role of the state in capitalist society will inevitably determine one's understanding of the role of planners themselves, either as technical operatives implementing democratic decisions, as managers and bureaucrats with ideals and goals of their own making, as social reformers effecting marginal redistributions in favour of the less well off, or as functionaries of the local state whose actions favour dominant classes or interests, giving legitimation to outcomes which are intensely unequal (see Kirk, 1980; Knox, 1982; McGuirk, 1991).

Planners often possess an implicit belief in a co-operative model of society: that society comprises groups with shared beliefs, values and aspirations, and that co-operation to the mutual advantage of all is normal. One frequently encounters planning policies which aim at facilitating the development of 'socially balanced and integrated communities' in order to maximise 'economic and social efficiency'. Planning literature and planners' documents are replete with phrases such as 'orderly development', 'proper planning', 'the common good' and 'public interest', without these ever being satisfactorily specified. There is a failure to recognise that such beliefs implicitly discriminate in favour of certain interests and that they are based on the belief that what is good for capitalism is good for all (Kirk, 1980).

However, if society is normally characterised by conflict between groups which do not share the same values and aspirations, and which are identifiable by their different resources, power and status, planning takes on an entirely different significance. Instead of its simply being a question of how generally agreed objectives are to be achieved, planning becomes a matter of why certain objectives should be pursued rather than others. Thus, as planning acts as a distributor of real well-being it becomes imbued with political significance. Rather than being technical, neutral problem-solvers acting in the 'public interest', characterised by rationality and political neutrality, in so far as they accept one ideology instead of another, planners represent certain social groups and classes rather than others. In Ireland, this appears to be almost entirely unrecognised by the planners themselves (McGuirk, 1991).

The structural role of planning must be understood within the context of the functions of the state under capitalism. As Sutcliffe (1981) points out, 'the synchronisation and general similarities of the world-wide planning movement are such as to suggest that town planning had a particular role to play in capitalist societies at a certain stage in their industrial development'. Major problems were being created by the anarchic quality of unfettered capitalist development. The built environment began to manifest the inherent contradictions of capitalist society which were generated by the production process (Beauregard, 1989; Scott and Roweis, 1977). As Gregory (1978, 120) affirms:

> the analysis of spatial structure is not a derivative and secondary to the analysis of social structure. . . . Spatial structure is not, therefore, merely the arena in which class conflicts express themselves, but also the domain within which and, in part, through which class relations are constituted.

Planning therefore emerged as a consequence of the need to provide some collective mechanism to help to control and guide urban land markets towards orderly and efficient development.

The historical emergence of town planning out of the coalition of nineteenth century interests which included the sanitary reformers, the philanthropic housing movement, the garden city movement, urban architectural conservationists and countryside preservationists, has conferred upon urban planning a vast ideological inheritance. Knox (1982) has identified five important aspects of planning practice which result from this inheritance. Each is present in contemporary Irish urban planning:

1. **Environmentalism**. The idea that it is possible to improve the physical, moral and social welfare of people by up-grading their physical environment has led to planners' concern for prescribing standards and formulae for achieving environmental and building quality.
2. **Aesthetics**. Planners' concern for the creation of visual order, harmony, scale and townscape can be traced to the civic design or architectural influence on modern planning and can be seen in the control over building height, design and alignment.
3. **Spatial Determinism**. The concern for separating urban functions through the practice of zoning, in order to eliminate incompatible

land-uses, derives from the spatially deterministic assumption that spatial order brings social and economic benefits. Similar assumptions underly the concept of the 'neighbourhood unit', which promotes the idea that careful layout of residential areas would lead to social interaction, the development of 'community' and stimulate feelings of security and stability. Yet the clear ideological significance of such goals is rarely recognised within the profession.

4. **Systems Approaches**. In attempting to introduce techniques such as operational research, systems analysis and cybernetics in the monitoring and modelling of the urban environment, planning is presented as a technical process. However, while the mathematics of modelling may be entirely correct, the assumptions upon which such models are based and the criteria for evaluation of alternative options depend on goals which are inherently political.

5. **Futurism**. Planning has long been imbued with a large dose of futuristic idealism. But the vision of the 'ideal' tends to be based on a particular culture from which the planning profession draws its functionaries, that of the middle class. It is a vision which assumes that a middle-class lifestyle is aspired to and is attainable by all.

The genesis of urban planning in Dublin

If one were to define the activity of urban planning as the administrative control over the character of development, one can trace the genesis of urban planning in Dublin back to the seventeenth century when the Duke of Ormonde, the Lord Lieutenant of Ireland, insisted that the properties which were then being developed on the northern bank of the river Liffey should face onto and be set back from the river instead of permitting their back-lands to run down to the quays (see Chapter 2). The effect of this stipulation was eventually to endow the city with its precious heritage of eighteenth and nineteenth century quay-side buildings facing one another across the river, 'grand, yet human in scale, varied yet orderly' (Wright et al., 1974, 271). Indeed, aesthetics has continued to remain a major element of urban planning in the city.

The Wide Streets Commissioners were also a significant influence on the way in which the city evolved. Although aesthetics played an important role in the projects which the Commissioners undertook, the establishment of the Commission resulted from the growth of traffic congestion in the vicinity of Essex Bridge and the need to create 'wide and convenient streets' through the congested quarters of the old city (Gough, 1991). Clearly, as early as the mid-eighteenth century, it had been recognised by the Irish parliament that to ensure that the urban arena could function in an efficient manner would require public intervention to ensure some degree of control over private property rights and the market forces which dominated development.

During the latter part of the nineteenth century, the practice of urban planning became embodied in two elements. The first was the increasing role of legislation which attempted, through a series of Public Health and Housing Acts, to secure better sanitation and living conditions for the labouring classes. This legislative approach was paralleled by the practical work of philanthropic organisations and the local authorities in slum clearance projects and the provision of dwellings for the labouring classes. In both respects, the character of urban planning mirrored the evolving trends in the control and improvement of urban conditions in England. Legislation was enacted to control nuisance and limit the effects of negative externalities, while physical endeavours were carried out often as a demonstration for other landlords of what could be achieved by private initiatives.

The similarities in the evolution of town planning practice in Dublin and in British cities remained true to a certain degree during the early decades of the twentieth century. Despite a prevailing view that they were of little relevance to the solution of Dublin's acute housing problems, some of the ideas embodied in the British town planning and Garden City movements slowly became influential in the city. Geddes initiated and led a movement for environmental reform in Dublin, while Unwin and W.H. Lever delivered lectures on town planning issues (Aalen, 1985). Their influence was embodied in the plans for a low density garden village at Marino, developed by the Corporation during the 1920s. The ideological and political consequences of improving conditions of accommodation were certainly not unrecognised at the time. As was noted in the British context by Jeffries (1918, 10), 'every garden suburb that comes into existence is a "pill-box" in the path of anarchy'.

Modern town planning in Dublin can be traced to a planning competition which, at the behest of Geddes, was initiated by the Lord Lieutenant and held in connection with the Civic Exhibition of 1914 (O'Brien, 1950). The winner was Patrick Abercrombie (with Sydney and Arthur Kelly), whose proposals were greatly influenced by the Ecole des Beaux Arts and involved such re-organisation of the city centre that its practical consequences there were very limited. However, the concept of moving the overcrowded urban population into low density suburban cottage estates at Crumlin, Cabra and Drumcondra had much greater long-term significance.

Almost all matters of urban land-use planning are the responsibility of the Irish local authorities. Although the Town and Regional Planning Act (1934), modelled on British legislation, had enabled local authorities to draw up a Planning Scheme for their area, it had not required them to do so. However, once devised, a plan had the force of law. The onus lay with developers to comply with the plan and local authorities were empowered to take legal and physical action to ensure compliance (Nowlan, 1989). There was provision for the payment of compensation and, where the value of property was enhanced by the operation or enforcement of any provision contained in a planning scheme, for betterment to be charged at a rate of 75 per cent of the increase in value. The Act also proposed the linkage of planning districts (boroughs and counties) to form planning regions, though it failed to formulate any operational procedures for dealing with disputes between contiguous authorities.

The Act was not well received by local authorities and was adopted only slowly. Business interests and property owners alike rejected it as an unwarranted inteference with private property rights. The betterment payment system remained untested, partly as a consequence of the fact that only one Planning Scheme, for Dublin City, was adopted and even there the betterment provisions were ignored (Nowlan, 1989). There existed neither pressure nor political will to implement the Act's provisions during the 1930s which were characterised by the 'economic war' with Britain, limited development pressure resulting from a depressed economy, declining population levels and high emigration. Moreover, the possibility of having to pay for compensation claims brought by property owners who were adversely affected by a Planning Scheme was further encouragement to do nothing. As Bannon comments:

> The inter-war period provided a hostile and difficult environment for planning. The domestic problems of the new state, the country's isolation, its rural dominance and the slow pace of industrialisation all contributed to a lack of momentum in most areas of public policy, including planning. (Bannon, 1989a, 69)

By 1941, a new sketch plan had been prepared for Dublin Corporation (Abercrombie et al., 1941). It supported the idea of increased residential land-use in the central area and policies to encourage a greater middle-class presence there. It also proposed the establishment of a green belt approximately 8 km. (5 miles) in extent, within which limited residential expansion would be permitted adjacent to existing villages. These would then function as satellite townships. However, in plans prepared by the City Engineer and Town Planning Officer during the 1940s, the concept of the satellite townships had already been abandoned in favour of fringe development because of the cost of developing transportation infrastructures to service the satellites.

Only Dublin Corporation eventually devised a full Planning Scheme. Following legal wranglings with developers over the Coporation's failure to adopt a plan 'with all convenient speed' as was required, and the threatened imprisonment of the Lord Mayor, Aldermen and Burgesses,

Dublin's Planning Scheme was drafted in 1957 and adopted by the City Council (Nowlan, 1989). It generated some 3,600 objections, mainly as a result of road widening proposals, a precursor of later conflicts over transportation issues.

By the early 1960s, the existing urban planning system was increasingly regarded as unworkable and even detrimental to development. Yet Ireland's changing socio-economic conditions, particularly the growth of development pressures resulting from industrialisation, rapid urbanisation and population expansion, were making an effective planning system essential. Advice was sought from the United Nations, consultants were appointed, and their report advocated 'an unashamedly expansionist role for planning in accommodating the needs of both industry and business' (Bannon, 1989b, 129). The recommendations were well received by a government which was intent on encouraging economic growth and were embodied in the Local Government (Planning and Development) Act of 1963. This Act repealed the earlier Town and Regional Planning Acts and, together with its amending legislation, forms the foundation for modern urban planning in Ireland.

The contemporary urban planning system

The basis of contemporary Irish urban planning lies in land-use zoning and development control. The 1963 Act confirmed the 87 local authorities as the appropriate planning bodies in the country. It imposed a duty upon every town and county council to adopt a development plan for its area. It granted powers of land assembly to the planning authorities and the duty to pay compensation.

Development plans comprise written statements and maps, covering such planning issues as the zoning of land-uses, traffic, areas of obsolescence and renewal, and the preservation and enhancement of amenities. The original emphasis of the Act was towards the active involvement of local authorities in development activities. In Section 77 of the Act, the authorities were empowered to develop or secure land for development, thereby permitting them to become involved in development and dealing in land. Indeed, the essentially negative or permissory functions of contemporary Irish urban planning practice stand in sharp contrast to the active role which was envisaged for it in the legislation, but the absence of financial facilities to undertake such activities, which ran the risk of impinging on private sector profitability, ensured that such powers could not be operated in a serious manner.

There was also provision in the Act for direct public participation. The Development Plan, which is devised by local authority planning departments, is presented to the elected members who comment on it and may make variations prior to adopting it in draft form. It is then placed on public display for a period not less than three months, during which time objections, comments and representations are invited. In addition, certain bodies, such as An Taisce (The National Trust) and Bord Failte (the Tourist Board), are consulted as of right in order to elicit their comments, and the plan is circulated to adjacent local authorities and the Minister for the Environment. All comments are reviewed by the planners and, where necessary, amendments are made to the plan. These amendments are again exhibited for public display and comments are requested. It is the elected members of the local authority who are ultimately responsible for the Development Plan's adoption, the Minister's having power only to ensure that the plans of adjacent authorities do not conflict on major matters.

It was intended that development plans would be subject to review every five years, but in practice the process of adoption and review has proved cumbersome and taken far longer. Dublin Corporation's first draft development plan, which was published in 1967, generated some 7,000 objections and was adopted only in 1971. The first review was put on public display in 1976 and adopted in 1980, while the second review, which was published in 1987, elicited some 15,213 submissions and comments. This led to around 1,200 changes being made. The plan was re-published in 1990, placed on display in early 1991 and adopted by the councillors of Dublin Corporation in December 1991. The plans for County Dublin have proved even longer in their gestation and refinement. The first plan was adopted in 1972. The first review commenced in 1979 and was adopted in 1983, while the second draft review was published and placed on display only in 1991.

Private sector developers are obliged to obtain planning permisssion for any proposed development, while the local authority Planning Department ensures that the proposals conform with the development plan. 'Developments' include not only new constructions, but building extensions above a certain size as well as changes to the functional use of buildings or land (excluding farmland). In addition to ensuring compliance with designated land-use zoning for the area, planners control the scale of the development scheme by regulating plot density and building height, and also examine all aspects of the external architectural character of the scheme. Until June 1982, the prerequisite of obtaining by-law approval for the building's plans ensured that structural and internal design aspects met local authority approval. Since that date, an essentially self-regulatory system of building codes has operated. The requirements of the roads engineers, however, regarding carriageway width often result in residential neighbourhoods which seem to have been created for cars rather than for people (Figure 5.1).

The procedures of development control appear to represent an arduous

Figure 5.1 Regulations established by roads engineers ensure that residential areas cater for cars rather than people.

barrier to development. Indeed, developers frequently point to the lengthy delays which can be occasioned by the process. Planners' requests for further information and their requirements for modification of applications can result in considerable delay in obtaining a decision. To a commercial property developer, where appropriate timing of development in relation to the vagaries of user-demand can mean the difference between profit or loss on a scheme, such delays can be infuriating and highly costly.

In the case of a refusal to grant planning permission, the applicant can appeal to higher authority. In the original Act of 1963, provision was made for appeals to be taken directly to the government Minister, though this has subsequently been altered in order to avoid charges of corruption or bias towards friends and party contributors. At very least, there always existed the suspicion that some development permissions were granted on spurious grounds. McDonald (1985a, 198) describes James Tully, Minister for Local Government and TD for County Meath, as a 'gutsy anti-intellectual' who had no time for planners. He quotes one of Tully's former officials as saying that 'almost every appeal that came from Meath was granted, especially for bungalows in the countryside,

Figure 5.2 Eglinton Road in Donnybrook. Planning permission for the office development was granted on appeal to the Minister for the Environment. A spate of questionable decisions led to the establishment of the planning appeals board.

because he apparently saw this as part of a service for his constituents'. One of Tully's more interesting legacies to the city resulted from his granting permission for the redevelopment of a house on Eglinton Road, Donnybrook, as a five-storey office block, as depicted in Figure 5.2.

A planning appeals board (An Bord Pleanala) was established by the 1976 Planning Act and commenced operation in the following year. However, the board itself has faced charges that its decisions have generally favoured development interests. The fact that its members were appointed by the Minister and frequently included a majority of individuals who possessed development interests and close ties with one major political party, long prevented it from being seen as a body independent of political influences. Even after the process for making appointments to the board was changed in 1983, when an elaborate procedure was set up to de-politicise appointments, the fact that the board still does not make public the planning inspectors' reports – the basis upon which its decisions are reached – has left it open to continued criticism. A further problem stems from the fact that in making its decisions, An Bord Pleanala is not obliged to conform to the adopted

Table 5.1 An Bord Pleanala decisions, 1984–90

Appeals against refusal		Appeals against conditions			Appeals by third parties		
Permission granted	Permission refused	Permission with same conditions	Permission with revised conditions	Permission refused	Permission with same conditions	Permission with revised conditions	Permission refused
30.0%	70.0%	15.9%	80.0%	4.1%	9.4%	71.0%	19.5%

Source: An Bord Pleanala, 1992.

Development Plans. This means that first-party appeals by developers are often successful. Table 5.1 indicates that between January 1984 and December 1990, about 30 per cent of appeals against outright refusal were reversed and 80 per cent of appeals against the conditions imposed by planners when granting permission resulted in a revision of such conditions (An Bord Pleanala, 1992).

A major feature of the Irish planning legislation is that it granted the right of appeal to third-parties, irrespective of whether or not they possessed a direct interest in the development proposal. This facility provides a vital opportunity for individuals and organisations which are concerned with broader physical and social environmental issues, such as An Taisce and residents' associations, to place on record their concerns regarding particular development schemes by appealing against planners' decisions to grant permission for development. However, the right of third-party appeal is clearly open to abuse. This extraordinarily 'democratic' provision in the legislation has been a source of constant complaint on the part of developers as a result of the considerable delays which can be engendered as a consequence of pernicious appeals – by individuals who appear to developers to possess no justifiable interest in a project, or even by other developers with rival projects under construction. However, fewer than 3 per cent of all planning applications receive third-party objections. Their number declined during the mid-1980s as a result of the property slump and the introduction of a fee for lodging an objection, currently amounting to IR£100, but grew steadily after 1987. Appeals brought by third-parties accounted for over a quarter (27.3 per cent) of the appeals lodged between January 1984 and December 1990. Table 5.1 shows that the most likely outcome of third-party appeals was for An Bord Pleanala to vary the conditions attached to a planning permission, being the outcome of over 70 per cent of such appeals. Permission was rescinded in about 20 per cent of cases and granted under the same conditions in the remainder. Needless to say, as the delay occasioned by an appeal may be as long as nine months and may prove costly to a developer, the system is open to abuse and the development lobby constantly presses for the abolition of the facility.

Since 1989–90, planning powers have been extended to include the provisions of the 1985 European Community regulations to protect the environment. This requires the submission of an environmental impact statement in the case of urban extensions of over 50 ha. (123.5 acres) or infill schemes of more than 2 ha. (4.9 acres), industrial projects of more than 15 ha. (37 acres), large holiday villages and hotel complexes and installations relating to certain chemicals, paints and pesticides. However, some developments which can be damaging to environmentally sensitive areas, such as the construction of golf courses on coastal sand dunes, need no planning permission.

Urban planning in practice

Urban planning in Dublin has been strongly criticised in recent years. Many of the limitations of Irish urban planning stem from its structural role as an activity of the capitalist state. Others, however, derive from the domination of the professional planning staff by a conservative city management which imposes central state requirements and ensures that planners' activities remain as narrowly defined as possible. Many such criticisms are voiced by the planners themselves, citing management's encouragement of bureaucratic inertia, its negative outlook and lack of imagination, its unwillingness to tackle politically unpopular problems or its failure even to implement certain parts of the legislation (McGuirk, 1991). The comments which follow are therefore an appraisal of planning in Dublin rather than of its planners.

Planning's permissory role

The fact that the planning department lacks spending powers severely hampers what it can achieve. As a spending department, even the city's Parks Department possesses more immediate power to shape the urban environment than do the planners. Planners must rely upon the private sector and the co-ordination of other local authority spending departments for the execution of plans. This clearly places planning in a very weak position in relation to development interests, especially at times of slump in the property development sectors when planners face political pressures to get any development going for the sake of employment in the construction industry. This means that planners either have to take what the developer is prepared to offer, making token adjustments here and there, or run the risk of the developer's abandoning the scheme altogether.

As in many capitalist systems, urban planning in Ireland can only operate if development proposals are forthcoming from the private sector. This dependency on capitalist development interests means that development plans must be drawn up in a way which complements market processes. Aspects of development plans which run counter to the logic of the market, be they highly desirable in community or built-environment terms, become mere 'wishful thinking' if public sector funds are not forthcoming to implement them. Significantly, in her survey of planners in the Dublin region, McGuirk (1991) found widespread acceptance of the facilitative role of planning towards private sector interests. Thus, irrespective of the formal channels which are open to the public for participation in urban planning, it is the ownership of private property, conferring the power to withdraw from the development process, which ensures that property interests have implicitly to be favoured. It is as though Development Plans are 'ghost written' by an invisible hand serving the interests of property (McGuirk, 1991).

Inevitably, the work involved in the statutory requirement to review periodically the development plan and to control development activities on a continuous basis has spawned a substantial bureaucracy of planners which is largely engaged in routine activities. This, together with the failure to finance the development powers which were granted under Section 77, has severely limited the ability of the system to act in a positive manner.

It could be contended, however, that the limited ability of urban planning to act in a positive fashion may be no bad thing. When planning and development powers have been effectively tied to the spending budgets of local authority departments, such as roads or housing, 'planning' has all too frequently shown itself to be unresponsive to local community objections. The 'planning imperialism' exhibited by the city's roads engineers (see Chapter 6) and the clearance of protesting residents from housing on Summerhill and Sean MacDermott Street prior to its demolition, reveal a degree of authoritarianism and unresponsiveness to public influence (Moore, 1989). As developments undertaken by government departments and by the local authority within its own planning area are largely exempt from development control, their activities are beyond the limited degree of public control which is provided by the planners themselves and through the third-party appeals system. This is regrettable, as the public sector has been responsible for some of the worst developments to have taken place in the city during recent years, including the construction of the Civic Offices at Fishamble Street/Wood Quay (Figure 5.3) and recent unsympathetic alterations by the Office of Public Works to the previously beautifully restored Royal Hospital at Kilmainham. It is therefore fortunate that urban planning in Ireland is merely permissory. Although made in a different context, a remark by

Figure 5.3 The Civic Offices at Fishamble Street/Wood Quay make no architectural concessions to their neighbour, Christchurch Cathedral. They occasioned the destruction of the site of a Viking settlement and caused a storm of international protest.

Smith (1977) provides a particularly appropriate description of public intervention in the urban environment in Dublin, as possessing all the finesse of 'a delicate heart operation performed with a spade.'

Joint ventures in which local authority urban planning has taken on a more entrepreneurial role have been limited. The ILAC Centre off Henry Street represents one such example, dating from the 1970s, in which development expertise and finance were provided by Irish Life Assurance while the local authority used its powers of compulsory purchase to facilitate site assembly to permit comprehensive redevelopment. The approach has not proved popular with private sector developers because of the perception that the public sector is an incompatible partner, being rife with naïve aspirations, lacking an understanding of development economics, and without any sense of urgency or that time is money (McGuirk, 1991). The joint venture to secure the redevelopment of the Custom House Docks has created a more favourable impression of joint ventures, but this scheme relied on the establishment of a separate development authority entirely divorced from the local authority (see Chapter 10).

Public participation

Participation in the Irish planning system is grounded in a pluralistic theory of society, in which competing groups vie with one another for influence but none is in the ascendancy. However, McGuirk (1991) has shown that in a system where influence depends on gaining acceptance of one's arguments at as early a stage as possible, the attempt to incorporate public participation into Irish urban planning has resulted in a system which tends towards a public relations exercise rather than the empowerment of people.

At first sight, the provisions within the legislation for public participation in urban planning seem considerable. They include the right of individuals and organisations to make submissions on the development plan and to lodge appeals against the decision to grant planning permission. McGuirk (1991) has shown how limited is public participation in practice. Inevitably, different community groups possess varying amounts of financial resources, expertise, knowledge and confidence, affecting their ability to participate. Those representing middle-class residential areas are more likely to have members with the confidence to deal with planning officers as equals, even including members with a professional involvement in planning or property development. They undoubtedly fare better than many other groups which feel that they are not listened to seriously. The former are also more likely to be able to afford to employ technical and legal assistance when required.

However, all the community groups are disadvantaged in comparison to business and development interests, with developers in a position to make the first contact with the planning authority through pre-application negotiations, and the public learning of the proposal only later. A notice in Dublin Corporation offices states:

> Discussion with officers of this department reflects our general policy of being as helpful as possible towards property developers and their agents in drafting proposals.

While not binding on the planning department, the informal negotiations which take place between planners and developers prior to the submission of formal applications enable developers to assess what the planners will give away in return for getting development going at a particular site and also allows developers to ascertain where political pressure needs to be applied (McGuirk, 1991). The content of such negotiations remains secret from the public; yet, once informal support is obtained, it becomes increasingly difficult for individual planners to alter course in response to public pressure.

Like the middle-class community groups, business and development interests are also in a better financial position to employ professionals to negotiate with planners on their behalf. These professionals speak the same language (and understand the same jargon) as the planners, tend to be drawn from similar class backgrounds and share the same views regarding the primacy and legitimacy of private property rights. Moreover, compared to development and construction interests, community groups possess few funds for the coffers of political parties.

Comments by businesses on the development plans themselves are also likely to be made at an earlier more influential stage, prior to their formulation. Indeed, before the drafting of the 1987 Draft Development Plan Review, business interests in the city actually had their views solicited by questionnaire survey from the planning department. Once embodied in the Development Plan, the plan becomes vested with unwarranted significance, is defended by those who spawned it and is altered only reluctantly. As Mazziotti (1982, 216) notes:

> . . . there exists an institutionalized bias in a society dominated by concentrations of economic and political power which makes the theory of pluralism nothing more than an euphemism for corporate capitalism.

The failure of planning to extend to real citizen participation is well summarised by the following quotation from the 'Manifesto for the City' (1987), drafted by a coalition of community groups and concerned citizens. Although the document fails to recognise the inherent structural limitations of the planning system or of the capitalist state, it is worth quoting at length:

> . . . public participation is minimal. Very little information is made available, usually the absolute minimum required to fulfil statutory obligations, and it is only released after the real decisions have been taken behind closed doors. Even exhibitions of the City Development Plan, on which ordinary people are entitled to make their views known, seem designed more to confuse than inform, with their indecipherable maps full of colours, dots and lines. If there was a genuine desire to involve the public, the planners would make their plans intelligible, with simple explanatory leaflets, widely circulated, and good publicity in the newspapers, on radio and television. But instead of reviewing the Development Plan for the entire city, a mammoth task which is usually undertaken once every decade, the plan should be reviewed on an area-by-area basis once every five years. . . . (Dublin Crisis Conference Committee, 1987, 22)

This ability to prevent serious public participation was accepted by one planner interviewed by McGuirk (1991, 266), who openly admitted that 'we are expert enough to make it complex enough for the average person not to understand'. Moreover, she frequently encountered an almost resentful view of public participation, that it was unnecessary because planners represented the 'common good' or 'public interest'. As one interviewee remarked, 'we are employed to do the job for the public. [Participation] is like buying a dog and barking yourself' (McGuirk, 1991, 266).

Planning the city

Political pressure

Influence which can be very difficult to resist is frequently brought to bear on planners' deliberations by local authority councillors and by individual members of the Dail. Pressure is also exerted by central government through the Department of the Environment, usually via the city managers. However, the degree of overt political pressure varies. Thus, as one Dublin planner noted, 'the construction lobby is stronger under Fianna Fail and the planning department is hauled over the coals more frequently' (McGuirk, 1991, 243).

The boom-slump cycle in property development also brings changes in the level of political pressure on planners. With the simultaneous collapse of all major property development sectors after 1982, local authority planners were encouraged to grant planning permission for almost any development in order to create jobs in a construction sector suffering from a 45 per cent unemployment rate. A circular in 1982 from the Department of the Environment advised planners that 'development should only be refused where there are serious objections on important planning grounds'. As another Dublin planner commented, it meant 'being asked by the DoE what the hell are you doing if you turn down any reasonable development' (McGuirk, 1991, 244).

Absence of a regional context

The fact that urban planning in Ireland is almost completely divorced from any other national, regional, economic or physical planning means that urban planning lacks strategic significance. The co-ordination of planning activity between neighbouring local authorities' development plans is attempted by a number of means. First, development plans are passed to neighbouring planning authorities. Secondly, in Dublin, a single individual acts as the Chief Planning Officer for all constituent local authorities in the metropolitan area.

However, neighbouring planning authorities may still pursue policies which run counter to each other's policies. For example, Dublin Corporation has attempted to preserve the city centre as the commercial and office core of the metropolitan area, thus protecting its income from commercial rates. Yet, in order to alleviate traffic congestion, it has tried simultaneously to reduce the reliance of office workers on the motor car. When granting planning permissions for office developments in recent years, the Corporation's planners have restricted the provision of car parking to one car space per 140 sq. m. (1,500 sq. ft.) of office space. Thus, a valuable incentive with which County Dublin has been able to lure office development away from the core has been the granting of office planning permissions with a far more generous parking allowance, as high as one car space per 19 sq. m. (200 sq. ft.). The growth of development activity in Clonskeagh, just beyond the jurisdiction of the Corporation planners in Dublin County, has partly been a reflection of such fiscal mercantilist policies.

In order to improve the role of strategic planning over a wider region than that of the individual local authority, nine Irish regions were delimited for planning purposes in 1964. *Ad hoc* Regional Development Organisations were appointed for each in 1969, comprising representatives from local authorities and government departments. Although lacking any statutory authority, these bodies did attempt to provide at least some degree of regional co-ordination, until they were abolished in 1987.

In the Dublin area, the Eastern Regional Development Organisation (ERDO) was composed of planning staff from the local authorities of Dublin County Borough, County Dublin, Dun Laoghaire, and counties Kildare, Meath and Wicklow. Its brief was to examine potential population growth in the East Region until AD 2011. Although in many ways it represents an admirably professional piece of planning, like many such plans which were produced in the UK during the 1960s, the Eastern Region Settlement Strategy (1985) was founded on population predictions which were hopelessly inaccurate. Rather than promoting residential development on derelict land in the inner areas, it favoured continued peripheral growth to accommodate the additional 500,000 people predicted by the year 2011. This resulted in the strategy's being seriously challenged by those who favoured the re-creation of a 'living city' (see Kelly et al., 1986; Dublin Crisis Conference Committee, 1987). Although the strategy was revised in 1988 to take account of the unprecedented reduction in Irish marriage and birth rates during the 1980s, the revision still reflected the preference of residential developers for peripheral expansion.

Compensation claims

A major problem facing planning authorities has been the obligation to pay compensation in cases where the 'reasonable development' of land was prevented through a planning decision. This meant that 'unsuitable zoning' was deemed to be a compensatable reason for the refusal of planning permission, thereby rendering the local authority liable to pay compensation for enforcing the regulations. Moreover, the fact that compensation is payable at market value, rather than at existing use-value, severely undermines the ability of planners to refuse planning permission, fearing the resultant large claims for compensation. Thus landowners are compensated for potential losses rather than actual losses. Although the total amount paid out in compensation has been relatively small, amounting to just IR£135,000 between 1964 and 1987, outstanding claims for compensation amounted to IR£12 million in 1987.

The constitutional guarantee safeguarding the interests of private property and the fear that legislation which tackles the issue of compensation would be found to be unconstitutional, is only a partial explanation of the failure of governments to address this matter for so long. Even the passage of the Local Government (Planning and Development) Act in 1990, applied only to land which was purchased after 20 October 1988, the publication date of the Bill, and had no effect on the long-term landbanks already owned by developers (McDonald, 1989).

Rezoning under Section 4 motions

The provisions of Section 4 of the City and County Management (Amendment) Act, 1955, empower the elected representatives to instruct the City and County Manager to perform particular executive functions. This provision was intended as a necessary safeguard to ensure local control over managerial actions, but was widely employed to vary the zoning status of specific areas of land.

Frequently against the advice of the professional planners, during the early 1980s Dublin county councillors voted to re-zone to urban functions over 2,020 ha. (5,000 acres) of land zoned for agricultural use in the 1972 County Development Plan, including a large tract of green belt lying between the new towns of Tallaght and Clondalkin. There may be good reasons for permitting such alterations to zoning, especially when the process of reviewing the Development Plan has tended to be so protracted. However, it opens the planning system to abuse by exposing the elected political masters of the planning process to charges of bias and of being influenced by landowning interests keen to achieve a higher zoning status for their properties.

The continued employment of Section 4 motions during the 1980s to enhance the zoning status of land according to the 1983 Development Plan resulted in considerable popular protest and led, in 1991, to amending legislation to ensure that such re-zonings could not be so readily abused. The new arrangements require that a Section 4 motion must be signed by three-quarters of the councillors representing the area concerned and, for adoption, it must be supported by three-quarters of all those who are entitled to vote.

Development density

Urban planning has registered some significant successes with respect to the control of building height and development densities, ensuring that Dublin remains a predominantly low-rise city. Some buildings do break the skyline, notably Liberty Hall, O'Connell Bridge House and Hawkins House, but these had commenced prior to the full operation of the provisions of the Planning Act of 1963. However, an adverse consequence of the low density of development in the central area, where plot ratios of 2.5:1 have been generally enforced, has been to push the wave of development pressure outwards into the surrounding areas. It was especially damaging for buildings located in the prestigious eighteenth century areas to the south and east of the central area where developers secured permission to redevelop sites. This situation has been exacerbated by zoning far too large an area of the city centre as suitable for commercial development, encouraging speculative site assembly for commercial redevelopment in fringe areas, displacing traditional residential or industrial functions and resulting in a deteriorating built environment with abandonment of building maintenance.

In suburbia, the imposition of low density criteria for suburban residential developments has been instrumental in creating a sprawling metropolis which is now very costly to service by public transport but where many residents are unable to afford the luxury of private transport.

Protection of buildings

A recent letter to the Irish Times by the chief architect at the Finnish Ministry for the Environment, who had recently visited the city, provides a salutary indication of just how unsuccessful planning appears to have been to the casual observer:

> During my spare hours I tried to find all the streets and places I had only seen in the books. I walked, among other places, along its quays and Dame Street. It is difficult to express my disappointment and sad feelings as I saw the horrifying state of buildings and the streetscape. I have been travelling around a lot, but I don't think I have anywhere else seen so many beautiful buildings – and right in the centre – left empty, left in the hands of vandals and the weather.
>
> It looked like Dublin's historic core was left to rot. . . . The way this beautiful and famous city has not been taken care of is excruciatingly sad. I would like to call this criminal neglect! How is it possible that any politician, any town planner, any citizen can accept that buildings are left like that? Is there no legislation for maintenance and care of buildings. Are there any town planning rules to favour the conservation of historic heritage? If so, why are they not being applied? (Santaholma, 1991).

Planning the city

Modern urban planning in Ireland has placed little importance on the conservation of the built environment. Indeed, the conservationist lobby, which has promoted the view that considerations other than commercial values should predominate in planning decisions, has long been regarded in Corporation bureaucratic circles as constituting an almost lunatic fringe and of 'trying to push the toothpaste back into the tube' (McGuirk, 1991).

Under the 1963 Local Government (Planning and Development) Act, the demolition of a building required no permission, normally constituting an 'exempted development'. Amending legislation in 1967 removed this exemption for buildings listed in the development plan as worthy of protection, while the 1969 Housing Act gave a measure of protection to residential buildings. However, the protection of buildings amounts merely to placing architecturally significant buildings on a list in the Development Plan, and planning authorities have been under no obligation to do even this. In the inner city areas of Dublin 1 and Dublin 2 which were developed in the eighteenth century, the 1980 Dublin City Development Plan listed 613 houses for 'preservation', of which only 23 were situated north of the river Liffey, with an additional 704 being included on list 2 for 'protection'.

A fleeting inspection of Dublin's eighteenth and early nineteenth century terraces and squares commonly reveals a sorry lack of completeness which mystifies overseas visitors, particularly those from countries which either lack such a precious heritage or where it has been carefully protected. Moreover, development plans reveal that until recently there has been a very limited conception among planners as to which structures are deemed worthy of protection. To the north of the river Liffey, Eccles Street, Gardiner Street Lower, Mountjoy and Parnell Squares have all seen major streetscape destruction, and Henrietta Street, though essentially intact to the west of the mews entries, remains in a very poor state of repair. South of the river, where the eighteenth century buildings retained their high status into the modern period and tended to be better maintained, widespread redevelopment for offices has wrought major change, destroying the integrity of many terraces. In particular, St Stephen's Green, Molesworth Street, Dawson Street, South Frederick Street, Nassau Street, Clare Street, Fitzwilliam Street, Mount Street Lower, Baggot Street Lower and Leeson Street Lower have all suffered the predatory attention of property developers:

> The small surviving stock of early 18th century panelled houses has been depleted by about half through the destruction of houses in Leeson Street, Molesworth Street, Fownes Street, Aungier Street and Bolton Street, which had the earliest surviving example of fresco decoration in Dublin. Important mid-18th century rococo plasterwork in Parnell Square and South Frederick Street and late 18th century Adamesque work in Harcourt Street and Eccles Street has [sic] been destroyed in large quantities. (An Taisce, 1985a, 4)

Figure 5.4 The west side of Mountjoy Square reveals the sorry state into which many of Dublin's once fine eighteenth century buildings have been allowed to fall.

Until recently there was no legal basis for the enforcement of building maintenance in Dublin such as one finds in some American cities. Presumably this was believed to represent a threat to private property rights, yet ignoring the blighting effect which dereliction inevitably has upon neighbouring property values. Nowhere is the absence of such a code of property maintenance more marked than on the west side of Mountjoy Square shown in Figure 5.4. However, the passage of the Derelict Sites Act (1990) has conferred powers on local authorities to ensure that land and buildings do not become derelict: to enforce the carrying out of remedial works – sanctioned by substantial fines or imprisonment, and the possibility of compulsory acquisition. It is too soon to appraise the effectiveness of this measure, and the fact remains that a large proportion of derelict land and buildings in the city is owned by Dublin Corporation itself.

Under such conditions, it has been all too easy for a developer who wished to redevelop a site bearing a listed building to remove roofing slates and lead flashing surreptitiously, thereby opening up the structure to penetration by water. Exposure to the elements quickly renders a building unsafe, whereupon the local authority's dangerous buildings officers were likely to order the building's demolition because of its condition, doubtless with grateful thanks from the developer.

Numerous architecturally important buildings have been demolished. An Taisce (The National Trust) estimates that between 1980 and 1985, no fewer than 80 listed buildings were demolished or permission had been granted for their demolition, with another 50 having suffered unauthorised material alterations detrimental to their architectural character (An Taisce, 1985a). Only three original houses on the south side of Mountjoy Square remain, despite the protected status of the previous buildings. Few eighteenth century properties now remain on St Stephen's Green, though here the battles with developers have been more keenly fought by the conservationists, notably over the destruction of buildings on either side of the entrance to Hume Street (see McDonald, 1985a). On the south side of St Stephen's Green, just 15 years or so after the development of Canada House, which had occasioned the demolition of four eighteenth century houses on the grounds that they were not structurally sound, it was with some satisfaction that conservationists noted that the new office block itself required repair as parts of its facade began to fall into the street.

Just as great a loss to the townscape has been the tendency to demolish a few buildings within a terrace on the grounds that, individually, they are not architecturally significant. There is still no statutory provision for the establishment of conservation areas, and this means that a single building, which might be important only in the context of its surroundings, was unlikely to receive protection. However, local authorities have designated certain localities as areas of conservation, and An Bord Pleanala has recently tended, on the grounds of neighbourhood conservation, to uphold local authority refusals to grant permission for the demolition of buildings which are located in such non-statutory conservation zones.

The public sector, as a developer, has not shown much greater sympathy towards Dublin's historic townscape than have private developers. In 1964, the Electricity Supply Board (ESB) was responsible for the demolition of 16 houses in Lower Fitzwilliam Street (Figure 5.5), thereby destroying the integrity of an eighteenth century streetscape which stretched along its eastern side for almost a kilometre (half a mile), and which was terminated in the south by views of the Dublin mountains. In its destructive course, the ESB was advised by Sir John Summerson who described the buildings as 'a sloppy, uneven series. . . . It is nearly always wrong to preserve rubbish and, by Georgian standards, these houses are rubbish' (quoted in McDonald, 1985a, 20). Even during the ESB's recent 'rehabilitation' of the eighteenth century buildings which it owns in Upper Mount Street, almost complete redevelopment became necessary when one of the 'protected' buildings collapsed.

Figure 5.5 Lower Fitzwilliam Street. The development of new head offices for the Electricity Supply Board resulted in the demolition of 16 houses and the destruction of one of the finest urban vistas in Europe.

As a city which is renowned for its reticent façades and splendid interiors, it is unfortunate that official policy was long dominated by the façade approach to conservation (Robinson, 1980). Only in 1976 was legislative provision enacted for the protection of interiors. Yet, until the 1987 City Development Plan Review, itself revised in 1990 and only adopted in December 1991, not one interior in Dublin was listed for protection, inadequate as such listing was. The consequent loss to the city's heritage is incalculable. The logic behind such a serious omission was that the planners did not actually know which interiors were worth protecting and that, being unable satisfactorily to protect the exteriors of listed buildings, they had little hope of intervening to protect unseen interiors. This was particularly regrettable considering the fine quality of craftsmanship which was often to be found in Dublin's eighteenth century dwellings and the unsympathetic treatment which it frequently received during the process of conversion to alternative functions at the hands of the public and private sectors alike.

Archaeological protection

If architectural and townscape protection has fared badly under the current planning regulations, Chapter 2 has shown that urban archaeological conservation has been disastrous. The treatment of the Viking site at Wood Quay – Fishamble Street – which was eventually excavated only in part and under severe time constraints before being bulldozed for the construction of the new Civic Offices, is an example of squandered opportunity. The medieval city wall has been rebuilt in part and stands incongruously beneath the new development.

Despite the negative outcome of the Wood Quay débacle, there still exists no requirement for proper archaeological excavation of sites prior to their redevelopment. At the time of writing, a hotel is being developed on a key medieval site to the south of Christchurch Place following only very limited archaeological investigation, despite the fact that it is believed to be as rich archaeologically as Wood Quay – being the site of the medieval Tholsel (town hall) and having remains which date from the tenth century.

It is hard to think of any other European urban administration which would show such scant concern for its heritage. One is reminded of the eighteenth century Irish parliamentarian Sir Boyle Roche, whose immortal words 'why should we do anything for posterity? What has posterity ever done for us?' succinctly encapsulate the attitude which seems to have long prevailed in Dublin Corporation circles.

The 1987 Draft Development Plan does recognise an 'Archaeological Zone' in the heart of the city, in which planning aims to prevent unsympathetic development and safeguard the archaeological remains. However, the fact that a significant proportion of this zone has also been designated as an area for rejuvenation and development does not bode well for the future. Fortunately, such has been the quality of some of the building in Dublin during the past 30 years that these sites will probably again present themselves for redevelopment before too long!

Location and development

While the record of planning authorities in protecting the built environment from the predations of developers has been poor, it has been abysmal with regard to engendering development in areas where it is actually required. Lack of funding has prevented local authorities from becoming development agencies, as envisaged under Section 77 of the original Act. On occasions, planners have attempted to influence the location of development by providing beneficial planning permissions, such as a higher than normal plot ratio in the case of Park House on the

North Circular Road, in order to lure office development away from traditional areas. These tactics have met with only marginal success because the relationship between profitability and location is so strong (see Chapter 7).

The shortcomings which are inherent in Irish urban planning and management systems have engendered periodic calls for integrated area-specific bodies to address problems, such as in the proposed Inner City Development Authority (Litchfield and Partners, 1979a; Society of Chartered Surveyors, 1986) or the short-lived Metropolitan Streets Commission (see Chapter 6). Increasingly, the failure of planning adequately to serve development interests has led to its being by-passed by central government. McGuirk (1991) found that while most developers recognised the need for urban planning, they believed that current arrangements were failing to deliver. A number of the city's office developers interviewed by McGuirk (1991, 279) opined that the Planning Departments in the Dublin area were replete with 'commies, reds and socialists'.

The perceived shortcomings are likely to have weighed heavily with the Government in its decision to establish a separate renewal authority for the Custom House Docks (see Chapter 10). In so doing, it expropriated virtually all local authority planning powers for the area concerned and vested them in the Custom House Docks Development Authority, which adopted a 'fast-track' system of planning control in the area. McGuirk (1991, 247) views the increasing degree of central government interference in urban planning as a reflection of:

> . . . a realisation at central government level that physical planning measures cannot deal with contradictions in the economic order as they are manifested in the built environment. The function of planning as a means of avoiding crisis in the built environment has increasingly been beyond its means. Hence, central government intervention aims at supporting development and dealing directly with conflicts in the development process. Rather than supplement its powers and run the risk of planners' imposing value judgements based on criteria of social justice, central government introduces its own measures, based purely on physical regeneration.

The Custom House Docks redevelopment scheme has been spectacularly successful in creating new buildings quickly. However, the vesting of planning powers in a pro-development body which is appointed by a government minister, runs the risk of challenging the legitimacy of the urban planning system itself, by exposing it as a tool for legitimating the unequal distributional outcomes of the development process.

The description by two Dublin-based planners provides a valuable insight into the contemporary role of planning in the city. One described it as 'the legitimation of the existing economic order: to give the impression of rationality that does not exist and of democracy that's not there', while the other believes that it now functions 'simply to facilitate the property market; to get development going and guide it' (McGuirk, 1991, 227–8).

Following the decision to abolish An Foras Forbartha (The National Institute for Physical Planning and Construction Research), Cliff Hague remarked that 'Ireland more and more becomes the place to send people to if you want to make the case for what would happen if you did abolish planning altogether' (Hague, 1987). Although this may be a somewhat harsh judgement, planning in Dublin is certainly a function which has become increasingly marginalised during recent years.

6
Strategic planning of land-use and transportation

Historically, the growing specialisation of functional operations in cities has been translated into geographical separation of land-uses, creating relatively homogeneous functional areas. Industrial functions comprise the productive base of the system, engaged in the transformation of raw materials or the assembly of components. Warehousing and retail land-uses involve the distribution of products either to consumers or for further processing. Private and public sector managerial and allocative operations characterise office functions, guiding and regulating the productive and distributive operations and dealing with legal matters such as ownership right, while the city's residential areas provide the required labour force to service the city's economy. These functional areas, retail streets, office districts, industrial zones and residential neighbourhoods, are linked via circulation space, comprising land and infrastructures used for the physical movement of goods and people. Thus, cities comprise a complex mosaic of different types of land-use and buildings accommodating specific functions.

Inefficiencies in the way in which circulation space discharges its role has serious consequences for the functioning of the urban system as a whole, imposing costs which may not only be difficult to quantify but which may remain unrecognised. For enterprises which compete in wider than local markets, sub-optimal performance of transport systems will be reflected in reduced levels of competitiveness resulting from increased production and distribution costs.

Irish urban policy has never been allowed to be ruthlessly dominated by logical argument, preference instead being shown for the easier medium of muddling through, hoping in the face of overwhelming evidence to the contrary that the *ad hoc* arrangements will eventually work. Nowhere is this truer than in the relationship between land-use and transportation planning. As land-use and transportation are intimately related, it is entirely logical that their planning should be inseparable. In Dublin, this relatively simple concept was long unrecognised. The duties of the transportation and land-use planners tended to be carried out as almost entirely separate pursuits, with land-use planning generally preceding transportation planning, and the latter being drawn up to accommodate resultant travel patterns (O'Cinneide, 1991). This will come as no surprise to anyone who travels around the city and encounters its traffic problems.

Legislation enacted in 1963 charged local authorities with the preparation of development plans for their areas. The two most influential strategic planning documents to have been produced for the Dublin metropolitan area were published in 1967 and 1971 and dealt respectively with land-use and transportation. Subsequent development plans have been deeply influenced by their recommendations. Unfortunately, no integrated land-use/transportation study was undertaken at this critical stage in the expansion of the city (Meldon, 1991). That omission has had very serious repercussions.

Settlement strategy and the Myles Wright report

The Myles Wright Report (1967), commissioned by the Minister of Local Government in 1964, represents a major turning point in the strategic development of the greater Dublin area. It concerned itself with a wide geographical zone surrounding the city, including County Dublin and parts of counties Kildare, Meath, Wicklow and Louth, and addressed the problem of accommodating a predicted population of 1.2 million persons in the wider Dublin region by 1985.

This settlement strategy contained several elements. It suggested that growth be directed towards a small number of pre-existing towns outside Dublin, notably Drogheda and Naas, with Navan and Arklow as secondary priority development centres. Growth was also to be continued in suburban County Dublin, accounting for over 260,000 additional residents between 1961 and 1985. It also foresaw a continued reduction in the resident population of the central city area, predicted to fall by over 73,000 between 1961 and 1985. The third element of the plan was more novel. It proposed the development of four finger-like linear new towns to the west of the city covering some 6,880 ha. (17,000 acres), at Blanchardstown–Mulhuddart, Palmerstown–Lucan, Clondalkin–Milltown, and Tallaght–Saggart, based on a number of small existing settlements. These four were to accommodate some 340,000 persons and would be separated from one another and from the city itself by green belts. Like the British New Towns planned in the 1940s, each was envisaged as a largely self-contained entity providing for residential, industrial and service functions. Unfortunately, their proximity to the city itself and the manner in which their development was carried out ensured that the likelihood of their achieving self-sufficiency was negligible.

The proposal that population growth should be accommodated mainly to the west of the city was a somewhat obvious choice given the manner in which the city is constricted by the Dublin Mountains to the south, by Dublin Bay to the east, while the airport to the north of the city represents a partial barrier to contiguous development there. It paid no heed to the existing public transportation infrastructure which might have favoured development along the coastal strip, already served by a railway line.

Although the report did include a transportation element, this was based on the motor car and the prediction that its role would become dominant in the future. Physical planning was therefore to be directed at accommodating its use. By according little attention to the role of public transport, reliance on the private car would become a self-fulfilling prophesy. It proposed the creation of a grid-like network for the suburban road system, encouraging journeys between the new towns and concentrically across the north and south of the metropolitan area. The proposals included latitudinal cross routes lying beyond the contemporary built-up area; a north-south route to the west of Phoenix Park; a new eastern by-pass crossing the Liffey to the east of the Custom House; and a further route along the line of the Royal Canal to serve the port. These would provide access to a new major north-south route lying to the west of the new towns and which would run from Athy to Drogheda.

The only significant contribution which was envisaged for public transport was for buses. These would provide a local service within residential neighbourhoods, and also transfer workers to the centre. However, as greater self-containment was achieved within the New Town areas, traffic flows on major radial routes were predicted to improve as the level of reliance upon the central area declined.

Implementation of land-use strategy

During the 1960s and 1970s, Dublin underwent a period of rapid population growth characterised by vigorous peripheral expansion. As the city's population rose from 718,300 in 1961 to over one million in

1981 it consumed about 400 ha. (1,000 acres) of agricultural land annually and transformed the city from 'a small, compact, high density city into a large sprawling decentralised metropolis around a declining inner-city' (Conlon, 1988, 167). The swiftest growth took place in sub-urban County Dublin, which registered nearly a threefold increase from 133,000 to over 420,000 during that period.

The land-use proposals of Myles Wright's advisory plan which related to Dublin were adopted in somewhat altered form in Dublin County Council's development plans of 1972 and 1983. Continued suburban development was to be permitted in County Dublin and the idea of developing new towns to the west was also accepted. However, their linear aspect was abandoned and the proposed four towns became three, with Lucan and Clondalkin being amalgamated to create Ronanstown. Unfortunately, following Myles Wright's advisory plan, neither County Dublin nor the Corporation envisaged any significant potential for increasing the residential function of the central area. Indeed, throughout the 1970s, Dublin Corporation continued through slum clearance policies to achieve a reduction of central area population densities. Industry was also encouraged to relocate to purpose-built industrial estates in the suburbs.

At a time of rapid population growth in the region, resulting from natural increase and a net inward migration to the city amounting to some 10,000 persons annually during the mid-1970s, the idea of self-contained new towns was seductive. When the British post-war new towns were developed, the necessary land was acquired by their development corporations at little more than agricultural use value. They had power to provide necessary infrastructure, develop housing, shops, offices and industrial premises. Other facilities such as health and community centres, swimming pools, sports centres, libraries and theatres soon followed. Furthermore, the development role of the corporations meant that there was close control of the scheduling of development activity and of the quality of development. In contrast, Dublin's new towns were to be developed with as little expense as possible being borne by the public purse. It was a new towns policy on the cheap, at least in the short term. Except in the case of necessary infrastructural development and the construction of public housing, reliance was placed almost entirely on the private sector to develop the new towns. Unlike in Britain, there were to be no development corporations. Land would have to be purchased at full market value by private and public sectors alike, bringing windfall gains to landowners. Moreover, planning was carried out by County Council planners working in offices located some 8 km. (5 miles) away in the heart of the city.

There are some similarities between Dublin's three new towns and London's Mark I post-war new towns. They are developed at a low density of 25 houses per hectare (10 per acre) and planned around separate neighbourhood units incorporating local services such as shops, a school, a church and a health centre. Main roads skirt the neighbourhoods, within which the residential estates are designed to prevent through-traffic (Killen, 1992).

Population growth in the 1970s generated a very buoyant level of demand for housing. At a time of annual price inflation exceeding 15 per cent (1979–82) and escalating house prices, people were eager to acquire almost anything that would give them a first foot on the housing ladder (Murphy, 1991). Houses were often sold 'off the plans' with queues forming before the opening of new show-houses. Almost anything could sell. Needless to say, the level of care and attention devoted by speculative residential developers to residential layouts, housing design and the quality of construction was often woefully poor (see McDonald, 1989).

The new towns were also poorly served by commercial facilities. Only in 1990 did Tallaght, the largest of the three western new towns with a population of over 70,000, receive its long-awaited shopping centre. Even then, it did so only because the Government agreed to designate a greenfield site as an 'urban renewal area', thereby allowing the scheme to benefit from tax incentives similar to those available for inner-city redevelopment areas (see Chapter 10). Of its type, The Square in Tallaght is a very well executed commercial scheme, winning the International Council of Shopping Centres award as best European large shopping centre in 1990. It stands in marked contrast with numerous other suburban shopping centres around Dublin which seem to have been designed under the principle that 'it'll do for the working class'. But The Square hardly constitutes a town centre and the other two new towns, Ronanstown and Blanchardstown, still lack their planned town centres.

Dublin's new towns were also starved of necessary public investment for social amenities and utilities. In 1979, at a time when Tallaght's population had swollen in less than 15 years from 2,500 to over 30,000, there were very few telephones in the whole town and urban services were administered from offices outside the area.

Moreover, population decentralisation took place at a faster rate than suburban job creation, leading to dependency on areas outside the new towns for employment. In 1981, only 20 per cent of workers resident in Tallaght were employed there (Dublin County Council Planning Department, 1987). Another consequence in these areas was high levels of unemployment. In late 1991 when unemployment stood at 20 per cent nationally, in some new town local authority estates such as north Clondalkin, the true rate is estimated to be nearly 70 per cent, about the highest level in the state. In north Clondalkin during 1992, nearly 65 per cent of households were dependent on unemployment assistance or other welfare allowances, 80 per cent of families having a weekly income of less than IR£150 and 48 per cent living on under IR£100.

It is intended that Tallaght will ultimately exceed 90,000 residents, having attained a population of 74,000 by 1989. The two other new towns have similar target populations but are currently smaller. Lucan-Clondalkin has grown from 5,000 persons in 1971 to reach 54,000 in 1989, while Blanchardstown grew from 3,000 to 39,000 in the 20 years up to 1989. However, the perception of the new towns as generally unattractive has hindered their development. Their image has certainly not been assisted by the presence of some very large public housing estates: about 40 per cent of Tallaght's dwellings have been developed by the public sector. Thus, the rate of housing construction in the new towns has declined recently as developers direct their attention towards more attractive areas of County Dublin and this now has serious implications for their completion (Dublin County Council, 1991).

Transport in Dublin

Dublin has been endowed with elements of transportation infrastructures which date from the canal, railway and motoring ages. The canals no longer have any significance in transport terms, the Royal and Grand canals which fringe the inner city to the north and south respectively on their way to the Shannon being too shallow and narrow for modern commercial operation. They made some contribution to the cereals trade of the late eighteenth and early nineteenth centuries, while the carriage of passengers was an additional source of revenue, the hotel at Portobello being a relict of that function. In the Dublin area their importance now lies only in their recreational use and, particularly in the case of the Grand canal, as an important water element of the linear park which fringes the south-east of the central business area of Dublin 2.

Horse omnibus services were established from the 1840s and served a route network of some 40 kms. (25 miles) by 1870. During the 1870s, these routes were all converted to horse tramways, additional routes served by steam tramways making their appearance during the 1880s. The tramway services were gradually electrified during the next two decades, the increased speed of such services facilitating the extension of services to places at greater distance from the city centre. By 1914, Dublin possessed a network of about 100 kms. (62 miles) of electrified tramway which was steadily replaced by motor omnibus services during the inter-war years (Killen, 1992).

Ireland's railway age commenced in 1834 with the construction of the line between Dublin and Kingstown (Dun Laoghaire). With the improvement in Dublin's own port, freight became less significant than the carriage of commuters and tourists, which the railway company actively promoted. The country experienced a degree of 'railway mania' during the 1840s, Dublin becoming the focus of a system of lines serving local, regional and national destinations. The termini, which were located at the periphery of what was then the built-up area of the city to avoid paying high city-centre land prices, were often designed on a grand scale in Classical, Gothic or Egyptian styles to convey to potential investors the impression of financial soundness. Towards the end of the century, the systems became linked, most visibly in the case of the City of Dublin Junction Railway, or 'loop line', which bridges the river Liffey immediately to the west of the Custom House.

Short-term economic considerations were responsible for the dismantling of a considerable proportion of the national rail network in the post-war years. The Harcourt Street line to Bray, serving an area stretching into south County Dublin, was closed entirely in 1958 for reasons of economy. This was very short-sighted as this hinterland was about to experience a massive increase in its resident population, particularly of middle-class white-collar workers dependent on commuting to the central business district for employment.

Thus, by the 1970s, buses provided the only available public transportation over most of the metropolis. However, the eighteenth century had endowed the city with a heritage of wide carriageways, used to well below their capacity during the 1950s and 1960s. In 1961, fewer than 55,000 private cars were registered in a city which had a population of nearly 720,000 people. During the next 20 years, car ownership rates increased dramatically. By 1981 there were 217,800 private cars registered in the Dublin area, a six-fold increase over 1951 and nearly four times the number present in 1961. Moreover, commuting fields had widened during the intervening period, bringing in additional vehicles daily from neighbouring counties. As a result, traffic congestion increased significantly during the 1970s. Scheduled bus speeds dropped, from 22.5 km./hour (14 m.p.h.) in 1970 to 11.25 km./hour (7 m.p.h.) in 1977. On some city-centre route segments, speeds fell to only 3.5 km./hour (2.2 m.p.h) (Transport Consultative Commission, 1980). By 1980 there were nearly 30 per cent fewer passenger journeys being made annually by bus than there had been in 1960. As a consequence, bus services were reduced and they moved from a position of profitability in 1970 to one of significant financial loss in 1980 (Killen, 1991).

Although the use of suburban railway services increased from the mid-1960s with the number of passengers more than doubling between 1965 and 1980, the major transfer among commuters has been to the use of private cars. In 1967, 34 per cent of journeys into the inner area of the city were by car. By 1989, when the total number of trips had increased by over 30 per cent, more than half were by car (Conlon, 1988; Killen,

1991). The inadequacy and cost of public transport services and the pursuit of policies which encourage car use, have resulted in a situation wherein nearly 100,000 persons now cross the Inner Cordon Ring (the recognised traffic boundary of the central area) by car each day.

Contemporary Dublin is thus perceived as having a serious transportation problem. In reality, this comprises a variety of conditions. To commuters, the problem is one of inadequate, uncomfortable and costly public transport services, congestion on the roads and difficulties in finding somewhere to park at journey's end. Businesses may view the problem in terms of congestion costs, difficulties encountered in delivering supplies along narrow streets only to find that the commercial vehicle loading areas are themselves filled with illegally parked cars. For inner-city residents, commuter parking is a nuisance or, when it takes place on pavements and at junctions, a safety hazard.

Transportation planning

Strategic transportation planning in the Dublin area has been guided by three significant reports: the Dublin Transportation Study (An Foras Forbartha, 1971, 1972), the Dublin Rail Rapid Transit Study (Voorhees and Associates, 1975) and the report of the Transport Consultative Commission (1980). Some recommendations of an earlier study by Schaechterle (1965) were incorporated in later reports and thence into policy, including proposals to widen the Liffey's quays, though his plan to convert the Grand canal into a dual carriageway was not adopted. Fortunately, Travers Morgan's (1973) traffic plan for central Dublin, which would have 'ringed and bisected the city centre with a maze of highways, underpasses, flyovers and spaghetti junctions' (McDonald, 1985a, 306) would have proved so costly that it was never feasible.

In order to quantify the various transportation implications of the City and County Draft Development Plans, An Foras Forbartha (The National Institute for Physical Planning and Construction Research) undertook a major transportation study of the Dublin region (An Foras Forbartha, 1971, 1972). The Dublin Transportation Study (DTS) involved a data-gathering operation and the use of statistical models to predict patterns of movement up to 1991. Like Myles Wright's report, the study's recommendations were overwhelmingly concerned with the improvement of transportation infrastructures to facilitate the use of the private car. In the outer suburbs where population densities were low, reliance was to be placed on the private car, with public transport playing a determinedly less significant role. Its proposals were based on a forecast that the number of cars in the eastern region would treble between 1971 and 1991, rising from 160,000 to over 500,000 by 1991, whereas the current

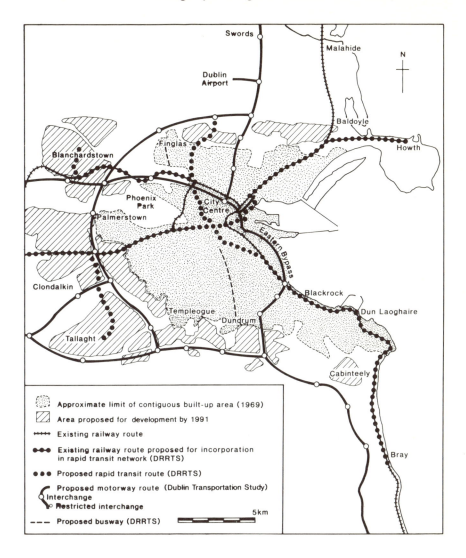

Figure 6.1 DTS and DRRTS transport planning proposals for the Dublin sub-region. *Source*: Killen, 1992.

level has reached only around half that number. Car ownership rates actually declined during the recession of the mid-1980s.

The study's major recommendation was for the construction of 110 kms. (70 miles) of motorways in and around the city, depicted in Figure 6.1. It proposed an outer motorway ring situated at about 10 kms. (6 miles) from the city centre to intercept the national primary roads

117

converging on the city. This would skirt the city to the north, run between the city and the new towns in the west, and fringe the southern suburbs. Another motorway (variously called the Port Access Route or Eastern Relief Route) running north-south and skirting the central area to the east would provide an eastern by-pass and provide the city with a complete motorway box. A further access route along the line of the Royal canal would also link the port and central industrial areas with the routes to the west.

Public transport was to play a predominant role only in the inner area and in moving people to and from the centre. The study proposed a phased improvement of the radial public transportation network including the introduction of high speed bus routes within the new towns, bus lanes on public roads and dedicated bus ways running from the centre to Tallaght, Finglas and Leopardstown-Foxrock. It supported the idea of radio control of buses which was then being investigated, as well as a previous proposal for the construction of a central bus terminal (Schaechterle, 1965). It also called for improved frequency of services on existing suburban rail links; suburban stations to be opened on existing lines; and the instigation of 'feeder-bus' services and car parking to serve suburban railway stations. It also suggested that there be an investigation of the feasibility of constructing a short underground passenger rail system in the central area to link existing rail systems. Strict control of parking in the central area was also envisaged.

However, even in the inner city, the DTS did not baulk at making important suggestions for the improvement of the road system. It proposed that at a radius of about one kilometre from the centre a number of existing roads lying to the south, west and north of the core be widened to divert through-traffic away from the core and improve the traffic flow.

The DTS has been criticised on a number of grounds: for the primacy given to technical objectives, reflecting the values of civil engineers rather than more widely defined 'quality of life' considerations which might have emanated from a broadly based inter-disciplinary team, for its lack of public participation and for failing to examine alternative land-use arrangements which might have enhanced the role of public transport (Crowley, 1991). Thus, it gave limited attention to the potential of public transport and failed entirely to provide any assessment of alternative public transport options.

This major shortcoming was to some degree remedied within a few years by the publication of another report, published in 1975 by consultants appointed by the state transportation group CIE. It recommended improvements to the public transport system and evaluated a variety of options. A re-appraisal of the role of public transport was further encouraged by the altered world energy situation occasioned by the oil crisis. The preferred option of the Dublin Rail Rapid Transit Study (DRRTS) was for the development of over 70 kms. (44 miles) of electrified railway (Voorhees and Associates, 1975). The three new towns would be linked to an underground central station, with a northern route running through Finglas to Ballymun. It was envisaged that the first stage would involve the electrification of the existing coastal route from Howth to Bray. In addition, it recommended that a dedicated bus way be constructed to Dundrum along the route of the defunct Harcourt Street railway line.

In 1980, a consultative commission set up by the Minister for Tourism and Transport reported on a series of low-cost options which could be implemented in the short term to alleviate traffic congestion in the city (Transport Consultative Commission, 1980). These included the use of bus lanes and resources to improve the enforcement of parking regulations.

Implementation of transport plans

Elements of each of the studies outlined above have influenced transportation policy in the city. Having accepted that it was the private motor car which was to be relied upon to provide the city's transport of the future, transportation planners have been obliged to devote the greatest attention (and expense) to the improvement of the road system.

The western section of the peripheral motorway (the Western Parkway) was opened in late 1990, with the northern and southern cross routes being due for completion in 1995. Considerable controversy, extending intermittently over more than ten years, has confronted the planned Eastern By-pass, which the roads engineers were reluctant to drop, even in the face of vehement opposition from conservationists. This scheme would create a major interchange on the site of the Booterstown bird sanctuary and run across Dublin Bay on the seaward side of Sandymount Strand. Following the local government elections in 1991 which returned a 'rainbow coalition' of councillors to Dublin Corporation unsympathetic to its adoption, it seems less likely that this section will proceed in the immediate future. However, the fear exists that the roads engineers, never ones to bow quietly to democratic decisions, may be able to resurrect the scheme through the aegis of the proposed National Roads Authority which is likely to be given powers to implement road improvement schemes even where these run contrary to local development plans.

The roads engineers have been more successful in pushing through their road widening plans in the heart of the city where they have been pursuing an urban roads policy long abandoned by more far-sighted

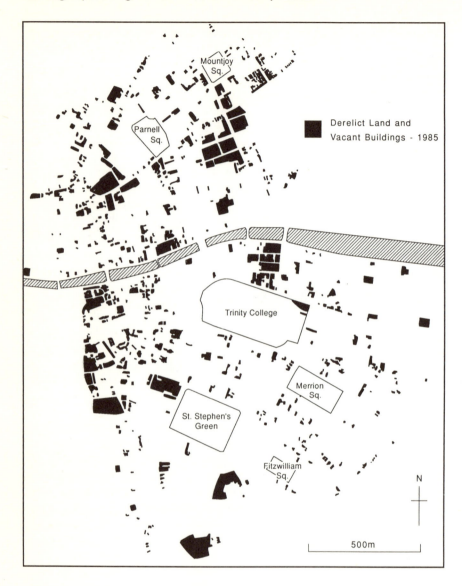

Mountjoy Sq.

Parnell Sq.

Derelict Land and
Vacant Buildings - 1985

Trinity College

Merrion Sq.

St. Stephen's Green

Fitzwilliam Sq.

N

500m

Figure 6.2   Derelict land and vacant buildings in central Dublin, 1985.

administrations overseas. Although the even more environmentally destructive proposals made by Travers Morgan and partners were never adopted, the remaining roads plans were costed in 1992 at nearly IR£1 billion. The dire consequences of 30 years of planning for the motor car are reflected in the extent of derelict land and vacant buildings in and around the commercial core, shown in Figure 6.2, much of which was associated with planned carriageway widening. In 1982, no fewer than 82 streets were earmarked by Dublin Corporation for road widening with an additional nine completely new roads projected for construction. By 1986, there were approximately 600 cleared sites and derelict buildings within the inner city, comprising a combined area of 65 ha. (160 acres). About 40 per cent of these sites related to the operations of the Corporation itself, including plans for road widening, housing, parks or community uses (Dublin Corporation Planning Department, 1986). Moreover, the fact that the roads engineers have no obligation to reinstate buildings means that there has usually been no replacement of the streetscape for many years following road widening.

Despite strong opposition, the inner relief route (the 'Inner Tangent') was incorporated in the 1971 Dublin Development Plan. Its route generated a trail of blighted property, derelict buildings and vacant land, extending westward from the south-west corner of St Stephen's Green, along Cuffe Street and Kevin Street, northwards up Patrick Street to pass insensitively in the form of a dual carriageway through the heart of the medieval core along High Street. 'Roads, instead of being diverted around the historic core, are being widened and pushed through the old city, destroying the medieval street system' (Bradley, 1984, 9). The route continues along Bridge Street and Church Street, thence eastward along North King Street, Parnell Street and Summerhill. Construction work, which has been pursued piecemeal over more than a decade, is now well advanced in some areas, with dual carriageways along Cuffe Street, High Street, Parnell Street and Summerhill; during 1991 work was taking place on Nicholas Street and Patrick Street. Such was the insensitivity of one proposal for the medieval core that 'as the plans were first devised, Christ Church Cathedral would have become a traffic island next to a high level motorway bridge' (Simms, 1987, 101). Although this idea was dropped, the road 'improvements' have created a soulless and windswept thoroughfare in the heart of the medieval city, separating medieval St Audoen's church from the early eighteenth century hall of the Tailors' Guild.

Similar devastation has been occasioned to other streets deemed to be candidates for road widening, particularly along Clanbrassil Street, where road widening proposals pre-date the 1950s. During the following 30 years of blight and property acquisition by the Corporation, construction work was minimal. When it was pointed out at an inquiry into the road widening plans for central Dublin that 80 per cent of the inner-city residents who would be most affected by the plans did not possess cars, the divisional roads engineer retorted 'Please God, some day they'll all have cars, if they wish' (McDonald, 1985b). The election of the new City Council in 1991, however, struck a severe blow against further despoilation by road improvements. Indeed, even the completion of the Inner Tangent route to the north of the river Liffey is now uncertain because Councillors decided to drop key sections of the route when the new Development Plan was adopted in December 1991.

The long-term plans of the roads engineers to set back the building line by some 6 metres (20 feet) along a number of the Liffey's quays to permit road widening have been a major cause of dereliction in this area. This was particularly evident at Arran Quay, Aston Quay, Bachelor's Walk, Ellis Quay and Essex Quay where, understandably, there was no incentive for owners to maintain properties which were destined for demolition and deterioration was inevitable. By the mid-1980s, what had previously been amongst the city's most precious townscape element had declined into a very sorry state of repair. Then, after years of blight and dilapidation, the plans to widen the quays were abandoned and special incentives to encourage property renewal had to be introduced by the Government to remedy this expensive mistake (see Chapter 10).

Apart from investment in road improvements, the quantity of parking space available in the central area of the city has also encouraged commuting by private car. Parking provision is generous by European standards with 38,000 car spaces in existence, including free on-street parking within the central business district. Moreover, existing parking regulations are hardly enforced, permitting the almost casual abandonment of vehicles in locations which are dangerous or seriously impede traffic flow. Surveys of parking in the central area have shown that well over 40 per cent of all on-street parking is illegal and that the likelihood of being apprehended was barely 2 per cent, even during rush hours on the major 'clearways' into the city (MacLaran, 1991b).

Despite the low level of car ownership in Dublin, there has been only very limited improvement of public transport. Investment has included the electrification of the Howth to Bray coastal railway line at a cost of IR£113M. This Dublin Area Rapid Transit (DART) scheme represents the first stage of the proposals incorporated in the DRRTS report. Because of its coastal route, half its catchment area lies in Dublin Bay. Nevertheless, it has attracted commuters away from using cars and has been shown to have been a cost effective investment (McGeehan, 1992). The report's other proposals, including the rail link spur to Tallaght, were rejected by the Transport Consultative Commission on the grounds of cost. For the past six years, an existing line to Maynooth, County Kildare, has been used to provide Blanchardstown with a somewhat skeletal rail service to the city centre and it is intended to use the main line to Cork to provide a service to Clondalkin by 1994/5. However, Tallaght, which is the fourth largest settlement in the state, remains ill-served by public transport.

In comparison with other European cities, public transport in Dublin is expensive. It also receives one of the lowest levels of public subvention in Europe, at 20 per cent, compared to 80 per cent in Holland (Perry, 1991). Cost-cutting has therefore been a management priority. The use of one-person operated buses has permitted labour force economies, but has increased journey times as boarding takes longer. In contrast, some recent improvements have helped to increase average bus speeds, including bus lanes and express bus routes, the video monitoring of traffic in the central area, the introduction of computer-linked traffic lights and bus priority at key traffic lights.

Córas Iompair Éireann (CIE), the state transportation company, also had plans dating from 1975 for the development of a central bus station. This was to comprise two separate developments linked by a pedestrian tunnel under the river, one occupying a 1.4 ha. (3.5 acre) site in the historic Temple Bar area between Dame Street and Wellington Quay, the other covering 2.4 ha. (6 acres) on the north bank of the river Liffey immediately opposite at Ormond Quay. Their location was determined in relation to the proposed development of a new north-south underground rail route running from the former stations at Broadstone and Harcourt Street, and another linking Connolly Station (Amiens Street) and Heuston (Kingsbridge). However, the plans for the southern teminus have subsequently been abandoned as a result of public sector financial stringency and pressure from conservationists (see Chapter 10).

Scant attention has been paid to the needs of cyclists in the city. There exist fewer than 10 kms. (6 miles) of cycle tracks in the whole city and no secure bicycle parks available to the public in the central area despite the fact that bicyle theft is very common.

Luckily, the paucity of public funds has resulted in the city's having been spared the worst excesses that roads engineers have perpetrated in other cities, with their urban motorways and multi-level interchanges. The completion of the Inner Tangent might have the intended result of diverting traffic away from the core, which would allow pedestrians to reclaim the streets. There still remain fine streetscapes in the city which, with vision and widespread pedestrianisation, could emerge from their current state of submersion as traffic arteries and parking lots to create a traffic-free core. However, there is now such mistrust of the roads engineers by conservationists that they are unwilling to believe that this would be the likely outcome of permitting the completion of the Inner Tangent.

The plans put forward during the mid-1980s by the short-lived

Metropolitan Streets Commission deserve close attention. Regrettably, this statutory body, which had been established by the Fine Gael Minister for the Environment in 1987 to improve the streetscape of the central city, was seen as threatening the power of the then Fianna Fail controlled Corporation and was rapidly abolished by an incoming Fianna Fail Government under the guise of saving money. Their suggestions included greater pedestrianisation even where this interfered with traffic flow, as at College Green, where it would have created a fine urban piazza enclosed by the buildings of Trinity College, the Bank of Ireland (formerly the Parliament building) and good quality nineteenth century commercial buildings to the south. However, given the lengthy battle which the Dublin City Centre Business Association had to wage in order to get Henry Street and Grafton Street pedestrianised, and the reluctance of the roads engineers to surrender a single square metre of roadspace, the prospects for creating an attractive and pedestrian-friendly heart to the city remain bleak.

Land-use and transportation strategies

In 1967, Dublin Planning Officer Michael O'Brien argued for the necessity for co-ordinating land-use and transportation policies (O'Brien, 1967). Regrettably, little effort seems to have been made along these lines. Taken together, the land-use and transportation planning strategies which have been adopted and operated in Dublin represent an excellent example of how urban strategic planning should not be undertaken. Even during recent years there has been ample evidence to suggest that there still exists only weak recognition among decision-makers of the intimacy of the relationship between land-use and transportation. The Eastern Regional Development Organisation's report (1985), which was to provide a revised settlement strategy, actually omitted to include transportation in its list of 14 criteria upon which land-use options might be appraised (Crowley, 1991).

Even more recently, a Dublin Transportation Review Group was established by the Minister for the Environment, comprising represen-tatives of interested Government departments (Environment, Justice and Transport), the local authorities, CIE (the state run public transport group) and the Garda (police). The Review Group subsequently appointed consultants to examine the previous 20 years of transport planning in the city, yet gave them no remit to investigate settlement strategy. A consultative panel including wide community representation has recently been established to assist the consultants and it seems that public transport will be given a greater degree of significance in any future strategy (Steer Davies Gleave, 1992).

Strategic transportation planning has been rendered more difficult by the fact that responsibility for the implementation of policy lies within a number of different departments of central and local government. At central government level, the Department of the Environment is responsible for the national roads network, the Department of Transport is concerned with public transport, while traffic control and parking enforcement lie within the remit of the Department of Justice and the work of the Gardai. In addition, at local government level, responsibilities for roads and for land-use planning lie in separate departments. Such absurd administrative fragmentation of responsibility inevitably results in a lack of co-ordination.

A sensible attempt was made by a Fine Gael-Labour coalition government during the mid-1980s to mitigate some of the adverse consequences of this administrative complexity by creating a Dublin Transport Authority (DTA), following the suggestion of the Transport Consultative Commission (1980). After it had been in existence for just six months, it was swiftly terminated by an incoming Fianna Fail government as an exercise in pruning public spending. One wonders how very short term such savings are likely to prove.

The recent history of the co-ordination of land-use and transportation planning situation is summarised by Enda Conway (1991, 73), a town planner:

> In the Dublin context we have worked out our land-use strategies, our land-use/drainage solutions, land-use/water supply solutions, land-use/education, recreation and commercial requirements etc. All of these have been worked out with the assistance of our professional colleagues. However when it comes to land-use/transportation the trouble begins.

The example of Dublin's orbital motorway illustrates the consequences of failing to plan strategically and in a co-ordinated manner for land-use and transportation. The Western Parkway, which proceeded in the absence of any planning studies of the land-use implications of the motorway, was to have a wide green space reserved to either side (McDonald, 1990a). However, it soon became evident that the motorway was having a major impact on the location of industrial property development and was in danger of being hemmed in by new construction (MacLaran et al., 1991). By 1990, sites alongside 'the golden mile' between Greenhills Road and the Naas Road were being sold for IR£455,000 per ha., twice the level of 12 months previously. In some cases, land prices in the area trebled in little over a year, land with planning permission fetching IR£1.24M per ha. (IR£0.5M per acre). Moreover, planning permission was being sought to develop a massive 140,000 sq. m. (1.5M sq. ft.) shopping and leisure centre at Quarryvale on the Galway road at its intersection with the Western Parkway, its scale relying on a regional catchment, based on accessibility to a projected population of 400,000 people living within a ten minute drive. Located at the north-eastern periphery of Clondalkin, this would almost certainly ensure that the development of the planned town centres for Lucan-Clondalkin and neighbouring Blanchardstown would have to be abandoned or drastically revised. Yet in May 1991, Dublin County Council voted to rezone the 42 ha. (106 acres) as appropriate for commercial development. In response, the developer of Blanchardstown Town Centre, where IR£3M of site-works had already taken place, abandoned development pending confirmation of the Council's intention with regard to the Quarryvale scheme. Meanwhile, in the vicinity of the Southern Cross motorway, considerable rezoning of land from open space to residential use has taken place under Section 4 motions.

Policy evaluation

In general, Dublin's transportation problem is perceived as being primarily one of traffic congestion causing inefficiency in the operation of the space-economy. Time is wasted, imposing costs on businesses and individuals. However, little consideration is given to broader issues in policy evaluation. Policies always possess different ramifications for different groups – be they property owners, inner-city residents, commuters or business owners – and the beneficiaries and losers from any transportation and land-use strategy should be identified. To the extent that policies redistribute real income between such groups, they are inherently political. Facilitating car commuting by ignoring illegal on-street parking benefits the commuter at the expense of compromising the safety and convenience of others – particularly of inner-city residents, the users of on-street public transport and short-stay visitors arriving by car. Just as there is no single conception of the nature of the problem, so can there be no single correct technical solution to transportation/land-use problems. Policies are imbued with political significance because they have differential distributional consequences.

Congestion, through the operation of market forces, encourages sub-urbanisation of economic activities. This is not necessarily to be condemned. If pursued in a planned fashion by public policies which promote (or undertake) the development of relatively self-contained and balanced suburban/ex-urban communities for both living and working, suburbs could be constituted as relatively independent entities. Indeed, this was the stated objective in the case of Dublin's own new towns. Such planning could result in a reduced dependency on daily commuting to the centre and produce a more energy-efficient city. This approach would also reduce the wasteful inter-suburban travel patterns which are of growing importance in Dublin and have long been evident, for example, in North America.

It could also be argued that there should be no major infrastructural investment in Dublin's transportation systems until the strategic land-use preferences have been determined. If taken in isolation from long-term strategic land-use policies, decision making about transportation may generate wholly inappropriate actions and undesired consequences. Similarly, the costly improvement of transport infrastructures should not be undertaken in the absence of short- or medium-term measures such as the enforcement of regulations. For example, in the absence of a strategic view of land-use preferences, costly improvements to transportation infrastructures which facilitate movement into the central area can have undesirable long-term consequences. Both road improvement programmes and developments such as the DART scheme increase the accessibility of the central business district. This enhances its attractiveness to business functions, raises the land values of central area sites and encourages property development pressures, land-use intensification and functional change (see Chapter 7). This can be clearly seen in the vicinity of Westland Row station, where there has been a major decline in industrial land-use and a proliferation of office development since the opening of the DART. It has brought windfall benefits to the owners of sites in the area, but has had detrimental repercussions for the working-class residents of the area who have experienced the displacement of the neighbourhood's industrial economic base. In turn, the development of new offices and shops is likely to bring greater levels of demand for passenger movement towards the city centre; but more commuting will inevitably generate renewed congestion and more demands for costly improvements to the transportation system. Thus it is essential that this cycle be broken by strategic land-use/transportation planning, the like of which Dublin has never experienced.

Moreover, whether costly public sector investment in transportation infrastructures should be undertaken in order to preserve and enhance central-area business functions, thereby protecting the property portfolios of investors, is highly questionable. The current debate between the need for road improvements or investment in public transit (such as light-rail systems) largely avoids these crucial issues and there is little evidence that any serious attempt to plan strategically is likely to be made in the foreseeable future. In its absence, the development of Dublin will continue to be shaped largely by market forces.

7
Creating the urban landscape

The city as built space

The very notion of towns as identifiably separate entities implies a distinction between urban and rural. Yet in our developed economies where capitalist market systems have penetrated the remotest parts of the rural environment, transforming its economic relationships and its traditional ways of life, it becomes difficult to place definite limits to the urban area. In such a context, any delimitation will necessarily be somewhat arbitrary. One useful way of viewing the urban environment is to regard it as marking a transformation in the use to which land is put, rural environments being characterised by land-extensive operations, while urban functions are largely land-intensive. Of course, within these two broad categories there are considerable degrees of variation in intensiveness, but it is a useful distinction because it focuses upon the very essence of 'the urban': the way in which land is used and the character of the built environment. Moreover, it directs our attention towards the powers which create built-space and the forces which transform it.

It is the myriad of decisions which lie behind the development of industrial, retail, office and residential properties in the city which shapes the geography of employment and housing. Because property development is responsible for structuring space, it has an important impact on human well-being. This is because access to employment of an appropriate type depends on where one can afford to live, and where those types of employment can locate. The built environment can therefore be viewed as a vast array of different types of buildings and infrastructure which represent a vast investment of capital that is tied up for lengthy periods in the form of bricks and mortar, steel, glass and concrete. The amortisation of this investment takes place only very slowly, so the built environment is relatively fixed and change is gradual.

At the periphery of the city, property development acts as the 'cutting-edge' of the advancing built environment, often operating on a very large scale by converting agricultural land mainly to residential or industrial functions. The scale of the industry's operations within the city is less extensive. Here, the fragmentation of land ownership, combined with the problems of obtaining clear legal title to permit redevelopment, mean that it is difficult for the private sector to assemble large sites for redevelopment.

Buildings are created with the intention of accommodating particular functions. As new types of function appear and develop (or die out) and as functions alter their building design requirements, these demands become reflected in changes in the built environment. Thus, the city expands laterally, grows vertically and adapts internally to the changing requirements of the users of built-space. Although certain types of built-space are developed by the state – such as housing and transport infrastructures which may be too risky for the private sector to undertake or which lie beyond the logic of individual capitalists to provide – it is the private sector property development industry which generally caters for such demands by equipping space for particular functions. The commodities which the industry creates are buildings constructed to fulfil a demand from users.

The private sector interests

New private sector developments result from the potential of property development to generate profits for those types of capital involved in the creation of the built environment. The major private sector interests involved in property development and the market relationships which bind them can be seen from Figure 7.1. In addition, there is a plethora of professional agents such as architects, structural engineers, planning consultants, estate agents and solicitors who operate on a fee-for-service basis. Obviously, the property sector comprises a considerable heterogeneity of interests which interact through different markets. These relationships are in a state of dynamic tension because of the inherent competition between the actors over development profits and because of differences in their economic power and the varied duration of their engagement in development.

Figure 7.1 depicts only archetypal roles and it is possible for a single individual, company or institution to take on a number of such functions simultaneously. If a construction company were to use its own funds to

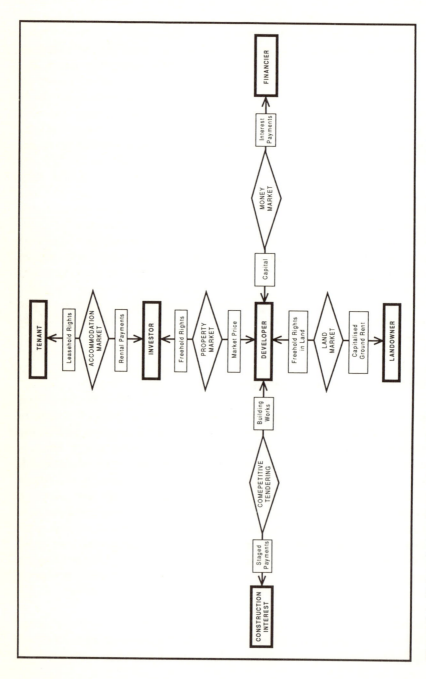

Figure 7.1 Major private sector relations within the property development industry. (After Malone, 1985a)

redevelop its own property for offices, it would be acting in the roles of landowner, developer and construction interest. If it were to retain the development for either owner-occupation or letting, it would also adopt the role of the investor.

As property development requires the profitability criteria of each participating interest to be fulfilled, the production of the built environment cannot be treated as an unproblematic reflex response to changing conditions of demand in the accommodation markets alone. Although the accommodation markets reflect the strength of demand for buildings, thus linking the development process directly to the cyclical trends in the wider economy, the fact that these conditions are mediated through the relations of production within the property sector means that the response becomes unpredictable. Moreover, for financiers and institutional investors, engagement in the property sector is but one of a number of possible options for pursuing capital accumulation. Thus, their participation can only be understood in relation to factors operating in the wider economy where current and predicted future returns from property and the analysis of investment risks are compared with equity markets, government stocks and cash on deposit. The prospective returns from property might be too low or too risky to warrant their participation at all.

Even in comparison with politicians or parking wardens, there can be few individuals, companies or institutions in Irish society who have attracted such an intense degree of opprobrium as have property developers. However, Figure 7.1 shows that the development function is pivotal. It is the developers who initiate the development process – by recognising an opportunity to profit from a perceived demand for certain types of building in particular locations. They negotiate with landowners for the acquisition of development rights to sites, either purchasing a freehold or leasehold interest in the property or entering into joint development arrangements to share development profits with the site owner. It is the developers who arrange the short-term financing for construction. They commission architects to devise a scheme, within certain cost constraints, which will be acceptable to the planning authorities. It is also they who engage the builders and use estate agents to seek suitable tenants or purchasers for the completed development. Thus it is the developer who carries the risk in undertaking a development, and this might not prove to be profitable. So, developers might appropriately be regarded as the impresarios of the built environment.

As in other cities, development interests in Dublin are highly heterogeneous in character. Some developers operate in a number of property sectors, others specialise in either industrial property, shops, offices or housing. Even excluding those developments which have been undertaken for owner occupation, the developers within a single sector can be very diverse (see Malone, 1985a, 1990). For example, Dublin's office developers range from individual operators and privately owned companies such as Hardwicke, John Byrne Group, Clancourt, Duke House, John Ronan and Durkan Bros., to companies quoted on the Irish stock exchange (Green Property and Power Corporation) or in Britain (MEPC, British Land and Oldham Estates). Since the mid 1970s these have been joined by the development departments of large financial institutions, particularly the insurance and life companies. Construction companies have also taken on the office development role, or have done so through development subsidiaries, reflecting the desire to gain greater access to development profits and the desire to create a more guaranteed work-flow rather than relying on contracts obtained through competitive tendering.

Property economics

The logic of the property development industry is to use the process of creating the built environment as a means of generating profit. Figure 7.1 shows that the industry serves two markets: an accommodation market supplying floorspace to fulfil a user-demand; and a property investment market supplying buildings to investors who receive the flows of rental income from tenants. Although the profits from property development ultimately depend on finding occupiers for buildings, the relative independence of these two markets can cause major problems for the industry, as will be seen later.

Developers can profit from a scheme in two main ways. They can retain a completed building and receive the flow of rental income, profiting so long as their income exceeds the flow of outgoings, primarily the cost of interest payments on debts incurred to purchase the site, to construct the building and pay the professional fees. Alternatively, buildings can be sold to an investor through the property investment market to realise a capital gain if the sale price exceeds the total development costs. Additionally, a variety of sale-and-leaseback arrangements can be made with investors to provide some element of capital gain without relinquishing all interest in future rental growth.

Briefly, the price at which a building sells is determined by the rental income which the building generates and the acceptable level of yield which this represents to an investor, according to the formula:

$$\frac{\text{Rental Income}}{\text{Yield}} \times \frac{100}{1} = \text{Capital Value (Price)}$$

$$\frac{\text{IR£100,000}}{5} \times \frac{100}{1} = \text{IR£2,000,000}$$

Thus, IR£100,000 represents an initial yield of 5 per cent on a IR£2.0M purchase price. Clearly, as rents double, capital values also double. If the prospects for future rental growth look good, more investment interest will be shown in property. The effect of increased competition between investors for a relatively fixed stock of investment property is to bid up its price. So the price one has to pay in order to obtain a given quantity of rental income rises. Its initial yield therefore declines. Thus, as capital values rise, initial yields fall or 'harden', perhaps to 4 per cent:

$$\frac{IR£100,000}{4} \times \frac{100}{1} = IR£2,500,000$$

So the sale price of a building may bear little relationship to its cost of construction, and this can generate a large pool of profit for which the private sector interests compete.

Yields

The level of initial yield which is deemed acceptable by investors is established in relation to the returns available from other forms of investment, their liquidity, future prospects and risk. Initial yields from prime property are often several percentage points below risk-free government stock, such investments being made in the hope that rents will rise in the future through the mechanism of regular 'upward only' rent review clauses incorporated in leases, ultimately outstripping returns from gilts.

However, real estate is far from being a homogeneous investment medium. Retail, office and industrial (factories and warehousing) premises each have different prospects for rental growth, liability to rental default and rates of locational and/or physical obsolescence. This is further complicated by variations in the construction quality and location of premises, high quality buildings in desirable locations being typified by lower acceptable initial yields.

As in the United Kingdom, direct ownership of commercial and industrial real estate in Ireland has been a far more important investment vehicle for life assurance companies and pension funds than is common in North America. It has recommended itself to investment managers for a number of reasons. First, in Ireland the equities market is small and, until the late 1980s, institutions were constrained from investing more than 10 per cent of their funds abroad. Property was therefore a useful means of portfolio diversification. Secondly, unlike a share certificate in a company which goes into liquidation, property is a real asset which retains at least some value and can be re-let should a tenant default.

Finally, rental income from commercial and industrial property has tended historically to grow in line with, or even outpace, the rate of inflation and such investments are therefore especially suitable for long-term investors such as life assurance companies and pension funds (Caldwell, 1985).

Investors in Irish property are even more varied than the wide range of developers noted above. Even if one ignores the state and the owner-occupiers, the latter themselves comprising a highly heterogeneous group, the major investors include Irish and overseas insurance and life assurance companies, property development companies, private pension funds and property unit trusts. Their scale of investment interest in property varies through time with respect both to the amount of property in portfolios and the mix of property types. Historically, property has comprised as much as 36 per cent by value of some portfolios, but its poor investment performance, compared to the high rates of return from equities and gilts during the 1980s, saw the value of property holdings decline to between 5 per cent and 10 per cent. Thus in 1985, while IR£700M was invested in equities and gilts, only IR£20M was directed towards property in Ireland (MacLaran, 1986).

In Ireland, the value of property portfolios might typically comprise 60 per cent in offices, 30 per cent in retail premises and the remainder in industrial units. However, for legal reasons and due to its limited potential for rental growth, residential property is rarely a major component of institutional investment. This mixture obviously changes through time, but large-scale juggling of the property mix within portfolios cannot be effected swiftly. Property in general is an illiquid asset and it can be particularly difficult to dispose of under-performing assets. Instead, switching is generally accomplished through additional acquisitions of those types of property for which the prospects appear to be good. As one might expect, the bulk of Irish investment property in the office, retail and industrial sectors is located in Dublin.

Rents

The basis for development profit is the amount of rent which can be extracted from the users of a given site. Rent is merely the economic reflection of the legally enshrined social relationship of 'property right' in which rental payments are made for the right to occupy land and/or buildings. Under given conditions of the market, the scale of rental payments which can be extracted from a plot or a building is determined by three elements: the class of the user, the type of function being accommodated, and the quantity of space generating rental income. Because land price (ground rent capitalised at the prevailing rate of interest) is determined in relation to the revenue-generating capacity of the site, there is a constant pressure to upgrade land-use to enhance the flow of rental income. This is undertaken in three main ways:

1. The class of occupier can be upgraded, low-class shops being displaced by those with a greater rent-generating capacity. Along the main shopping streets in Dublin's central business area, there has been a gradual disappearance of local retailers in favour of international multiples such as Marks and Spencer, Saxone, HMV, Laura Ashley and Next , or franchises such as Benetton, The Body Shop and The Sock Shop. Only where an owner-occupier or a tenant with a long lease has resisted the temptation to sell-out to more profitable types of outlet do the smaller retailers retain a somewhat incongruous foothold.

   This process of displacement is akin to 'gentrification' in housing markets, though lacking the transfer of tenure which usually characterises the change from working-class tenants to middle-class owner-occupiers. In the retail property market it has led to the progressive reduction in the heterogeneity of business types occupying prime locations. In 1960, there were 36 different types of business present in Grafton Street, Dublin's prime shopping street to the south of the Liffey. By 1985 there were only 26. Types of business which disappeared from the street between these dates include an antique shop, an art dealer, three booksellers, three chemist's shops, a children's clothes shop, a china shop, a cinema (replaced by an arcade of boutiques), three grocery shops, a shoe repair shop, a specialist tobacconist, two men's tailors and an ironmonger's shop. These were displaced by four financial institutions, two fast food outlets, four hairdressing establishments, two jewellers' shops, six shoe shops and 11 women's fashion stores (Browne, 1986; Lisney and Son, 1989).

2. A second method is to change the type of function being accommodated, which is the basis for the conversion of agricultural land to urban functions as well as upgrading within the city. Retail and office functions normally have a higher rental capacity than either industrial or residential uses. Current technology of industrial production and warehousing favours expansive (land-using) single-storey buildings. Moreover, industries are producing or handling physical commodities which often compete on world markets and therefore have to be price-competitive with foreign imports. However, in the case of both retailing and office-based professional and financial services, there is a greater measure of locational monopoly as customers and clients are geographically constrained in their choice of shops or services and this can be reflected in the

ability of retail and office functions to pay higher rents for favourable locations.

To the south of the Liffey, this has led to the conversion of many of Dublin's eighteenth century residences into offices. Merrion and Fitzwilliam Squares had an adult residential population of 572 in 1960, but by 1985 this had fallen by 65 per cent to fewer than 200. In 1989, only 6 of the 161 buildings on the two squares were still wholly devoted to residential uses, compared with 27 in 1966, the number which had been partly residential declining from 70 to fewer than 40 (Naughton, 1990).

The conversion of residential buildings to commercial functions has often resulted in the wholesale abandonment of the upper floors of buildings, even near to the city's main shopping streets. The cost of alterations in order to meet rigorous fire regulations, the unwillingness of commercial users to share entrances with residents, the cost of providing separate entries, the problems associated with disposing of buildings with sitting residential tenants and the operation in the past of the residential Rent Restriction Acts, have all contributed to buildings' being left partly unused.

Upgrading also involves the conversion of industrial premises – as at Bolands bakery, now the site of a 12,075 sq.m. (130,000 sq.ft.) office building – and has resulted in the adaptive reuse of public buildings for office functions, such as Sir Patrick Dun's Hospital and a number of city churches.

3.   Another method of enhancing the flow of rental income from a site is to increase the quantity of lettable space. This might involve the internal modification of an existing building's volume, reducing the space devoted to stairways and halls which do not produce rent. This remodelling process has far less visual impact on the townscape, but it has often resulted in the loss of important internal architectural elements. It is also possible to redevelop a site completely, replacing the building entirely by a space-efficient structure, simultaneously attempting to increase the plot ratio by accommodating a much larger building. In Dublin, this has resulted all too frequently in the replacement of structurally sound buildings of considerable architectural and townscape merit either by 'Anywheresville' architecture, slavishly following the most recent international fad, or by degraded pastiche designs which seem to mock their eighteenth century neighbours.

Profit and location

To developers the urban landscape represents a profitability surface which is highly differentiated geographically, and there exists a tendency to direct development to prime locations where capital and rental values are at their highest and where initial investment yields are at their lowest. For example, to purchase a 10,000 sq.m. building renting at £160 per sq.m. in the prime area of Dublin 2 or Dublin 4, an investor might be willing to accept an initial yield of 6 per cent in the belief that rental growth will be strong, and pay up to £26.67 million in order to acquire it. A similarly-sized building on Mountjoy Square (Dublin 1), would command a rent of perhaps IR£80 per sq.m., while the initial yield required by investors would be considerably higher, perhaps 8 per cent, reflecting the riskier location. The effect on the building's capital value and potential for profitability is enormous. Although land costs may be much lower in the second location, construction costs would be similar and short-term development finance may even be more costly, penal interest rates being charged to reflect the riskier character of the development. For example:

Dublin 2 or Dublin 4:

$$\text{Capital value} = \frac{\text{IR£1,600,000}}{6} \times \frac{100}{1} = \text{IR£26.67M}$$

Mountjoy Square:

$$\text{Capital value} = \frac{\text{IR£800,000}}{8} \times \frac{100}{1} = \text{IR£10.0M}$$

This has resulted in the directing of development towards the prestigious areas of Dublin 2 and Dublin 4 where the quality of existing buildings was generally high. Here, rental values are at their peak because of high user-demand, while levels of acceptable initial yields are lower because of lower levels of risk and the location's capacity for rental increase and capital growth. The past 30 years have therefore witnessed a progressive attack on those parts of Georgian and early Victorian central Dublin which were previously the best preserved areas.

In contrast, areas to the north of the river Liffey and to the west of Dublin Castle, where much of the fabric of the city was in a state of serious dilapidation and in need of refurbishment or redevelopment, long failed to attract interest from commercial property developers because of their poorer potential returns. The scheme depicted in Figure 7.2 on the south eastern corner of Mountjoy Square has been in the process of development for about 20 years but was abandoned several years ago prior to completion.

Figure 7.2 Only three Georgian houses remain on the south side of Mountjoy Square. The remainder are 1980s replacements. The abandoned, partly completed office block has been in the process of development for some 20 years, a reflection of weak user-demand in this location.

Site assembly and secondary areas

A prerequisite for any development is, obviously, access to land. Developers of suburban housing often invest a proportion of company profits in building up a land bank for future development. Windfall profits can accrue if they are able to purchase large tracts of cheaply priced 'white land' (zoned for agricultural purposes), obtain a re-zoning classification to urban functions and then divide it for sale to smaller builder-developers who lack the financial muscle to speculate in this fashion. Redmond (1987) has indicated that speculation and trading in peripheral land takes place in Dublin and can generate substantial profits.

However, in the central area, landownership can be very fragmented. In Dublin, where much of the central area was first developed in the seventeenth and eighteenth centuries, plots are generally small. Yet there are substantial economies of scale to be gained from large redevelopment schemes. Moreover, as Lamarche (1976) has shown, the ability to negate

Figure 7.3 The scale of modern property development is often highly intrusive. The development on the right replaced six 'protected' eighteenth century houses along South Frederick Street.

undesirable neighbourhood conditions increases with the scale of development. Thus, developers in central Dublin have usually preferred to undertake redevelopment projects on sites which are the product of assembling a number of original plots. In doing so, they have begun to transform the grain of the city's structure and this has resulted in the intrusive imposition of unsympathetically large-scale redevelopments on the existing townscape, as in Figure 7.3.

This preference for larger sites has also created a niche for specialist site assemblers. They operate by recognising the development potential of sites and buying up neighbouring properties at prices which reflect their current uses rather than their development potential, profiting from their sale to a developer at an inflated price. Site assembly generally proceeds surreptitiously so that property owners do not realise what is happening and inflate their asking prices. During the assembly of the site for the Harcourt Centre office development on Harcourt Street, houses purchased early on in the assembly process fetched IR£80,000 each whereas the last pair were reputed to have been bought for IR£600,000 (McDonald, 1985a).

In addition to the problems of acquiring a multiplicity of freehold rights, there may be several layers of leasehold rights which have been granted historically as tenants have granted sub-leases to sub-tenants, and sub-tenants have granted further sub-leases. This means that it can be very difficult and time-consuming to gain clear legal title to a site because all the interests must be bought out.

The case of the St Stephen's Green Shopping Centre at the southern end of Grafton Street clearly illustrates the problems. Site assembly here commenced in the mid 1960s and required about 15 years to buy out more than 150 property interests to create a 1.82 ha. (4.5 acre) redevelopment site. Originally conceived as an office development, by the time assembly was complete, the office market had crashed and planning permission had to be sought for a retail development. Similarly, MEPC's 12,050 sq.m. (130,000 sq.ft.) Ardilaun Centre, an office development on the west side of St Stephen's Green occupying a site of 0.8 ha. (2 acre) which is 'wrapped around' the Unitarian church, was completed only in 1982. Even though some plots were obtained from the local authority which had been exercising its powers of compulsory purchase in order to buy up properties in the area for road improvements, this small redevelopment site took ten years to assemble and required several years subsequently to sort out the legal problems of ownership title (Greene, 1986; McDonald, 1985a).

Because of the length of time required to assemble sites, almost inevitably a substantial period of time elapses prior to redevelopment. During such time, building maintenance tends to cease, there being little point in maintaining buildings which are destined for demolition. Moreover, a building which is incapable of beneficial occupation, such as one which has had its roof removed, is not subject to rates. Thus, the process of site assembly is often very destructive of the city's fabric, dereliction being the almost inevitable result, blotting the landscape for many years and having greatest impact where the buildings form part of a terrace.

Properties along Bachelor's Walk underwent site assembly for a period of almost 20 years. This is a location with considerable commercial potential, lying as it does between the city's two major shopping areas of Henry Street and Grafton Street. However, it was also important in architectural terms, possessing a number of listed buildings which dated from the eighteenth century, including one, at number 7 Bachelor's Walk which was built in the 1730s and retained particularly fine interior wood panelling and was widely recognised as one of the most important domestic-scale buildings on the quays. From the early 1970s, a succession of developers attempted to assemble the properties for a large-scale development of shops and offices. During the intervening years, buildings deteriorated and in some cases were demolished to provide revenue from

Figure 7.4 Bachelor's Walk. The Liffey's quays have been blighted by road widening plans and suffered from site assembly for property development.

illegal surface car parking. A series of fires hastened the process of dereliction, a fire in number 5 Bachelor's Walk necessitating its demolition. This demolition had the effect of destabilising the house next door, which also had to be pulled down, followed by another fire in number eight which brought down part of its roof (McDonald, 1990b). Figure 7.4 reveals the very sorry state of Bachelor's Walk in 1992, a quay frontage which not many years previously had been one of the most attractive features of the city.

As a postscript to this saga, it is ironic that as a result of a fall in confidence in the retail property market during 1989 and the recognition that the remaining properties would still require considerable time to assemble, the properties were put up for sale in 1990 in a number of separate lots by their owner, Arlington Securities, a subsidiary of British Aerospace. Doubtless, much money had been made over the years by the property transactions while others probably lost out. But the real loser is the city itself.

Because of site assembly difficulties in the core of Dublin's central business area, developers have often turned their attention towards acquiring larger sites under single ownership in secondary areas marginal to the core. Frequently, these have accommodated industrial functions, so developers reap the additional benefit of cheapness compared to prime locations. Moreover, if the scale of a redevelopment project is sufficiently large, developers may be able to extend the prime zone to incorporate the new scheme.

Some of the developments by Irish Life provide good examples of where this has taken place, as with Irish Life's 36,000 sq.m. (390,000 sq.ft.) of offices on Lower Abbey Street, and its 15,000 sq.m. (160,000 sq.ft.) office development at Harcourt Square. An even larger project comprising 46,450 sq.m. (500,000 sq.ft.) of offices at George's Quay, a secondary location previously accommodating industrial and warehouse premises, remained undeveloped for nearly ten years following the collapse in the office property market, but its first phase is now under construction.

In common with most European cities, Dublin has experienced the suburbanisation of industrial functions, responding to the changing technologies of those industries in favour of single-storey buildings with extensive car parking and loading areas. Important inner-city industrial functions which have been lost from central Dublin include Jacob's biscuit factory, William and Woods (a subsidiary of Nestlé) and Boland's bakery, which left their cramped inner-city sites at Bishop Street, Parnell Street and Lower Grand Canal Street for more expansive premises at the periphery. The demand for land from alternative functions has enabled industrial users to capitalise the value of their inner-city properties and defray substantially the costs of relocating to modern premises in more profitable locations.

Jacob's Biscuits successfully sold its 1.6 ha. site on the south-western fringe of the central business district for over IR£1 million to a British property company, thus helping it to finance its move to Tallaght in 1976. Part of the site now houses the Government Stationery Office. However, site disposal can be fraught with difficulty depending on timing within the development cycle. It took nearly ten years for William and Woods to sell its 1.92 ha. (4.75 acres) site on the north-west margins of the central business area. Despite having signed an option to sell at IR£2M at the height of the office boom, the collapse of that market resulted in the company's eventual disposal of the site only six years later at a price of IR£1.25M (Kearney, 1986). Most of this site was subsequently cleared and operated as a surface car park. Although outline planning permission was obtained for a retail-office complex incorporating 34,400 sq.m. (370,500 sq.ft.) of office space, there is no immediate prospect of development because of insufficient demand.

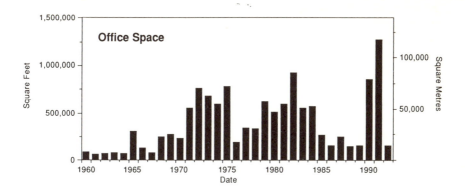

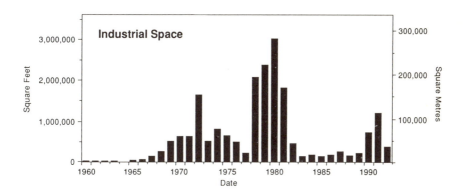

Figure 7.5 Development cycles in the office and industrial property sectors.

Development cycles

Property development tends to be cyclical. Periods of frenetic activity are punctuated by phases of relative quiescence, resulting in boom-slump cycles which seem to characterise every major sector of the property market, including office, industrial, retail and residential development (Beamish, 1990; MacLaran and Beamish, 1985; MacLaran et al., 1987; MacLaran, 1989a; MacLaran et al., 1991; Malone, 1985a, 1990; Redmond, 1987). Figure 7.5 shows the cyclical character of development in Dublin's office and industrial property sectors.

As real estate development is undertaken to satisfy a demand for accommodation, the stimulus to property development is normally a rise in the user-demand for buildings. As Bill Nowlan, the Property Manager of Irish Life, observes: 'just as you don't buy an envelope unless you want

143

to post a letter, people don't want buildings unless they have a function to accommodate' (Nowlan, 1986). However, buildings are in a relatively fixed supply and, unlike most other products, they take a long time to produce; so developers not only have to respond to current demand, but they have to try to predict the future demand for buildings. As the supply of built space is relatively inelastic, increased demand chasing a fixed supply results in an increase in the levels of rent which buildings can command. Their sale price, therefore, also increases, which increases the potential profitability of development, but it will take a substantial length of time for any new development to reach completion. Even a project which is 'ready to go', where the land has already been assembled and clear legal title and planning permission obtained, will take time to construct. During this phase there is likely to be a sustained period of rising rents which encourage increasing numbers of schemes to be undertaken as developers attempt to cash in on the boom.

The problem is that no mechanism exists to ensure that the production of buildings will exactly match the scale of demand. Moreover, once construction has commenced, it becomes very difficult to abort developments even when it is apparent that demand may be faltering. As Maurice Greene, the Managing Director of MEPC (Ireland) (now Dublin City Properties) notes:

> This is one of the problems with development. When we are all there with the ear to the ground, we are all getting the same vibes and all are saying 'we're going to build in central Dublin' or wherever, and too many rush in, then this overheating occurs and there is the over-supply. The problem is that the gearing of the whole development process is so slow that once it's started it's like, perhaps, running a ship. You can't just slam on the brakes and stop. The whole process has to keep going. It's very hard to respond instantly to problems like that. So if people are geared up and rolling towards a development, they have tended in the past to say that 'ours is a bit better than the fellow on the left, and certainly a lot better than the one on the right, and ours is going to be the one that wins. (Greene, 1986)

Inevitably, some lose out. Once an over-supply of space appears, some developers are unable to secure a purchaser or tenant for their buildings, facing them with having to meet interest payments without receiving any rental income. Vacancy rates increase, rents stabilise or fall, new developments are shelved and the market enters a period of slump. Those developments taking place during the ensuing downturn tend to be either for owner-occupation or are pre-let.

It was noted earlier that property development serves two separate markets: the accommodation/user market; and the property investment market. However, the operation of the investment market can drive the development cycle towards over-development on a scale which is wholly unjustifiable in terms of user-demand, severely exacerbating the fluctuations which result from the business cycle. As space shortages occur and rents begin to rise, investor confidence in property also rises. With large quantities of funds suddenly switching into the property market, the price of the limited stock of property available on the investment market rises to highly inflated levels. Investors become willing to accept lower initial yields in the hope of obtaining increases subsequently through rent reviews. The effect on capital values can be dramatic, and developers rush in to satisfy this enhanced investment demand.

This can be illustrated by reference to Dublin's office market during the period 1988–90, but Beamish (1990) points similarly to the effect of investment-led development in industrial property during the late 1970s and early 1980s. Following a period of major depression in the office market when prime rents had been static at around IR£100 per sq.m. for over six years, shortages of prime space began to emerge in 1989. With the supply of newly completed space being reduced from its historic high of 85,105 sq.m. (916,124 sq.ft.) in 1982 to just 13,005 sq.m. (140,000 sq. ft.) in 1988, vacancy rates in modern (post-1960) offices fell to below 3.5 per cent. Rents for new lettings rose rapidly. By late 1988, the inducements offered by developers to prospective tenants had disappeared and by mid-1989 rents for the few newly completed prime developments reached IR£150 per sq.m..

Such a dramatic rise in rents during a period of less than a year, with all its implications for the capital values of buildings, generated a new mood of confidence in office property as an investment. As investment fund managers were all monitoring the same market indicators, there was a tendency for institutions to make similar decisions and switch funds into property. During 1989 the Dublin office market witnessed a ten-fold increase in the value of investment transactions in office property to over IR£116M, initial yields strengthening from 6.5 per cent to below 6 per cent (MacLaran and Hamilton Osborne King, 1990a). (Declining initial yields, it should be remembered, are a sign of confidence in the future of property as a medium of investment.) So, instead of buying into property when the market was weak and prices were low, acting logically in a counter-cyclical fashion, there was a tendency for investment managers to 'follow the market' revealing behavioural tendencies reminiscent of a herd of sheep. The largest investors involved in making acquisitions during this upsurge in investor interest were Irish institutions and they were joined by foreign insurance companies. Commercial property development and investment companies were also active acquirers of buildings as were industrial companies for which property investment was a peripheral activity.

The effect of this investment demand for office property and the over-confidence generated by its short-term performance, was to stimulate a massive burst of development activity. Its scale was wholly unwarranted by the level of user-demand, take-up having averaged little over

18,580 sq.m. (200,000 sq.ft.) of new space annually during the previous four years (1986–89). However, the length of time required for construction ensured that rents continued to rise throughout 1989 as only 14,400 sq.m. (155,000 sq.ft.) of new space reached the market that year. By December 1989 the vacancy rate for modern office space had fallen to 3.35 per cent, with only 9,660 sq.m. (104,000 sq.ft.) of the vacant 35,300 sq.m. (380,000 sq.ft.) being newly completed. During 1990, the rush of new developments began to reach completion. The office market was swollen by over 78,965 sq.m. (850,000 sq.ft.) of new space in that year alone, with a further 117,000 sq.m. (1.26M sq.ft.) being added in 1991. Thus, in a period of just two years, the stock of post-1960 office space in the city had expanded by 18 per cent.

The consequence of such a frenetic burst of development activity was to raise vacancy rates. In mid-1990, vacant space amounted to 39,480 sq.m. (425,000 sq.ft.), of which 22,296 sq.m. (240,000 sq.ft.) was newly completed (MacLaran and Hamilton Osborne King, 1990b). By December 1991, the vacancy rate exceeded 10 per cent. Some 125,000 sq. m. (1.35 million sq. ft.) of office space lay vacant, of which almost 60 per cent was brand new (MacLaran and Hamilton Osborne King, 1992a). Rents began to stabilise and then to fall in real terms as development entered another decline. Thus, although it is often opined that location is the key factor in property development, it is clear from the above that timing is also important.

Business functions and locational requirements

Retailing in Dublin

The geography of retailing activities and the desirability of different locations are influenced by a number of factors. These include accessibility, environmental obsolescence, growth potential, the mutual cohesion and compatibility of retail functions and the minimisation of competition.

The highest prices for urban land are commonly found in retailing areas at the city centre. Historically, this was the focus of the intra-urban, inter-urban and possibly also the national public transportation systems affording accessibility to a wide catchment area of consumers. Accessibility also underlies the development of retail functions along highways where they can intercept customers from passing vehicular traffic. In central areas of cities there exists a close relationship between retail rents and the volume of pedestrian traffic. In Dublin, prime retail streets such as Henry Street and Grafton Street possess the highest volumes of pedestrian flow and also command the highest rents (Figure 7.6). Shopping streets are, nevertheless, subject to environmental

Figure 7.6 Flower sellers and buskers add interest to pedestrianised Grafton Street, the city's most prestigious retailing street.

obsolescence, the volume of retail sales tending to fall if levels of pedestrian volume decline. This has happened at South Great George's Street and Capel Street during the twentieth century as the central business area has migrated eastward.

Retail businesses prefer to locate in areas which possess a potential for growth, either in terms of an increasing population or growing incomes. The suburbanisation of Dublin's population, particularly of the middle class with its rising real purchasing power, together with enhanced personal mobility associated with increasing car ownership, have all encouraged the suburbanisation of retailing. It has led to the development of suburban shopping centres catering for the motorist, though suburban shopping centres in Dublin have tended to be small by comparison to their American counterparts. The first such centre in Dublin, located at Stillorgan, dates from 1966 and since that date, no fewer than 51 planned shopping centres of over 1,858 sq. m. (20,000 sq. ft.) have been developed (Figure 7.7), amounting to more than 278,700 sq.m. (3 million sq.ft.) of floorspace (Parker and Kyne, 1990).

Initially, developments tended to be located in the post-war suburbs previously reliant on inadequate traditional village shops and by 1980,

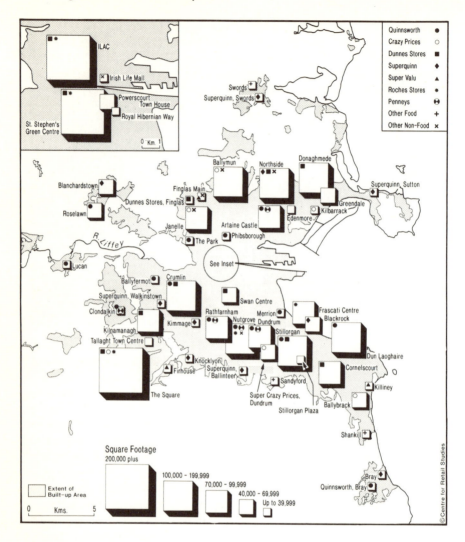

Figure 7.7 Purpose-built shopping centres in Dublin. (Source: Parker and Kyne, 1990)

the pattern of development was of relatively small (2,000–12,000 sq.m. (22,000–130,000 sq.ft.)) centres located three to five miles from the city centre and about two miles distant from one another (Litchfield and Partners, 1980).

More recent trends have led to the provision of in-town shopping centres, commencing in 1979 with the opening of the Irish Life Mall comprising 2,400 sq.m. (26,000 sq.ft.) of retail space in a retail-office complex in Lower Abbey Street. This was followed in 1981 by Irish Life's redevelopment of an area between Henry Street and Parnell Street as the ILAC Centre, comprising 20,400 sq.m. (220,000 sq.ft.) of lettable retail space, and the opening of the Powerscourt Town House Centre in the same year, a high quality rehabilitation by Power Securities of Powerscourt House (1774) in Clarendon Street and its conversion into an attractive multi-level shopping centre.

In 1988, two further inner-city retail schemes were opened. Friends Provident's development of the Royal Hibernian Way is located on the former site of the Hibernian Hotel in Dawson Street (1,580 sq.m. (17,000 sq.ft.) lettable), while British Land redeveloped the south side of South King Street as the St Stephen's Green Centre (21,180 sq.m. (228,000 sq.ft.)). These, together with certain environmental and infrastructural improvements, have confirmed the central area's attraction and significance as the single most important shopping location in the metropolitan area. The pedestrianisation and repaving of Henry Street, Grafton Street and North Earl Street, strenuously promoted by the City Centre Business Association, has resulted in greatly improved environmental quality. Private sector provision of multi-storey car parks on the edge of the shopping area has also facilitated access for customers.

The development of retail schemes in the suburbs has also continued, particularly of smaller centres in the catchment areas lying between existing centres. This process of in-filling has been associated with schemes characterised by a far greater attention to design and architectural detailing, as in the 5,353 sq.m. (57,000 sq.ft.) Blackrock Shopping Centre completed in 1984 (Parker and Kyne, 1990).

Although the development of planned shopping centres in the inner suburbs started in the 1960s with the development of the Phibsborough Shopping Centre (1966), developers became increasingly willing to turn their attention to such localities during the 1980s, as indicated by the completion of the Swan Centre (Rathmines) in 1983, the Park Shopping Centre (Prussia Street) in 1985 and the Merrion Centre (Nutley Avenue) in 1986. Meanwhile, other centres were begining to reach the stage at which major refurbishment and improvement work was becoming increasingly necessary, renovation having taken place at the Rathfarnham and Northside shopping centres which date from 1969 and 1970 respectively.

The emergence of retail warehousing on industrial estates is a trend which arrived relatively late in Ireland, is still of quite limited importance and is confined essentially to the sale of furniture, electrical and do-it-yourself items. The range of products obtainable is therefore more restricted than one would find in many British cities and far less extensive than in many small European or American towns. However, 1991 marked the opening of the first dedicated retail warehousing park, developed on the Naas Road by The Royal Liver Friendly Society. It represents an important step in the retailing market and is likely to be the first of several such developments.

Some large-scale retail developments have either been developed or are planned for the western suburbs, and these are likely to have a major impact on the geography of retailing in the region. The completion in 1990 of The Square, a 55,740 sq.m. (600,000 sq.ft.) multi-level shopping scheme in the centre of Tallaght, comprises over 130 shops, nine restaurants and a 12-screen cinema complex. This has provided much needed retail and leisure facilities for the new town, which currently has a population in excess of 74,000 people, while the new Western Parkway around the city has created an extended catchment area.

The proposed developments of Blanchardstown's Town Centre and the major retail complex planned for Palmerstown would doubtless further erode the economic base of the central area, which will have to turn its attention to improving its drawing power, trading on its character and the heterogeneity of the built environment. Part of this programme should include major extension of the pedestrianised zone and limiting vehicular access into the core area for public transport alone. If this is not undertaken, retailers will increasingly recognise the advantages of trading from the controlled environment of planned shopping malls, as they have done in America, and question the benefits received from the ever increasing burden of city-centre rates.

Up-to-date information on the relative performance of central area retailing is unavailable, but between 1966 and 1977 retail turnover in the city centre grew by over 17 per cent in real terms, but this was outstripped by the 67 per cent growth experienced in Dublin as a whole. Thus, in the intervening period, the city centre's annual turnover as a proportion of the whole of Dublin declined from 39 per cent to 27 per cent (Dublin Corporation Planning Department, 1985a). As in British cities, it has been the trade in convenience goods which has suburbanised most rapidly, the city centre accounting for 70 per cent of the total durable goods trade in the late 1970s, but only 10 per cent to 15 per cent of the trade in convenience items (Litchfield and Partners, 1979b).

Office functions and office development

Offices are commonly able to out-bid other functions above the ground-floor level in centrally located buildings. Beyond the immediate vicinity of the city's major shopping streets they commonly comprise the dominant ground floor function in buildings located in the prestigious areas. One can identify at least three types of office function within both private and public sectors:

1. Those related to the day-to-day control of manufacturing activities which are typically located within industrial plants and therefore increasingly possess a suburban location.
2. Those relating to routine office employment including support services (filing, computer operations etc.) which generally do not require to be centrally located. Offices of this type are often the first to depart from the centre. The location of the Bank of Ireland's computer centre at Cabinteely, near Foxrock, is an example of this trend.
3. Offices such as the branches of banks and building societies which have a requirement for over-the-counter contact with the public tend to locate at ground floor level in the retail core and increasingly at accessible suburban locations. Their locational demands are more akin to retailing establishments than to other offices.
4. Private and public sector offices which accommodate headquarters, regional directorate functions and professional services, commonly require ease of contact between staff within the establishment as well as with other office services external to the company. These have therefore tended to be located in multi-level buildings near the centre of cities. The functions of personnel employed in these offices involve both programmed contacts of short duration relating to the direct exchange of information, and longer, more widely ranging meetings covering policy issues.

Any office may have a variety of professional, managerial and skills requirements, needing, therefore, to draw employees from widely dispersed residential areas. Traditionally, the central areas of cities offered accessible locations for the assembly of a workforce from a wide range of geographical locations, especially if public transport is used for the journey to work. This reinforced the central city as the key location for office activities – and central Dublin is the major nucleus of office functions in the state – but these activities have also been suburbanising in recent times. With improvements in telecommunications and the growth of personal mobility among office workers, suburban office locations have become increasingly attractive. In Dublin, some headquarters functions have also moved out.

Suburban office locations are of varied types. Individual offices may be located at geographically scattered locations, either in converted buildings or in purpose-built developments such as those of the First National Building Society at Booterstown. There are also office centres attached to existing suburban nodes (e.g. Blackrock) and modern office parks, similar to industrial estates but generally developed with far higher levels of attention to landscaping quality. A number of office parks located in the vicinity of one another may ultimately form a new office cluster in its own right, for example at Sandyford-Leopardstown and at Clonskeagh.

Push factors have been significant in inducing office suburbanisation. The costs of locating in the central area can be considerably higher than in the suburbs. In February 1992, prime rents for new buildings in central Dublin stood at IR£170 per sq.m. (IR£16 per sq. ft.) compared to as little as IR£107 per sq.m. (IR£10 per sq. ft.) in some suburban office parks. Congestion in the central business area and a lack of parking for employees and clients have encouraged firms to relocate towards inner-suburban locations where there is widespread availability of free on-street parking (MacLaran, 1990). Furthermore, the strict limitation of parking provision in office developments in the core has encouraged developers to construct schemes just beyond the Corporation's boundary in County Dublin.

Within the central business district, since the inception of the DART system, there has been a distinct movement in the location of modern office developments into the area to the east of Westland Row (MacLaran, 1991a). While such an outcome was not foreseen, it indicates how public sector investment in transportation infrastructures can influence locational patterns. It also shows the way in which public investment can be employed to bend market processes towards a defined planning goal, but such goals should be identified prior to the implementation of investment strategies.

Approximately 1.18 million sq. m. (12.7 M sq.ft.) of modern office space was developed in Dublin between 1960 and 1992, responding to the growing demand for space to accommodate the increasing number of office workers in the city. Figure 7.5 shows clearly that the completion of this space has been achieved in three major development cycles and one can perhaps identify a tendency for the cycles to become increasingly accentuated.

The cycle has important effects on both developments and developers. During slump conditions, a greater proportion of the developments are either undertaken by owner-occupiers, are pre-sold by developers to owner-occupiers or are pre-let to prospective tenants before construction commences. This eliminates the risk of failing to find an occupier when the building is complete. Those speculative schemes which do proceed are more likely to be located in the heart of the central business area, the industry expanding its field of activity geographically into riskier fringe or secondary locations during boom periods in the cycle when confidence is high (Malone, 1985b; MacLaran, 1989b).

There is also a marked tendency for commercial property companies rather than the institutions to pull back from development during the downturn in the cycle (Malone, 1985b; MacLaran, 1989b). Institutional developers are more likely to be undertaking developments for owner-occupation and their timing is therefore unrelated to external conditions of demand for accommodation. Indeed, developments carried out during the slump benefit from the lower building costs which are the result of depressed conditions in the construction sector. Moreover, institutional developers almost invariably have a stronger financial position than commercial development companies. Investor-developers generally do not need to borrow funds to undertake developments, drawing instead upon internal cash resources and the flows of premium income which they derive from long-term savers. This creates less commercial pressure on institutions to achieve a swift economic return from property development. Getting the timing right is therefore not so crucial for institutional investor-developers as for companies operating on short-term borrowings.

During the early 1960s, much of the office space which was developed in the Dublin area was for owner-occupation and located either in the Dublin 2 postal district (the south-eastern wedge of the inner city lying within the canal ring) or extending beyond the Grand Canal into the residential area of Dublin 4. It was attracted to Dublin 4 by the pleasant physical environment, its prestigious character and the presence of large dwellings occupying substantial sites. However, this incursion of modern offices transformed parts of the district, particularly Burlington Road and Pembroke Road.

Demand for office space was boosted during the 1970s by a rapid rise in demand from the public sector (central and local governments, public agencies and semi-state organisations such as the Electricity Supply Board (ESB) and the telecommunications services). Indeed, throughout most of the 1970s, the public sector took up on average about 55 per cent of lettable space placed on the accommodation market, accounting for as much as three-quarters in some years. It utterly failed to use the strength of its market position to encourage development in locations which were in need of redevelopment rather than in those requiring protection.

During the second boom in office development which peaked in 1982, the public sector continued to play a major role in the lettings market. However, its involvement was highly erratic, ranging from a take-up of just 5,575 sq.m. (60,000 sq.ft.) in 1983 – when it accounted for less than a quarter of the lettings market – to over 23,225 sq.m. (250,000 sq.ft.) in both 1980 and 1981 – when it comprised three-quarters of user-demand for leasehold space. It became impossible for private developers to adjust their scale of activity to match such wildly fluctuating requirements. Moreover, as a result of the parlous state of the public sector's finances, there was a government embargo on further state lettings and it withdrew almost entirely from the lettings market after 1983.

The public sector has also played a significant role as a developer of office space for its own use, accounting for around 10 per cent of all modern office space constructed since 1960 and over two-thirds of the 130,000 sq.m. (1.4 million sq.ft.) which it owns. The most important public sector developer has been the Office of Public Works, responsible in recent years for the excellent reconstruction of 2,790 sq.m. (30,000 sq.ft.) of offices at Dublin Castle and the conversion of buildings at the former Jacob's biscuits factory in Bishop Street for use as the Government Stationery Office and store.

The bulk (almost 60 per cent) of modern office space which has been developed in the city has been sited in Dublin 2, where over 671,000 sq.m. (7.2 million sq.ft.) of office space is located in over 240 properties. However, as half of this was developed prior to 1976, it is now showing its age, and many post-1960 buildings in the district have undergone substantial refurbishment. The second most important office district is Dublin 4, with 175,000 sq.m. (1.9 million sq.ft.) in 54 buildings. Its stock is generally newer than that of Dublin 2, mostly post-dating 1975. A further 140,000 sq.m. (1.5 million sq.ft.) of modern office space is located in some 30 developments in the north inner-city area of Dublin 1. These again mostly post-date 1975, with a significant proportion being accounted for by the Irish Life Centre and the more recent Custom House Docks scheme (see Chapter 10). Blackrock and Dun Laoghaire comprise the only major office node outside Dublin 1, 2, and 4 with some 30 developments accounting for 48,000 sq.m. (516,000 sq.ft.) of space dating mainly from the period of the second office boom.

Developments outside these locations have been in the form of isolated blocks or in landscaped office parks, such as the IDA – promoted South County Business Park between Foxrock and Sandyford. A relatively early development of associated office premises was also undertaken by the construction company McInerney at Leopardstown Office Park on the eastern edge of the Sandyford Industrial Estate. This location has subsequently attracted further office development and over 11,150 sq. m. (120,000 sq. ft) of office space are now located in the vicinity while in the inner suburb of Clonskeagh, the construction of a number of office campus developments in the neighbourhood of Smurfit's headquarters (1979) is creating a new office cluster here.

Most development schemes in Dublin have been small, from 929 to 2,323 sq.m. (10,0000–25,000 sq.ft.). However, although fewer than 20 of the 400 or so modern office developments are larger than 9,290 sq.m. (100,000 sq.ft.), these account for 30 per cent of all post-1960 office space and total over 353,000 sq.m. (3.8 million sq.ft.).

Unsurprisingly, the character of office buildings has changed over time. The 1960s brought the influence of the modern movement in architecture, albeit in a rather degraded form, and the decade saw the construction of buildings such as O'Connell Bridge House (D'Olier Street),

Figure 7.8 The Central Bank looms over adjacent properties in the Temple Bar district between Dame Street and the river Liffey.

Fitzwilton House (Wilton Place), St Stephen's Green House (Earlsfort Terrace), Liberty Hall (Eden Quay) and Hawkins House (Hawkins Street). None of these has greatly enhanced the urban environment, the latter having been described as 'easily the most monstrous pile of architectural rubbish ever built in Dublin' (McDonald, 1985a, 41).

Dublin fared little better at the hands of developers and architects during the early 1970s, the international penny-pinching style of the developers being reflected in buildings simply designed to serve their money-making purpose as generators of rent. Little thought was given to the context in which development was taking place. The decade opened inauspiciously with the completion of the new ESB headquarters in Fitzwilliam Street which had required the destruction of 16 early nineteenth century terraced houses. Much of the redevelopment of Lower Mount Street also took place during the decade, as did the destruction of 'a marvellous group of relatively sound, important, splendid irreplaceable' eighteenth century buildings on St Stephen's Green, either side of the entry to Hume Street, and their replacement by 'poor quality pastiche buildings' (Barry, 1975, 55). Although the destruction of Dublin's eighteenth century streets was wrought mainly by private sector developers, much of the space was taken up by the public sector. The public sector also failed as a developer by neglecting to ensure that its own schemes fitted successfully into the traditional small scale of the city's streetscapes. This is typified by the controversial 8,360 sq.m. (90,000 sq.ft.) Central Bank building in Dame Street, depicted in Figure 7.8, which is a fine building in the wrong location, towering over its neighbours and dominating the whole area.

During the decade, as institutions became increasingly interested in office property as an investment, they frequently found themselves unable to acquire a sufficient supply of speculative office schemes of a quality which would retain their value in the longer term. They therefore either became involved with the developers at an earlier stage in the development process, or were induced into undertaking speculative developments themselves. This closer involvement with projects has generally improved the architectural quality of recent developments.

The 1980s brought to completion the new Civic Offices at Wood Quay (Figure 5.3). This 12,075 sq.m. (130,000 sq.ft.) development has attracted much derisive criticism for its architectural style which resembles a multi-level gun emplacement and which makes no concession to its immediate neighbour, Christchurch Cathedral. There was also a continued improvement in the internal specification of buildings, increasingly incorporating raised floors to facilitate new office technology. Architects continued to design both modern and pastiche schemes, but from the mid-1980s there was a rapid growth in 'own-door' office developments resembling town houses and which proved popular with smaller businesses. By the end of the decade, elements of post-modernism were becoming fashionable.

Within the central area, development locations also widened considerably, especially following the establishment in 1986 of Dublin's inner-city Designated Areas (see Chapter 10). Here, in decidedly secondary or even tertiary areas on the fringe of the central business district, virtually untouched by development of any sort during the twentieth century, there was a burst of office construction during the late 1980s and early 1990s encouraged by financial incentives. Office users, however, were more conservative in their locational preferences and vacancy rates in the Designated Areas exceeded 30 per cent by the end of 1991, three times the norm for the city as a whole (MacLaran and Hamilton Osborne King, 1992b).

Industrial functions and industrial property

Fewer generalisations are possible regarding the locational requirements of industrial functions as these include a wide range of activities (processing, assembly and service operations, storage and warehousing) and have developed over a lengthy period. Generally, industrial functions require geographical locations which permit ease of assembly of goods and raw materials for processing, assembly or storage. They also require accessibility to an appropriately skilled workforce. Long-established industries may now possess locations which were based on previously significant factors, such as an orientation towards canal or rail-based transportation, but have grown to a size at which it becomes economically difficult to relocate the plant to a more efficient location. However, many industrial functions have been suburbanising.

It has been public policy to encourage firms to relocate to single-storey buildings on purpose-built industrial estates at the periphery, the zoning practices of urban planners having encouraged out-migration by deeming industrial functions to be 'non-conforming land-uses' in central areas. The costs of acquiring inner-city property, and the fact that *in situ* expansion has often been precluded by zoning policies, have militated against expansion there and congestion costs have helped to push industrial functions out.

Industrial property includes both factories and warehouses. Figure 7.5 shows that the creation of modern industrial buildings in Dublin since 1960 has taken place during three major development phases which produced over 1.86 million sq.m. (20 M sq.ft.) of industrial space (MacLaran et al., 1991). The strategies of the developers and the institutional investors have been of vital significance in the developing industrial geography of the city during this time. However, unlike the development of retail and office property, the supply of industrial property has also been very heavily influenced in a direct way by the actions of government and semi-state bodies (Beamish, 1990).

Dublin's first boom in industrial property development during the late 1960s and early 1970s reflected a period of rapid economic expansion in Ireland which generated a demand for new industrial premises. The completion of industrial space doubled annually between 1966 and 1969, reaching a peak in 1972 with 150,000 sq.m. (1.65M sq.ft.) of floorspace. The availability of large suburban sites, the lower costs of suburban green-field developments compared to central areas, together with the added profits to be won from land conversion from agricultural to urban functions meant that new industrial premises were located on suburban industrial estates rather than in the inner city.

The first boom ended as a result of deteriorating economic conditions around the time of the world oil crisis in 1973. Emerging economic problems caused a reduced demand for new premises and an over-supply of industrial space emerged. Escalating interest rates and building costs also squeezed developers, who responded by cancelling developments, sometimes even leaving buildings unfinished. By 1977 the output of industrial space had reached its lowest level for ten years with only 18,500 sq.m. (200,000 sq.ft.) reaching completion.

The second boom in industrial property resulted from a combination of factors: a resurgence in world trade during 1976; the improved international competitiveness of the Irish economy; and a series of expansionary budgets, lifted the economy out of recession. The IDA's incentives for industry contributed to a climate of optimism which encouraged industry to expand. By late 1977, space shortages in the industrial property sector had begun to emerge, forcing up rents at double the rate of general inflation during 1978. Conditions of low interest rates and an abundant supply of labour power in a construction industry with an unemployment rate of 22 per cent, facilitated a second development boom. A tenfold increase in the completion rate of industrial property occurred in 1978. The boom lasted just four years and reached a scale of output far in excess of that which was achieved during the previous cycle, rising to over 278,700 sq.m. (3 million sq.ft.) in 1980 alone. However, by the end of the boom, so great was the oversupply of industrial property on the market, that it took more than seven years to reduce the surplus to a level at which development activity was able profitably to recommence during 1989.

This second boom had been marked by the emergence of modern industrial property as a vehicle for institutional investment. In 1980 alone, investors acquired over 92,900 sq.m. (1 million sq.ft.) in 78 units. Increasingly, life assurance companies and pension funds recognised the value of standard industrial units as a useful outlet for their growing premium income, noting the rapidity with which industrial rents were rising during the late 1970s, outstripping the general inflation rate and also the rate of rental increase for offices and shops. Industrial property had long been considered more vulnerable to rental default due to recession, while the lower land value content and high rate of building depreciation also militated against it as a suitable long-term investment. However, institutions minimised these problems by concentrating investment in standard warehouse units rather than factories, warehousing accounting for over 80% of their portfolios of industrial space by 1985. It was this gearing of development to the scale of demand emanating from the investment market rather than the user-market which prolonged the boom and drove it to such heights of over-production.

In addition, largely through the activities of the Industrial Credit Corporation (ICC), a state-owned bank, and the IDA, substantial amounts of European Investment Bank funds were directed into industrial property in the city (Beamish, 1990). By the early 1970s, it was becoming evident that the IDA's regional policy of not promoting industrial growth in the Dublin area while encouraging new industries to locate in the regions, was achieving a measure of success. It soon became apparent, however, that Dublin had suffered badly from the recession of the mid-1970s and it therefore became essential for the IDA to reverse its bias against Dublin and from 1976 it commenced promoting the city as an industrial location. This strategy was undertaken mainly in response to political pressures which required visible activity in Dublin at a time when key Dail seats came under threat. Thus, it commenced acquiring land for industrial estate development and undertook the direct provision of factory premises, recognising that the 'spec-built tin cans' of the private developers were of such poor quality that they could not induce international high technology employers to locate in Dublin (Beamish, 1990).

It also entered into joint development ventures with private developers in which the IDA would guarantee to find tenants for properties, thereby underwriting the leases and acting as the guarantor for rental income. The IDA's own development programme allowed it to offer high-specification buildings, either of a standard design or custom built, generally between 1,858–3,720 sq.m. (20–40,000 sq.ft.) but extending in certain instances to over 9,290 sq.m. (100,000 sq.ft.), developed on low density schemes incorporating copious room for expansion and landscaping. The private sector was reluctant to provide this type of package, having traditionally developed low specification industrial sheds of between 460 sq.m. and 1,858 sq.m. (5,000–20,000 sq.ft.) in size, located on high density sites. Moreover, the IDA was prepared to provide options to purchase on a staged basis.

The impact of IDA involvement can be gauged from the fact that by 1983 it had been associated with the development of nearly one-third of the factory units developed in Dublin since 1960 and was the largest owner of industrial space in the city, accounting for some 163,500 sq.m. (1.76 M sq.ft.). The ICC had also assembled a large portfolio of industrial properties, valued at IR£20M in 1984 making it the second largest freeholder. Interestingly, the third largest owner was yet another state-owned institution, the Irish Life Assurance Company (MacLaran and Beamish, 1985).

One market segment which the IDA showed itself prepared to enter had previously attracted virtually no private sector interest. This was its provision of industrial space in the inner city. Although the response of the IDA might be described as being too little and too late, creating just 37,000 sq.m. (400,000 sq.ft.) in 75 industrial units in the inner city by 1982, the operations of the IDA stand in sharp contrast to those of the private sector. By 1982, the IDA had invested over IR£16M in industrial premises in the inner city, representing 39 per cent of the industrial units in its portfolio, though the small size of these units meant that they accounted for only 16 per cent of its city-wide portfolio of floorspace. However, this compares with the general neglect of the inner city by private developers, the inner city having attracted fewer than 4 per cent of their factory units since 1960. Thus, the IDA has been responsible for developing well over four-fifths of all the factory space built in the inner city since 1960.

Private sector developers have tended increasingly to concentrate their activities to the south of the river Liffey, which has attracted 65 per cent of modern industrial space (MacLaran et al., 1991). The south-west, which possesses good communications with the national market, alone accounts for over half (53 per cent) of all post-1960 industrial space, amounting to 975,000 sq.m. (10.5M sq.ft.). The north-east, with good links to Belfast and proximity to Dublin Port and Dublin Airport, has attracted over 450,000 sq.m. (4.89M sq.ft) of modern industrial space. However, it is disturbing to note that less than 185,000 sq.m. (2 million sq.ft.) of industrial space has been developed in the north-western sector. This represents barely 10 per cent of the total. Yet it is an area of large working-class housing estates including Finglas and the new town of Blanchardstown whose population expanded fourteenfold between 1961 and 1979.

Industrial properties completed since 1987 have shown a general improvement in quality of design and construction materials, resulting mainly from the lead shown by the IDA and the influence of the institutional investors. The office component has tended to increase, some units having an office element in excess of 45 per cent. There has also been a trend towards improving the quality of that office component to include atrium reception areas, suspended ceilings, modular lighting fittings, carpeting and even platform floors to accommodate cabling systems for computer operations. Clearance heights of the eaves have also tended to rise, with 6 metres (20 feet) being regarded as the norm, developers responding to the greater attention being paid by users to the cubic capacity of warehousing rather than simply to floor area.

Building construction materials and the quality of insulation have improved, marked by the abandonment of asbestos in favour of metal deck roofing and a greater use of profiled, insulated and often coloured metal cladding for walls. These, together with high technology glazing, give the appearance of an altogether higher level of attention to design and build quality which sets many of the recently completed industrial properties apart from the bulk of their predecessors. Outside, there has also been a trend towards the provision of more extensive car parking and greater attention to the quality of landscaping, and these elements have resulted in a reduction in site coverage, typically to around 35 per cent to 40 per cent. Security arrangements have also been enhanced.

There has been a tendency towards the blurring of the functional categories of industrial space. This is true with respect to the functional character new buildings which are being accommodated on industrial estates, and with regard to the division of space within buildings. Some buildings might more appropriately be classified in the 'science park' category where the production of high value components and the greater proportion of managerial, administrative and research, and development personnel leads to a demand for higher quality accommodation from occupiers with greater rental capacity (MacLaran et al., 1991).

Considerations

The redevelopment of the built environment is a costly process. The logic of private sector activity is to undertake developments which will give the highest possible return. In the past, these have usually comprised office and retail schemes, which offer high rental capacities, rental growth potential and limited ownership or management costs. However, it is also the potential profits which can accrue from such high value developments which underpin the high cost of central city land. Thus, the only form of developments which seem to be justified are office and retail schemes, the land market effectively zoning out industrial functions because of their limited rental capacity. While the potential profitability of certain types of development is instrumental in determining the price of land, equally the high price of central area land determines what can profitably be built. This creates a 'hope value' in neighbourhoods surrounding the central business area where property owners hope to receive a high price for land which they believe might attract a high value redevelopment and are reluctant to sell at a lower price. In Dublin, the area zoned for commercial development has been very broad geographically and has resulted in a wide band of underutilised land on the margins of the central business area where property owners have held unrealistically optimistic ideas about property values. However, as property owners recognise the unlikelihood that such widespread redevelopment for commercial uses will ever be required, they have turned increasingly to residential functions as an option, the proposal by Bord Gas Eireann to redevelop an 8 ha. (20 acre) derelict site in the docks to include 1,400 dwellings being an example of growing realism.

8
The population of Dublin

The population of the Republic of Ireland is ethnically very homogeneous. There are historical influences which include Norse and Anglo-Norman elements, as well as those of Scottish, English, Dutch and French Huguenot stock, but visitors are often struck by the absence of visibly distinct ethnic minorities. Not only is the population homogeneous ethnically, it is also overwhelmingly Roman Catholic, the proportion having increased from 92.6 per cent of the population in 1926 to 95.4 per cent in 1981. This population is characterised by a high level and frequency of formal religious observance. An estimated 1.25 million people, more than a third of the population of the Republic, attended the Papal Mass in Dublin's Phoenix Park in 1979.

The second striking feature of the Irish population is its youthfulness. In 1986, over 38 per cent of the state's population of 3.54 million people was aged under 20 years. A quarter of the population was less than 14 years old and only a minority was aged over 28. Figure 8.1 presents the changing age structure of the Irish population since 1961, during which time it expanded by 25 per cent. The greatest proportionate increase occurred in the age group from 20–24 years, which grew by more than 80 per cent over the 25 year period, with other young adult groups (aged between 15 and 39) all marked by increases of over 35 per cent. During the late 1970s and early 1980s, rapidly expanding job opportunities for the growing labour force enabled many young adults to stay in Ireland, even encouraging a net inward migration during 1981. In contrast, and alone among all the categories, the age cohort between 45 and 54 years actually registered a decline of over 6 per cent. Changing attitudes favouring smaller families are reflected in the limited growth of the youngest age group. Indeed, the number of children in the country aged

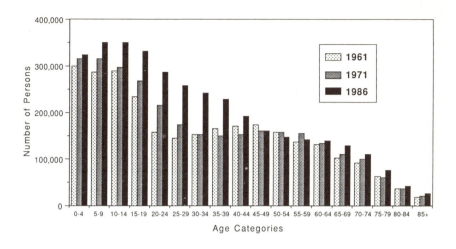

Figure 8.1 The changing age-structure of the Irish population.

under 5 years actually declined by nearly 29,000 between 1981 and 1986, representing an 8 per cent reduction. At the other extreme, there has been a 37 per cent increase in the number of persons aged over 85 years between 1961 and 1986.

The Irish population's youthfulness has ramifications for job creation in the economy as a whole. In recent years, the growth of jobs has generally failed to keep pace with the numbers of young adults entering the workforce. A continued shortfall in the creation of employment has implications for social stability, particularly in Dublin's new towns where such a large population is now reaching adulthood. This is especially serious at a time when the traditional outlet of emigration, which rose almost continuously during the 1980s to reach 46,000 (net) in 1989, has been dramatically curtailed by severe recessions in Britain and the USA.

The country's historically high birth rate, the emigration of economically active age groups and the high rate of unemployment have resulted in a very high dependency ratio. In 1986, only 30.36 per cent of the population was in paid employment. Thus, for every employed person in the state, there were 2.3 dependents and this dependency ratio is reflected in high levels of personal taxation to support state welfare and education services.

Urbanisation and the recent growth of Dublin

The economic transformation of Ireland during the twentieth century has been reflected in the changing geographical distribution of its population. Following a century of almost continuous decline, the total population increased slowly during the 1960s from its historically low level of 2.8 million in 1961. It grew by 5.7 per cent in the decade, and rose rapidly during the 1970s. Indeed, during that decade, population growth was the highest in western Europe, expanding by over 15 per cent (Walsh, 1978).

These processes of population change were associated with continued urbanisation. From being an overwhelmingly rural society at the outset of the twentieth century, it has become predominantly urban. At political independence, less than a third of the Irish population had resided in urban areas (32.3 per cent in 1926), defined in the Irish census as centres with a population greater than 1,500 persons. The urbanised proportion increased to 41.5 per cent in 1951 and by the mid-1960s over half the population was urban. This was partly a consequence of substantial rural population decline which continued until 1970, whereafter even rural population numbers increased as a consequence of longer-distance commuting.

By 1986, 56.4 per cent of Ireland's population was urban, though there was considerable variation regionally. While the population of Leinster, the eastern province, was 72.4 per cent urbanised, less than half (48.1 per cent) of Munster's population was urban, and in the province of Connaught and that portion of Ulster contained in the Republic of Ireland the urban components were only 26.4 per cent and 21.6 per cent respectively.

In contrast to slow expansion during the nineteenth century, Dublin's population has grown rapidly this century. The population of the Dublin sub-region (Dublin County Borough, County Dublin and Dun Laoghaire) doubled between 1926 and 1991, from 506,000 to 1,024,000, and the proportion of the Irish population for which it accounted also increased substantially, from 17 per cent to almost 29 per cent. Dublin has become a primate city within the Republic of Ireland. Its population is three times the combined totals of the four next largest towns of Cork, with 174,000 persons in 1986, Limerick (77,000), Galway (47,000) and Waterford (41,000).

Population growth in Dublin was especially marked during the 1960s and 1970s, during which time it increased by nearly 40 per cent:

The stark reality is that the Dublin built-up area has grown by a greater number in the past sixty-five years than in its entire history up to the 1920s! What is of particular note is that almost 60 per cent of this growth took place in the twenty years from 1961 to 1981. . . . By 1981 the Dublin built-up area accounted for 47.8 per cent of the urban population of the state and Dublin had twice the population of the next nineteen large urban centres in the country (Bannon, 1988, 134–5)

Table 8.1 Recent population growth in the Dublin area

	1961	1966	1971	1979	1981	1981[a]	1986[a]	1991[a]	
Co. Borough	537,448	567,802	567,866	544,568	525,882	544,833	502,749	477,675	
Dun Laogh.	47,792	51,811	53,171	54,244	54,496				
Co. Dublin	133,092	175,434	231,182	384,853	422,786	178,116	180,675	185,362	D.L.-Rathdown
						165,264	199,564	208,666	Belgard
						114,951	138,479	152,726	Fingal
Dublin	**718,332**	**795,047**	**852,219**	**983,665**	**1,003,164**		**1,021,467**	**1,024,429**	
Ireland	**2,818,300**		**2,978,200**		**3,443,400**		**3,540,600**	**3,523,400**	
Dublin as %	25.5%		28.6%		29.1%		28.9%	29.1%	

(a) Figures relate to the newly defined areas following the Local Government (Reorganisation) Act, 1985. Direct comparison of Census data is rendered impossible over the longer run as the population figures have not been adjusted by the Central Statistics Office for census years prior to 1981 to take account of the revised boundaries.

Source: Central Statistics Office, Census of Population, Vol. 1, 1971, 1981, 1986, Preliminary Report 1991.

The population of Dublin

Table 8.1 illustrates the scale of recent population growth within the Dublin sub-region in relation to the state as a whole. Although migration from rural areas has played some part in this growth, the major contributor has been natural increase, the excess of births over deaths. The prescriptions of the Roman Catholic church and, until the 1970s, the unavailability of artificial methods of birth control, encouraged large families and helped to ensure a growing population and demand for residential land. The church, as a significant institutional suburban landowner, has coincidentally profited from this through land sales to housing developers. Religious orders, which owned over 600 ha. (1,500 acres) in Dublin in 1987, were involved in an estimated IR£20M worth of property deals between 1987 and 1991 (Murphy and Sheehan, 1992).

Between 1961 and 1981, while natural increase accounted for an additional 246,770 people, net in-migration to the sub-region amounted to just 38,062. This, nevertheless, reversed the net loss during the previous decade through migration of nearly 70,000 persons, a trend which had been common to the country as a whole. By 1986, the situation had again reversed, resulting in net outward migration from the Dublin area of 36,583 persons, though this was more than balanced by natural increase of nearly 55,000 persons. Preliminary population data from the 1991 census indicates that Dublin's population increased only very marginally during the previous five years, at a time when most counties outside the Dublin commuter belt lost population and the total population of the state actually declined by 17,000. As a result, Dublin's share of the national population increased marginally.

Within the Dublin sub-region, the relative contributions of natural increase and migration to the changing balance of inner-area and suburban populations differ. Table 8.1 reveals the rapid growth in the population of County Dublin, having recorded an 83 per cent increase between 1971 and 1981. This was accounted for only in part by natural increase, amounting to just 72,828 persons. The larger contributor was the substantial net inward migration of 118,776 persons. Meanwhile, despite a net excess of births over deaths in the County Borough amounting to 52,450 persons between 1971 and 1981, it still experienced a net population loss of nearly 42,000 people, resulting from net outward migration of over 94,000 persons.

The growth of Dublin's population occasioned a period of massive extension to the built-up area. The policy of diverting population growth towards the western new towns, the profitability of land conversion from rural uses and the ease of developing in greenfield locations combined to produce residential expansion at the fringes of the city instead of much needed redevelopment within the core. During this almost unbroken phase of peripheral expansion, the resident population of the inner city (bounded by the Grand and Royal canals) continued to decline. Some inner-city wards began to lose population from as early as 1911. From its peak at 269,000 persons in 1926, when the inner city accounted for two thirds of the population of the built-up area, the number of inner-city residents declined by more than half to 132,000 by 1971, when it comprised 10.6 per cent of the total, falling thereafter to 83,200 persons in 1986.

By 1961, this process of decline had also begun to affect the inner suburbs of the County Borough, including some public housing areas which had been developed during the 1920s to accommodate people moving out from the central city. Table 8.1 shows that after 1971, population decline became a continuing feature of the County Borough as a whole. By 1991, despite its geographical enlargement, the County Borough's population had registered a loss of nearly 67,000 persons in just 12 years and was declining annually by over 5,000 persons. In contrast, the population of County Dublin continued to grow by over 5,000 per year, having expanded by over 88,000 persons, or nearly 20 per cent, since 1981. Thus, the city's notorious tenements have now largely disappeared and the typical Dubliner has been transformed into a suburbanite living in a house with a garden.

Household composition and demographic structure

In addition to population growth, the demand for housing has been boosted by a continuing trend towards smaller households. Since 1971 there has been a decline in the average size of households in Ireland from 3.94 in 1971 to 3.54 in 1986 (Census of Population, 1971 and 1986). This has accompanied a reduction in the average size of families, the total fertility rate, representing the average number of children to which a woman can expect to give birth during her lifetime, having fallen rapidly from 4.0 in 1971 to 2.3 in 1987. Declining average household size also reflects the growing tendency for young people to establish separate households from their parents, while at the other end of the age spectrum the elderly are increasingly likely to continue living independently of their families rather than in three-generation households (Blackwell, 1988).

In the Dublin area, declining average household size has been even more rapid than in the country as a whole. From having an average of 3.98 in 1971, slightly above the national average household size, by 1986 the local figure was somewhat less than the national average. Within the metropolitan area, average household size has tended to fall in both the County Borough and suburban Dublin County areas, though Table 8.2 indicates that the reduction has been more marked within the Borough.

The population of Dublin

Table 8.2 Changing household size in Ireland and in the Dublin area

	1971	1981	1986
Dublin Co. Borough	3.85	3.34	3.26
Dun Laoghaire	3.57	3.23	
County Dublin	4.32	4.01	3.73
Dublin Area	**3.98**	**3.59**	**3.48**
Ireland	3.94	3.66	3.54

Source: Central Statistics Office, Census of Population of Ireland, 1971, 1981, 1986.

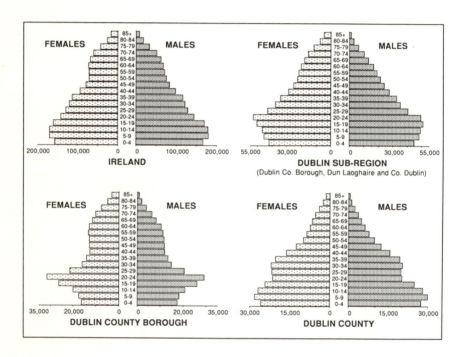

Figure 8.2 The demographic structure of Ireland and Dublin, 1986.

Figure 8.2 permits a comparison between the population structure of the Republic, the Dublin sub-region and both the County Borough and County Dublin in 1986. The sub-region as a whole had a slightly lower proportion of young children and of elderly people than did the Republic, differences also existing with respect to the sub-region's sex structure. While the number of males in the state matched or outnumbered the females in each age category up to the age of 54, in the Dublin sub-region males were outnumbered in all age groups after the age of 20.

Dublin has a very youthful population. In 1986, over 45 per cent of the population was aged under 25, with 27 per cent being less than 15 years of age. As late as 1961, nearly 15 per cent of households comprised seven or more persons, with nearly 9 per cent having eight or more members. This has subsequently declined, so that in 1986 only 8.6 per cent of all households were of seven or more persons while just 4.1 per cent had eight or more people present.

There also exist substantial contrasts between the demographic structure of the County Borough and Dublin County. In suburban County Dublin, the population was predominantly youthful with the under-25 age group accounting for almost half the total (49.5 per cent), whereas in the County Borough it was 44 per cent. One of the three sub-areas of the County, Dublin Belgard, which includes the two new towns of Lucan-Clondalkin and Tallaght, had a population with a median age of around 24. A quarter of its population was aged under nine years and 45 per cent were less than 20 years old.

There were proportionately fewer children aged under 15 years in the County Borough, where they represented only a fifth (21.9 per cent) of all residents, compared to County Dublin where that age cohort accounted for over a third (33.6 per cent) of the population in 1986. In County Dublin, on the other hand, young adults were more weakly represented while the County Borough also possessed a significant presence of people aged over 60 years.

In both the County Borough and suburban County Dublin, males comprised the greater proportion of each age category until early adulthood, whereupon a switching of the relationship takes place as a consequence of high levels of adult female migration from rural areas towards Dublin (Walsh, 1991).

The dramatic variations which existed between small sub-areas of the metropolis are illustrated in Figure 8.3, which adopts broad age categories to depict the differences in the age structure between selected areas. They include the mature and predominantly owner-occupied suburbs of Clonskeagh, Blackrock and Foxrock, the owner-occupied suburb of Rathfarnham which has experienced considerable recent speculative housing development around an older core, two inner-city areas, two established areas of public housing at Crumlin, dating from the 1930s, and Finglas, developed in the 1960s, and the three western new towns of Tallaght, Clondalkin and Blanchardstown.

The newer suburbs of County Dublin had a youthful population profile, over 48 per cent of residents being aged under 25 years in 1986. The western new towns in particular were characterised by large proportions of children, with 40 per cent of the residents being under 15 years

The population of Dublin

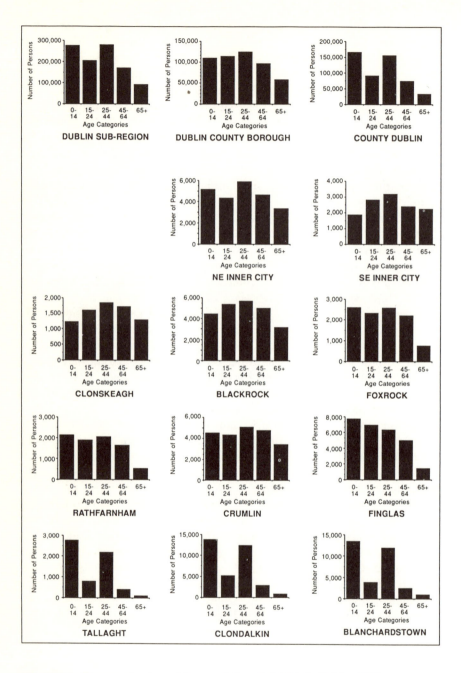

Figure 8.3 The age-structure of the population of districts in Dublin, 1986.

Figure 8.4 Children distracted from their street party in Killinarden. In 1986, half of the residents here were under 15 years of age.

of age. In some new town neighbourhoods, such as Mulhuddart in Blanchardstown and Killinarden in Tallaght, this proportion exceeded 50 per cent (Figure 8.4.).

The population profile of Finglas exhibited a greater degree of maturity than did the new towns and is more reminiscent of the newer owner-occupied areas such as Rathfarnham. Crumlin, with its higher proportion of elderly residents was beginning to take on the profile of a mature district, but was differentiated from owner-occupied areas such a Clonskeagh by its having a higher proportion of children. The two inner-city areas also offered something of a contrast in that the south-east inner city comprised far fewer children and had a greater presence of elderly residents.

Social status in the city

Inheritance is the most common determinant of social status in Dublin. In a survey of inter-generational social mobility among male adults in Dublin, 40 per cent had retained the social standing of their parents, a

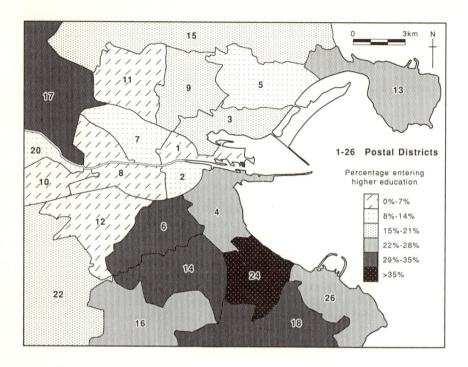

Figure 8.5 Variability in rates of participation in higher education. (After Clancy and Benson, 1979)

third had moved to a higher status and slightly over a quarter had fallen below that of their parents (Hutchinson, 1969). However, there was considerable variation in the degree of mobility when comparing different levels in the hierarchy. The four lowest status groups were predominantly recruited from amongst themselves and half of those comprising the lowest status group had been born into it:

> It appears that in Dublin rather more than half the socially mobile men moved no further than the category of status lying adjacent to that of their fathers, either above or below it. There is little evidence of dramatic gains or losses of status, partly because the system itself appears to preclude them. Downward mobility in the higher, or non-manual, categories, tends to occur internally: there is little crossing of the line separating them from the manual categories. Similarly, it is comparatively rare for men moving upwards in the lower manual categories to succeed in crossing the same frontier to occupy a position at the non-manual levels. (Hutchinson, 1969, 32)

As the level of educational achievement remains a significant determinant of employment status, it is noteworthy that differential participation rates in higher education between social classes in Ireland strongly favour the continued transmission of class position from one generation to the next (Hutchinson, 1969). Around a quarter of school-leavers enter some form of higher education, with slighly less than 10 per cent being admitted to university in 1986 (Clancy, 1988). The children of higher professionals, salaried employees, lower professionals, farmers, employers and managers all had above average participation rates, with those from higher professional backgrounds participating at a rate which was three times what would be expected from the overall class composition of school-leavers. In contrast, children from families of manual workers were significantly underrepresented. For the children of unskilled manual workers the probability was just 16 per cent of what would be expected from their representation within the population. Figure 8.5 maps the frequency of entry into higher education by postal districts, indicating low levels of take-up within the inner city and over large areas of the northern working-class suburbs.

The Irish census defines six categories of social class and a seventh where class is unknown. These are detailed in Table 8.3. It is apparent from Figure 8.6 that in the County Borough there was an overrepresentation of lower status social classes represented by groups 5 and 6, resulting from the suburbanisation of more highly qualified white-collar employees, while classes 1 and 2 were overrepresented in County Dublin.

As was the case of demographic status, the figure also shows that there were sharp differences between the class structure of small sub-areas of the city. The inner-city areas were characterised by a predominance of lower-skilled residents with few residents from classes 1 and 2. In the north-east inner city, higher groups comprised fewer than 10 per cent of the population, while almost 40 per cent were drawn from classes 5 and 6. The local authority housing areas of Crumlin and Finglas, which had been characterised by contrasting demographic structures arising from their different development dates, recorded very similar class structures. Fewer than 10 per cent of their residents were from classes 1 or 2 and over a third were either semi-skilled or unskilled manual workers. Two of the new towns, Tallaght and Clondalkin, also possessed similar class distributions, with skilled manual workers accounting for around one-third of the residents in each. The third new town, Blanchardstown, had a greater representation of higher social groups, classes 1 and 2 accounting here for almost a quarter of the population.

The profiles of the middle-class suburbs of Blackrock, Foxrock and Rathfarnham provide a considerable contrast. Here, classes 1 and 2 accounted for over half the population, exceeding two-thirds in the case of Foxrock, with lower social groups being weakly represented and reaching only 10 per cent of the total in Blackrock.

The population of Dublin

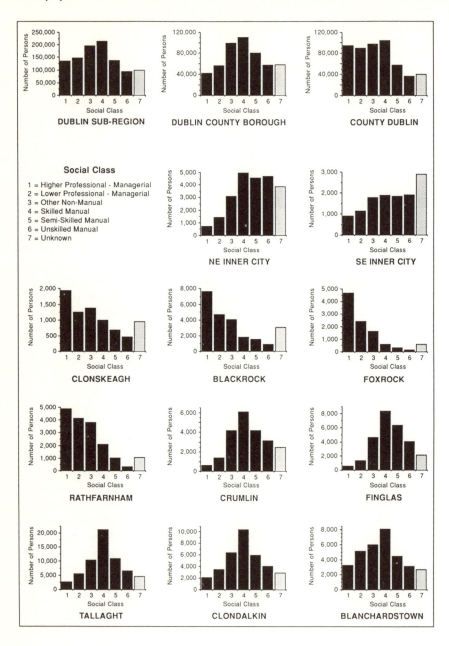

Figure 8.6 Social class structure within Dublin.

Table 8.3 Census definitions of social classes in Ireland

Social Class	Description
1	Higher professional, higher managerial, proprietors employing others, farmers with 200 or more acres.
2	Lower professional, lower managerial, proprietors without employees, farmers with 100–199 acres.
3	Other non-manual, farmers with 50–99 acres.
4	Skilled manual, farmers with 30–49 acres.
5	Semi-skilled manual, farmers with less than 30 acres.
6	Unskilled manual.
7	Unknown.

The social geography of Dublin

It is possible to categorise households according to their economic status and to stages in the life cycle. These factors determine the household's spending power, influence the amount of accommodation which it requires and the type of neighbourhood which is sought. Different types of accommodation, with regard to tenure, price, size and neighbourhood amenities, tend to be geographically segregated (see Chapter 9). Thus, the population of a city becomes sifted and sorted into distinct patterns. The social forces which differentiate households – in terms of social status, position in the life cycle and sometimes by additional criteria such as ethnicity – thereby become reflected in the population's geographical patterning. Thus, the city takes on the character of a residential mosaic, and the factors which underlie such patterns are known as the city's 'ecological structure'.

'Factorial ecologies' can provide a very useful method of investigating a city's ecological structure. They use data describing the social character of small sub-areas within the city and subject them to multivariate techniques, such as factor analysis or principal components analysis, in order to explore the regularities which underlie the patterns of a city's population distribution.

Unfortunately, a major reservation about such studies in the Dublin context is that the available small area census statistics refer to wards or district electoral divisions (DEDs) which have fairly large populations, averaging over 3,500 persons in the sub-region as a whole. These therefore tend to be socially quite heterogeneous internally, especially in the County Borough where patterns of development are more finely grained and where social mixing tends to be greater. Nevertheless, a brief examination of some of the major findings of such studies is worthwhile.

As in many previous studies of the ecological structure of cities in North America and Britain, researchers have discovered two main differentiating factors which underlie the spatial organization of neighbourhood types in Dublin. These include social class or socio-economic status, and family status or the household's stage in the life cycle (pre-child, child-rearing, child-launching, 'empty nesters', etc.). Interestingly, in common with many studies of British cities, an identifiable 'housing factor' has also been found to be a significant basis of neighbourhood differentiation in Dublin.

An important early investigation of the city's ecological structure was undertaken by Brady and Parker (1975) based on 196 tracts of the 1971 Census. They examined the city's ecological structure by employing a balanced range of 56 variables covering socio-economic status, demographic and household structure, population change and housing. Five factors, representing composite elements of the original variables, were found to account for 71 per cent of the variation in the data matrix.

The most important differentiating factor was identified as 'housing conditions', picking out the city's 'twilight areas', associated particularly with small households living in privately rented unfurnished dwellings. The second factor was interpreted as a measure of socio-economic status, identifying residential areas of manual workers, and characterised by high levels of housing occupancy and local authority housing. A third factor differentiated areas according to their 'family status', in broad measure contrasting suburban districts with their high marital and fertility rates with, in particular, the flatland areas of the inner suburbs. Another two minor factors proved to be significant, one denoted as 'residual communities', typified by inter-war housing and an ageing adult population, and the other proving to be a sub-grouping of socio-economic status representing professional workers.

Perhaps, in view of the rapidity of population growth in Dublin during the 1970s, it is not surprising that when Brady and Parker (1986) re-examined the city's factorial ecology based on the 1981 census data, considerable differences emerged. A total of 54 variables drawn from each of the 200 DEDs were employed. These measured aspects of the population's age and life cycle structure, its marital status, household size, educational attainment, employment status and structure, and the age, quality and tenure of housing.

Differences from the previous study could be accounted for only in part by the different variables which had been used. The most important variation was that the separate housing factor which had been identified from the 1971 data had now been subsumed into the other social factors. Four major factors now dominated. The first was unambiguously a 'socio-economic status' factor, the ten most significant primary variables being detailed in Table 8.4. High positive loadings were produced for the significance of professional workers in the population, higher educational attainment, the presence of students, and the prevalence of married

Table 8.4 Dublin's factor structure, 1981

Factor 1: Socio-Economic Status (accounting for 34.5 per cent of individual variance)

Variables with ten highest loadings	Loading
Semi-skilled manual workers	−0.942
Secondary level education	+0.940
Primary level education only	−0.938
Unskilled manual workers	−0.910
Persons per room	−0.898
Population aged 15 and over unemployed or seeking first job	−0.898
Labour force at work	+0.889
Employers and managers	+0.880
Salaried employees	+0.867
Unemployed aged under 25	−0.851

Factor 2. Family Status (accounting for 30.1 per cent of individual variance)

Variables with ten highest loadings	Loading
Persons per household	+0.871
Family units with the youngest child aged between 5 and 14 years	+0.800
Housing built between 1940 and 1970	+0.792
Population aged under 19 years	+0.783
One and 2 person households which are not family units	−0.775
Two person household units	−0.771
Family units with no children	−0.762
Housing built prior to 1919	−0.741
Households with 1 or 2 people aged over 64 and living alone	−0.708
Households with fewer than 3 rooms	−0.654

Source: Brady and Parker, 1986.

women in the workforce. In a city where owner-occupation is so dominant, it is not surprising that its relationship with the socio-economic status factor should not prove to be particularly strong. However, renting from the local authority did load heavily on the factor, but in a negative direction (− 0.820).

The 'socio-economic status factor' is mapped in Figure 8.7 and was found to vary little from the situation in 1971, areas maintaining their relative positions during the intervening period. The map reveals an area of generally low status centred on the inner city and the docks, extending in a westerly and south-westerly direction towards the peripheral new towns of Tallaght and Clondalkin, though rising here to middle-ranking status. In the new town areas, where the DEDs tended to be large and heterogeneous, comprising a range of social groups and the presence of both private and public housing, their internal variety is obscured and the towns emerge as middle ranking in terms of socio-economic status. In contrast, there existed a wedge-shaped zone of almost uniformly high

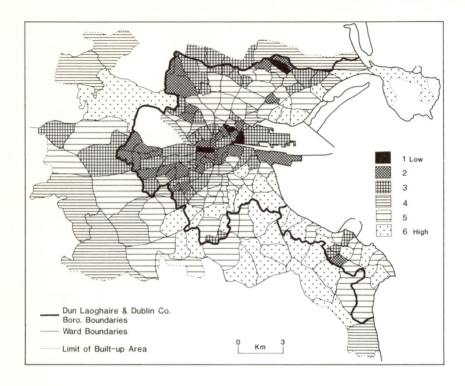

Figure 8.7 Factor I, socio-economic status in Dublin, 1981. (Source: Brady and Parker, 1986)

status stretching outwards from the central area in a southward and south-easterly direction, punctuated by a few scattered public housing areas and the older parts of Dun Laoghaire Borough. To the north of the river Liffey the picture is more complex. Generally, though, quite high status areas fringe Dublin Bay, extending outwards from Clontarf to Howth and these also characterise the northern inner suburbs which separate the low status inner city from a belt of lower status areas comprising the northern fringes of the built environment.

'Family status', indicating stages in the life cycle, was identified as the second most important factor. The factor reflects the development of different parts of the city through time and the way in which the property market has operated to allocate housing in particular neighbourhoods to people at broadly the same stage in the life cycle. It distinguishes between stable areas which are engaged in child rearing and family life, and those declining older areas which are characterised by small households, few children and an ageing population (see also Brady, 1987).

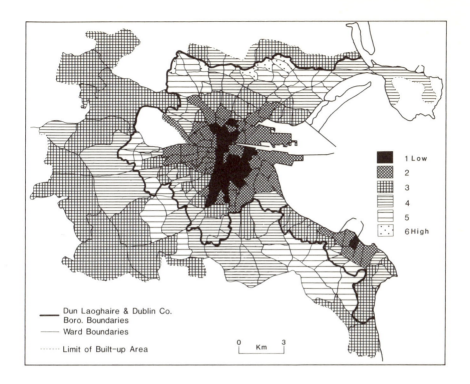

Figure 8.8 Factor II, family status in Dublin, 1981. (Source: Brady and Parker, 1986)

Figure 8.8 maps the distribution of family status in Dublin. Although the pattern is complex, it is possible to recognise a degree of concentricity of arrangement in its spatial expression. Family status generally rises as one moves out from the core, but there is an outer ring of new communities of rapid and substantial recent population growth which are identified in their study by a separate third factor, the 'new residential communities' at the periphery of the city appearing as distinctive because of their very youthful age structures. The fourth axis of differentiation, despite being termed a 'rented sector' factor, is in part an extension of the family status dimension identifying social characteristics typifying those living in privately rented housing.

Two other useful investigations of Dublin's social character have been completed which make use of data from the 1971 Census of Population and attempt to identify social areas within the city. They differ from the aforementioned factorial ecologies in their allocation of each DED to a single cluster or social area type rather than focusing on an analysis of the different factors which underlie the city's ecological structure.

However, they do provide a good description of the social geography of the city at that time.

The earlier study by Hourihan (1978) identified five factors underlying the social geography of the city. These were socio-economic status, a life cycle dimension, a housing dimension, and two further life cycle components one of which identified young unmarried persons and another which related especially to elderly people living in deprived circumstances in older rented dwellings. These factors and the technique of cluster analysis were then used to delimit seven social areas of the city, which were as follows:

1. The central inner city. This is typified by low socio-economic status, multiple-use housing, a higher than average proportion of elderly residents and a declining population size.
2. A zone in transition which shares most of the characteristics of the first area but which was distinguished from it by its heavier concentration of elderly residents.
3. An area of young unmarried people, corresponding closely to the flatland districts of the city.
4. The Corporation housing estates. These are concentrated to the north and south-west of the city. The population is of low socio-economic status and has generally reached the post-geniture stage in the life cycle, many of the areas recording a loss of population.
5. The inner suburbs. This belt of older suburbs which almost ring the city was characterised by high status and a well balanced population demographically, but was experiencing population loss.
6. The newer high status outer suburbs. These differ from the previous social area in having a low representation of both young adults and elderly, residents then being at a dominantly middle-aged stage in the life cycle.
7. Recently developed suburbs. These were the most recently developed, occupied almost exclusively by middle-class young married couples with children.

Bannon, Eustace and O'Neill (1981) had a similar objective in attempting to identify social areas in the city, but employed a different methodology to impart a greater degree of precision and sensitivity to the analysis. Extracting 42 variables for each of the 193 DEDs of the 1971 census, they used a two stage cluster analysis to generate six broad social area types, each of which comprised a range of sub-groups. The distribution of the six area types is mapped in Figure 8.9 and their characteristics are enumerated in Table 8.5. It is not surprising that close similarities should appear between the two latter studies, for although the choice of primary variables differs and they employ different methodologies, the

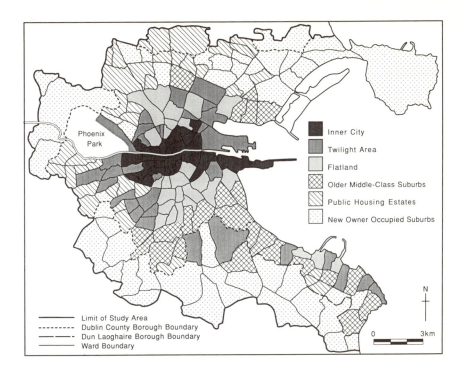

Figure 8.9 Social areas in Dublin, 1971. (After Bannon, 1981)

same census provides the data. Indeed, the differences really appear only in detail.

The first area, comprising the inner city and south docklands, suffered from acute social disadvantage, characterised by a concentration of unskilled employees, high levels of unemployment, a large proportion of dwellings with only two rooms, numerous elderly persons living alone and low levels of car ownership. The inner-city cluster was bounded by a discontinuous ring of housing built during the first half of the twentieth century. This was the least well-defined cluster, but was identifiable by its ageing population, small households and below average numbers of children or professional workers. The third cluster comprised a group of districts exemplified by late nineteenth century housing, a high representation of small households, small dwellings, furnished flats and an above average representation of females and those in the 15–24 age group. Typical of such flatland areas, there were few children present. Further away from the centre, cluster 4 comprised the older middle-class suburbs. These mature districts of large detached and semi-detached villas, comprised the highest status areas in the city. They either possessed easy

181

The population of Dublin

Table 8.5 Dublin's social areas and sub-areas

Social area	Characteristics	Sub-area types (cf. main social area type)	% Total pop.
1. Inner city	Low income, multiple dwellings, acute social disadvantage	a) Lowest social status area b) Skilled, family housing area c) Privately rented housing	11.0
2. Twilight areas	Areas of older housing and population, few children or professionals	a) Terraced housing estates b) Areas transitional to flats c) Newer areas d) Elderly, institutional populations	15.4
3. Flatland	Multi-occupancy, late nineteenth century, small households and small dwellings	a) Older, furnished flats b) Emerging flatland c) High status flatland	12.6
4. Old middle-class suburbs	Older middle-class population, substantial dwellings	a) Southside high status b) Northside high status c) Newer high status	9.7
5. Local authority suburbs	Local authority housing, large families, manual employees, unemployment	a) Older mixed tenancies b) New estates c) New flat complexes d) Newer mixed tenancies	22.3
6. New owner-occupied suburbs	Young and growing populations	a) Low status areas b) Older, mixed areas c) High status areas	29.0

Source: After Bannon, Eustace and O'Neill, 1981, 81–2.

access to the central business area or occupied desirable situations fringing Dublin bay or Killiney bay. Its social character was determined by the predominance of professionals, a paucity of residents with manual occupations and a well below average incidence of all measures of social malaise. The fifth cluster comprised the peripheral post-war local authority housing areas, concentrated mainly in the north of the city. As one might expect, these areas were typified by a high representation of manual employees, larger than average family size, a high incidence of unemployment and few elderly residents. Finally, the sixth social area was characterised by the presence of larger recently developed houses, often possessing six or more rooms, and in owner-occupation. It shared many of the features of the older middle-class districts but distinguished itself in terms of the number of young children (aged 0–4), high rates of fertility and also by the presence of skilled manual workers who formed a significant residential element.

In a slightly different vein, an examination of areas of deprivation in County Dublin was undertaken for Dublin County Council (Dublin County Council Community Department, 1987). It is neither a factorial ecology, nor does it make use of multivariate techniques. Instead, it examines areas of need in terms of their performance on three groups of indicators relating to socio-economic position, dependency and housing. However, it is worth noting here as it is based on an analysis of otherwise unavailable data for each of County Dublin's 311 suburban enumeration areas for the 1981 census. As each district comprised only 300–400 households, this investigation represents an examination of the detailed spatial variations present within the large suburban DEDs which is masked in the previous studies because of the size of the units. It therefore provides a more sensitive description of areas of need. In particular, it identifies significant areas of acute and multiple deprivation within the western new towns, whereas the far larger DEDs comprising these districts appear as middle-ranking suburbs in Brady and Parker's (1986) study because of the evening-out effect caused by the planned proximity of middle-class owner-occupied housing and local authority dwellings.

9
The residential environment

Housing is by far the largest element geographically of the city's built environment. It is through the operation of the housing markets and the allocation criteria of the public housing sector that households attempt to match their requirements for accommodation with the types of housing which are available. The interaction of demand for housing and the conditions of its supply create the varied character and patterning of the city's residential areas. This chapter focuses on the manner in which accommodation has been created and allocated.

The quality of housing is a major factor determining personal well-being. Poor accommodation can have a serious impact upon levels of physical and mental health, so the provision of adequate accommodation is a basic requirement for the attainment of a satisfactory quality of life and the successful reproduction of the labour force. Residential environments provide a diversity of types of accommodation where the city's labour force is housed and succoured. It is here that it recuperates from daily toil, if it is able to find any work at all! Here, too, it reproduces itself from generation to generation. It is within the diversity of the city's residential neighbourhoods that children are socialised into patterns of behaviour, modes of thought, values and aspirations equipping them for their future positions in the workforce. It is predominantly from the middle-class areas of the city that the future business owners, managers and professional workers will be drawn, while clerical and manual workers tend to be recruited from working-class districts. Residential areas may therefore be regarded as the 'labour-factories' of the city.

Housing the people

Dubliners are generally very well housed in terms of basic household amenities. In 1981, within the Dublin area as a whole, nearly 45 per cent of the housing stock had been built during the previous 20 years and 67 per cent post-dated 1940. In suburban County Dublin almost three-quarters of the dwellings had been completed since 1961, and 90 per cent dated from after 1940 (Central Statistics Office, 1986). With such a high proportion of modern housing, it is unsurprising that the city fares well in terms of the standard indicators of housing quality.

In 1981, the latest year for which entirely reliable housing statistics have been published, nearly 94 per cent of dwellings in Dublin possessed a fixed bath or shower, over 95 per cent had a hot water supply to a fixed tap, and more than 99 per cent were equipped with a flush water closet. This is a dramatic improvement on the situation prevailing in 1946 when only two-thirds of households in the city had exclusive access to an inside water tap, and fewer than half possessed a fixed bath or shower.

As a consequence of large-scale residential development in recent years, there has also been a large reduction in the number of small dwellings within the housing stock. Dwellings of three or fewer rooms comprised 55 per cent of all dwellings in 1936, when as much as a fifth of the stock was single-roomed. By 1981, only 18.8 per cent of Dublin's housing possessed three rooms or fewer, and only 5 per cent was single-roomed.

Levels of overcrowding had been very severe during the early twentieth century, Irish families often being very large. As late as 1936, there were 9,386 households of four persons or more living in single-roomed dwellings in Dublin. By 1981 fewer than 300 households lived in such conditions. Although there has been a decline in the incidence of severe overcrowding during the twentieth century, levels of dwelling occupancy still remain quite high, especially in the County Borough. Here, in 1981, 43,000 people (over 8.5 per cent of the resident population) were living at a density of two or more persons per room. If a more realistic definition of overcrowding is adopted, one is obliged to recognise that some problems still remain. At that time, in the Dublin area as a whole, over 28 per cent of the population was living at a density of over one person per habitable room, though this compares favourably with a level of 47 per cent in 1961.

The predominant character of suburban development has been that of low-rise detached, semi-detached and terraced houses with gardens. These have generally been built at a low density of 20–25 dwellings per hectare (8–10 per acre) with a mandatory provision of 10 per cent for public open space (or 0.4 hectares (1 acre) per 100 dwellings in Dun Laoghaire), such criteria probably stemming from a reaction against the levels of overcrowding which typified the city's tenements. Apartments account for only 12 per cent of all dwellings in Dublin. They constitute a significant element of the dwelling stock only in the County Borough area and in Dun Laoghaire, amounting to 18 per cent of dwellings, while in the suburban areas of County Dublin they comprise a mere 3.3 per cent of the stock.

Residential development is closely controlled by the planning system, including regulations to control housing densities, the provision of open space and gardens, width of carriageways and roadside grass verges, set-back and building lines. Unfortunately, developers have tended to interpret planners' minimum development requirements as maximum standards to which they will develop, and this has led to the creation of a suburban environment characterised by an overpowering monotony. This is especially true in the neighbourhoods catering for low-income owner-occupiers and in public housing districts where cost constraints have played an important role. Nowhere is this blandness more evident than in the three western new towns.

In a city in which car ownership rates are low by European or North American standards, where in 1986 only 55 per cent of households had a car and in which public transit is of mediocre quality and costly, low suburban densities have had detrimental consequences for the mobility of a large number of people, especially for women, children, the elderly and the poor. Car availability rates among households are higher in suburban County Dublin (72 per cent in 1986), but among unskilled and semi-skilled manual workers ownership levels fall to below 35 per cent and for skilled manual workers they barely exceed 45 per cent.

A further problem which results from the built form of the recently developed suburban areas is that of the structural quality of the dwellings themselves. A large proportion of recent housing has used the 23 cm. (9 inch) concrete cavity-block as the main structural element. This has poor properties of heat insulation and relies upon the quality of external rendering to obtain damp-proofing. By permitting the use of such materials, long-term structural problems may await many owners.

The supply of housing

As one might expect in a capitalist economy, housing in Ireland is supplied essentially as a commodity, as a means of generating profit for those interests associated with its supply. These include landowners, landlords, housing developers and building contractors, development financiers, and institutions such as banks and building societies which provide long-term mortgage finance. In addition, a plethora of professionals such as architects and solicitors, auctioneers and estate agents,

Table 9.1 Tenure of private dwellings in Dublin and in Ireland, 1961 and 1981

	Dublin[a] 1961	Ireland 1961	Dublin[a] 1981	Ireland 1981	Co. Boro. 1981	Dun-L 1981	Co. Dublin[b] 1981
Owner occupied[c]	41.6	59.8	65.6	74.4	57.5	62.3	78.1
Privately rented (unfurnished)	24.1	14.9	4.4	3.8	6.2	6.6	1.4
Privately rented (furnished)	5.9	2.3	6.3	6.3	15.5	12.4	3.7
Local Authority	25.6	18.4	17.2	12.5	18.8	16.0	15.5
Other	2.8	4.6	1.9	3.0	2.0	2.7	1.3

a) For the purposes of comparability between the Census of 1961 and 1981, the term Dublin refers to Dublin County Borough, Dun-Laoghaire Borough and all of County Dublin.
b) The 1981 figures for Co. Dublin refer to the county's aggregate town areas.
c) Including tenant purchase and vested cottages schemes.

Source: Central Statistics Office, Census of Population of Ireland, 1961 and 1981.

surveyors and valuers, are required to service the industry and lubricate the market. Most have a vested interest in the promotion of owner-occupation and in maximising demand in relation to supply in order to ensure rising house prices.

What one is far less likely to expect from one of the poorer countries of western Europe is the high proportion of housing which is owner-occupied, currently estimated nationally to exceed 80 per cent (Blackwell, 1988), having increased from 60 per cent in 1961. Table 9.1 sets out the tenure structure of housing in the Dublin area and shows the growing dominance of owner-occupation. In a period of just 20 years, it expanded from a minority position to account for almost two-thirds of the stock by 1981, the latest year for which reliable data are available. This represents an increase of over 105,000 owner-occupied dwellings, or almost 150 per cent in 20 years. In suburban County Dublin, owner-occupation exceeded 78 per cent in 1981.

Rather than simply representing the outcome of some mystical desire of the Irish to be property owners instead of tenants or, as has sometimes been asserted, the consequence of a tradition of peasant proprietorship, this situation results at least in part from the housing policies which have been pursued by the Irish state. These have taken fully on board the interests of the private sector by making the encouragement of owner-occupation a stated aim. This is set out clearly even in the following highly generalised outline of policy goals:

The basic aim of the Government's housing policy is to ensure that, as far as the

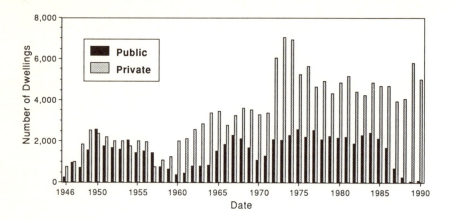

Figure 9.1 Public and private sector housing development since World War II.

resources of the economy permit, every family can obtain a house of good standard, located in an acceptable environment, at a rent or price they can afford. A secondary aim is to encourage owner-occupation. (Department of the Environment, 1980)

In contrast to the growth of owner-occupation, the significance of private renting in Dublin has diminished dramatically from about 30 per cent of the stock in 1961 to just over 10 per cent in 1981. Although the number of local authority dwellings in Dublin rose marginally from around 44,000 to 46,000, the local authority sector has also experienced a relative decline, accounting for less than a fifth of the stock in 1981. This has not only been the product of inactivity in public sector housing development, but results from sales to sitting tenants, which inevitably tend to be the better dwellings. Thus, during the past decade, public housing in Ireland has become increasingly synonymous with 'stigmatised housing for a residualised minority' (Blackwell, 1988, 89) reminiscent of welfare housing in the USA. Clearly, over the 20 year period, choice was becoming more and more constrained, obliging people to seek housing almost exclusively within the owner-occupied sector – the fringe sectors of housing co-operatives and housing associations being very poorly developed in urban Ireland.

Redmond (1987) has shown that the supply of new housing in Dublin since World War II has been markedly cyclical and that these have been dominated by private sector developments which account for nearly 70 per cent of the 223,480 dwellings completed from 1946 to 1990 (Figure 9.1). A small proportion of this stock has been sold to landlords for the purpose of letting on the private market, an element which was encouraged during the 1980s by taxation benefits for landlords (Section

23 and Section 27 allowances). Most, however, was destined for owner-occupation. Development by the local authorities constituted little over 30 per cent of all dwellings completed since 1945, though this proportion has varied through time. Public sector output averaged nearly 45 per cent of completions from 1946–59, comprising over 50 per cent in 1950 and 1954 and surpassing 65 per cent in 1957. It accounted for little over 20 per cent between 1960 and 1964, averaged 36 per cent over the following five years, declining subsequently to comprise less than 30 per cent of completions between 1970 and 1985. More recently, public sector financial stringency during the 1980s resulted in the collapse of public sector completions, falling to less than 2 per cent of output by the end of the decade.

Owner-occupation

Because owner-occupied housing accounts for the great majority of all dwellings in the city, catering for households with a very wide range of incomes, it is not surprising that this stock is highly varied in price, size and quality, though it is almost uniformly good in terms of the provision of basic sanitary facilities (Figures 9.2. and 9.3). Added diversity is imparted by the fact that a significant number of owner-occupied dwellings were developed by the public sector.

In contrast to the late 1970s when there were frequently queues of people awaiting the first opening of show houses on new developments and when it would almost have been possible to sell a cement-rendered cardboard box, purchasers had to be wooed during the slump in demand in the mid-1980s. In the search for product differentiation in such straightened circumstances, builders increasingly turned away from the degraded neo-classical designs of the previous boom, with their fibreglass stick-on porticos over the front door, frequently turning instead to mock Tudor styles (or 'Tudor *flavour*' as one scheme was advertised) with false beams on front elevations. However, the changed market did lead to an improvement in the attention which had to be paid to landscaping.

Financing and affordability

Entry into the owner-occupied sector depends on a number of factors. With the growth of owner-occupation throughout the twentieth century, inheritance of a property is becoming increasingly common and an important method of transferring wealth between generations. More commonly, access depends on the availability of either sufficient capital to fund outright purchase of the dwelling or the possession of an

Figure 9.2 Typical design for mid-priced speculatively developed housing during the late 1970s to early 1980s. Note the little distance between houses.

Figure 9.3 Recent speculatively developed owner-occupied housing in Stillorgan, County Dublin.

adequate and stable flow of income to satisfy the criteria of mortgage lending institutions. Even in the latter case, considerable capital will be required in order to enter the sector. The value of the loan (usually 75 per cent to 90 per cent) will be required to be topped-up to the level of the purchase price of the property. There will also be the need to pay for life insurance cover and building insurance, to pay for the necessary legal fees, the structural and valuation survey of the dwelling, and, in the case of properties which are not brand new, the government's stamp duty on the transaction. Entry to the sector, and transfers within it, clearly involve costly processes.

The evolution of owner-occupation as a mass housing market has been facilitated by the expansion of the Irish building society movement, especially since the 1960s. With origins grounded in the nineteenth century self-help movement of the skilled working class, these friendly-societies have since developed into major financial institutions, and have in recent years been obliged increasingly to pursue interest rate and lending policies grounded strictly on market criteria (Murphy, 1990). Between 1970 and 1988, Irish building societies' assets grew from IR£87.1M to IR£3,804.9M, representing a sixfold increase in real terms.

The rising scale of funds flowing into the societies during the 1970s permitted the extension of owner-occupation to a wider range of income groups. Until 1989, societies were effectively single product financial institutions being highly constrained in the type of lending which they could undertake. The expansion of owner-occupation was therefore necessary for their success. By advancing capital so that households could purchase dwellings, usually through annuity mortgages which were repaid with interest over 20 or 25 years, the societies also permitted housing developers to realise profits from their construction and land conversion activities. In some cases, block-mortgage schemes were operated between some societies and particular developers, greatly facilitating the disposal of the developer's product, especially at times of mortgage scarcity (Murphy, 1990).

When funds have flowed freely into societies, they have extended their lending facilities to more marginal groups in terms of household income and into geographical locations which at times of mortgage scarcity are regarded less favourably. Interestingly, Murphy (1990, 1992) found that at times of credit scarcity, building society managers viewed the large peripheral one-class housing estates at the bottom of the owner-occupied sector as areas to be avoided in their lending practice. The very types of area which their own previous expansionary policies had helped to produce became targets for a type of 'red lining' through restricting the number of advances which they made towards properties located there, by valuing such properties at a substantial discount or by advancing lower proportions of the property's price. Thus, residents in parts of

Dublin's new towns have discovered that the first rung on their housing ladder has become a rather more permanent position than they had intended, as they realise that selling is very difficult.

Building societies dominate the Irish mortgage market. With the exception of two years, they have accounted for over half the mortgages advanced annually in the country since 1970. Nevertheless, other institutions also lend for the purpose of house purchase. Life assurance companies played a significant role throughout the 1960s but declined rapidly during the early 1970s. However, the tying of building society interest rates and lending practice to market criteria encouraged banks to take an interest in the domestic mortgage market, targeting upper-income recipients in particular. By 1990, commercial banks accounted for 34 per cent of the value of all new loans advanced. Local authorities have also been in the mortgage market since 1966, advancing smaller sums to those on below average incomes. The intensity of their lending involvement has been somewhat erratic and has declined of late, having accounted for over 22 per cent of the value of new loans in 1987 but just 2.8 per cent two years later. This coincides with the inception of a new scheme whereby the building societies and banks agreed to service demand from low-income applicants in return for local authorities' guaranteeing the loans, thus permitting the private sector agencies to recoup any losses which arose as a result of default.

Another factor accounting for the high proportion of owner-occupation is that a significant proportion of the housing stock which was developed as public housing has subsequently become owner-occupied due to the policy of selling such dwellings to sitting tenants. After 1973 considerable inducements were offered to encourage purchases by tenants, and by 1981 over 18,000 dwellings were being acquired from local authorities in Dublin. In 1989 alone, 2,373 houses were purchased from the city's local authorities compared to the development of just 80 dwellings in the whole of the city by the public sector and 4,981 private sector completions (Department of the Environment, 1991b). Nationally, by 1987, over 180,000 public sector dwellings had been purchased in this way, compared to a remaining national public sector housing stock of 119,000 at that date.

In a market which is so heterogeneous, average figures mean little. However, in 1990, the average price of a newly developed house in Dublin was IR£63,600, and the average price for older dwellings was slightly under IR£59,000. Table 9.2 shows the range of prices paid for new and older properties which were sold in Dublin 1990.

There is a further problem when examining temporal changes in the affordability of owner-occupied housing, because statistics are not controlled for shifts in the composition of the dwelling types which are being developed or traded. Recorded price movements may, therefore,

Table 9.2 House prices in the Dublin area, 1990

	New houses (%)	Transactions involving older dwellings (%)	All houses (%)
<IR£25,000	0.1	6.3	4.6
IR£25–35,000	0.7	19.6	14.8
IR£35–40,000	3.9	9.1	7.9
IR£40–60,000	37.7	34.0	34.8
>IR£60,000	57.6	31.0	37.9

Source: Department of the Environment, 1991b.

simply reflect changes in the types of dwelling being sold. Nevertheless, while new house prices outpaced the rate of consumer price inflation between 1968 and 1980, rising at a real rate of 3.7 per cent annually, between 1980 and 1987 new house prices declined by 27 per cent in real terms. Blackwell (1988) suggests that even when account is taken of the changing character of the stock being traded, this decline was still notable, at 19 per cent. Housing was clearly becoming more affordable. For a greater part of the 1980s, earnings rose more quickly than new house prices. The ratio of new house prices to average net industrial earnings fell from 5.8:1 in 1981 to 4.4:1 by 1987. Net repayments as a proportion of after-tax income on an averagely priced new house fell from 43.3 per cent in 1981 to just 15.3 per cent in 1986 (Blackwell, 1988).

Generally, residential accommodation for those in employment is quite affordable. In mid-1991, when male pre-tax industrial earnings averaged approximately IR£14,000 per annum, it was still possible, in the new town of Clondalkin, to purchase an ex-public sector three-bedroomed terraced house for as little as IR£22,000, or a three-bedroomed semi-detached property for only IR£24,000. However, in some areas of the city, particularly in the southern inner suburbs, house prices rose dramatically between 1988 and 1991. These mature areas with their leafy streetscapes and pleasant parks offer good accessibility to the central business district and to the city's leisure and cultural amenities. The demand for properties in these areas generated a rapid increase in site values, which developers needed to recoup through high sale prices and more profitable design configurations. Somewhat to the consternation of officials, a number of developers opted for 'back-to-back' housing, sometimes euphemistically called 'vertical apartments', in which party walls (and noise) are shared with three neighbouring dwellings. Although this arrangement does provide dwellings with their own separate entrance from the street, it precludes through-ventilation of the building and may compromise safety in the event of fire, one's exit being effected on one side of the building only. Nevertheless, in 1991, 16 back-to-back terraced cottages, part of a larger residential in-fill development in the prestigious inner-suburban district of Ballsbridge, were all sold within hours of going on sale to the public, despite their having been priced at IR£69,950–IR£73,950 and comprising only 47 sq. m. (510 sq. ft.) of living space. At IR£1,476 per sq. m. (IR£137 per sq. ft.), their costs exceeded the price of own-door offices in the city's central business area.

The promotion of owner-occupation

The encouragement of owner-occupation includes the retention of tax relief on mortgage interest payments, despite the abolition of Schedule-A tax on the imputed income from property which was the original basis for such an allowance. This is a highly inefficient way of targeting public funds towards housing consumption. It is effectively a never-ending subsidy to owner-occupiers of a house. Each time the house is sold and a new mortgage is taken out, the new mortgagee becomes entitled to an annual tax allowance of up to IR£1,600 (IR£3,200 for a couple) for mortgage interest paid. Those with higher levels of income on higher marginal rates of taxation obviously benefit the most. However, the construction industry, which has been the greatest beneficiary from the subsidy because it allows people to pay a higher price for accommodation, has strenuously opposed its abolition.

Encouragement has also included the exemption from capital gains tax of any profits which may accrue from the disposal of one's main residence, and direct government subsidy of the mortgage rate to cushion the effects of high interest rates. During the mid-1980s, there also existed a grant of IR£5,000 to public sector tenants who surrendered their tenancy in order to move into the private sector.

National policy has also favoured new construction rather than refurbishment. First-time-buyers of new dwellings are entitled to a cash grant, currently IR£2,000, and prior to their abolition, new housing was entitled to the remission of a proportion of domestic rates. Contracts to buy newly built dwellings have also been exempted from stamp-duty. For most houses in Dublin, this would be at a rate of 4 per cent or 5 per cent of the purchase price in 1991, and 6 per cent for dwellings priced over IR£60,000. However, this remission has recently been rescinded for larger dwellings. These policies have not only stimulated owner-occupation, but because speculative residential developers favour greenfield developments, they have also promoted massive suburban expansion.

Undoubtedly, owner-occupation would not have been so successful had it not created real benefits for owners – yet Murphy (1991) has shown that owner-occupancy can involve severe financial difficulties for those at the lower end of the sector. Moreover, during the mid-1980s, the real value of properties in many areas declined, sometimes involving a fall in monetary values to below the amount of the outstanding mortgage. Cases of mortgage default and even of property abandonment occurred. In a weak market for second-hand houses, owners often invested additional capital in their declining asset in order to cope with staying on, constructing extensions to provide additional space or installing double glazing to reduce street noise.

Public sector housing

In the market sector there is nothing to ensure that the profitable supply of housing will necessarily fulfil personal need. Public housing, therefore, acts as a safety-net for a proportion of those who lack sufficient resources to gain access to private sector accommodation of a suitable standard. However, in the past, this has generally not included catering for the needs of single persons. In Ireland, public housing has always been regarded as a residual sector providing for special needs, whereas in the United Kingdom, and in Scotland in particular, it has accommodated a far wider range of social groups by developing housing for general needs.

During the mid-1980s, the availability of a grant of IR£5,000 for tenants willing to relinquish their tenancies inevitably stimulated the departure of higher-income recipients able to finance mortgage repayments. During the first year of the scheme's operation, half of all applications for such grants came from the three new towns of Blanchardstown, Tallaght and Clondalkin (Dublin Corporation, 1986). The effect has been to deprive many public housing areas of their community leaders and has contributed to the negative image of public sector housing as providing accommodation merely for a residual minority of the population (see Byrne, 1984). The policy also created difficulties for public sector housing managers who had to cope with increasing numbers of vacant dwellings which were often subjected to major vandalism, individual properties sometimes having to be renovated on several occasions.

The public sector housing stock

The shifting emphases of public sector housing policy have endowed the city with considerable heterogeneity in its stock with regard to quality and style. At its best, local authority housing can be well located and of very high quality, while at its worst, especially when it is poorly maintained, it hardly merits the payment of any rent whatsoever.

The earliest of the schemes, completed between 1885 and 1920, were small in scale, typically less than 2 ha. (5 acres) in extent, comprising either apartment blocks or two-storey cottages built at a high density on small in-fill or slum clearance sites in the inner city. Substantial numbers of the latter still remain, though many have since been purchased by their tenants. The similarity of the built form of both these types of dwelling to those which were being developed by philanthropic bodies was remarkable.

During the inter-war period, the Corporation's housing strategy comprised two main elements. The first involved the development of houses in suburban areas where densities ranged from 32 to 70 dwellings per ha. (13 to 28 per acre). Houses tended to be small, the average net floor area of a 1930s 4-roomed cottage containing 3 bedrooms and a living room being only 52.5 sq.m. (565 sq. ft.). The second element was the continued construction of flats in the inner city, developed at higher densities averaging 116 apartments with 750 persons per ha. (47 dwellings and 305 persons per acre) (Colivet, 1943). The policy was reviewed in the Report of Inquiry into the Housing of the Labouring Classes of the City of Dublin (1939/43) which concluded that building flats was uneconomic and noted that their all-in cost was twice that of suburban cottages and more expensive than the earlier high-density, low-rise inner-city cottages.

Shortages of building materials immediately after World War II delayed any significant public housing development until the early 1950s. However, over a thousand dwellings were renovated, including eighteenth century buildings at Summerhill, though these have since been demolished to provide for road-widening and new Corporation housing. Rehabilitation was largely abandoned during the next decade due to its high cost and the need for large-scale developments.

Despite the findings of the Report of Inquiry which had cast doubt upon the wisdom of developing inner-city flats, throughout the 1950s and 1960s, Dublin Corporation continued its dual policy of building inner-city apartments, as at North Strand and North William Street, and low-density suburban houses, thereby contributing greatly to the sprawl of the city. Some low-cost housing schemes were developed during the 1960s, as at Cherry Orchard (Ballyfermot), but these have generally failed to stand the test of time and must be regarded as having offered no long-term economic advantage over traditional schemes.

Fortunately, the Modern Movement in architecture and the use of system-building both played very minor roles in the city's public housing.

Figure 9.4 System-built high-rise public housing at Ballymun, located on the northern periphery. It was completed in 1969 and is undergoing refurbishment.

Ballymun, pictured in Figure 9.4, comprises a scheme of system-built high-rise apartments and is an important exception. It was developed at a relatively low density (50 dwellings per hectare (20 per acre)) by the National Building Agency in the 1960s on low cost peripheral land 5.5 km. (3.5 miles) from the city centre. The seven 16-storey towers and eight-storey deck-access blocks which provide accommodation for 16,000 people were believed to offer a quick solution to the city's continuing housing problems. However, the much greater cost per dwelling of developing high-rise blocks can rarely be justified on economic grounds except at inner-city locations where land values are at their height. There never was any economic justification for their construction at the periphery. The flats failed to deliver their promise of a 'quick fix' to the city's housing problems. At a cost of over IR£22,000 per flat and total-ling some IR£62M, a refurbishment and security enhancement scheme for the 2,814 flats was commenced in 1991. By then, the area was reputed to have an unemployment rate in excess of 50 per cent and a tenant turnover rate of around 30 per cent per annum.

Darndale was an experimental low-rise development. Here, private sector architects, influenced by the British town of Andover, created a

Figure 9.5 Corporation housing at City Quay. Since the mid-1970s, the Corporation has developed 2,400 high-density low-rise dwellings in the inner city.

scheme on the northern fringe of the city at a higher than normal density (75 houses per hectare (30 per acre)). It incorporated Radburn planning principles of complete separation of pedestrians and traffic as well as the concept of 'defensible space' propounded by Newman (1969), providing a good example of the application of architectural determinism and neighbourhood theory (Redmond, 1986). Developed as a reaction to the perceived failure of the Ballymun complex, Darndale, with its sizeable working-class families, has been described as having become 'a claustrophobic pressure cooker, made even more intolerable by multiple deprivation' (McDonald, 1989). Moreover, although the desired high densities were achieved, it soon became apparent that the low-cost criterion could not be met, and what resulted was far removed from the neighbourhood which the architects predicted would be 'interesting, vital and full of character' (Street, 1974). Darndale is also currently undergoing a major refurbishment of the dwellings and alteration of its lay-out to improve the level of informal supervision of public space.

Growing disenchantment with the Corporation's policy of building only flats in the inner city led, in October 1973, to a statement by the Minister for Local Government that he would not be prepared to sanction the development by local authorities of flat-blocks of more than three storeys, except in locations where this was imperative for streetscape preservation. Effectively, Dublin Corporation was being directed to revert to its earlier policy of higher-density low-rise housing for the inner city. Since that date, the Corporation has been responsible for the development of around 2,400 high quality inner-city houses in a wide range of locations at densities of 65 to 75 dwellings to the hectare (26 to 30 per acre), as in the housing depicted in Figure 9.5 at City Quay. No cost benefit analysis ever preceded this decision, which turned out to be one of the best which has ever influenced the character of public housing in the city. Excluding the cost of land, the new style of townhouses cost approximately 50 per cent more than the cost of developing suburban cottages. Moreover, when comparing the last of the schemes of Corporation flats with the first of the medium-density low-rise schemes which were built almost contemporaneously, the latter were actually found to be cheaper per person housed (McNulty, 1983; McDaid, 1988).

By the late 1970s, shortages of sites in the County Borough obliged the Corporation increasingly to locate in suburban County Dublin more than 70 per cent of the 1,550 new houses which it developed annually (Dublin Corporation Planning Department, 1985b). Urban managers, reacting to the problems of Dublin's overcrowded tenements, encouraged architects to adopt site plans in which low densities were those most desired. Design recommendations and layout criteria have contributed to the development of monotonous and sprawling low-density suburbs which, many would claim, lack any true feeling of urbanism. Straight, wide streets of standard (generous) dimensions to speed traffic flow, grass verges and pavements of uniform width, gardens each of similar length and housing built at a low density, have created a depressingly barren landscape.

It is possible to see embodied in the built environment of Killinarden (a neighbourhood of 6,600 people in the new town of Tallaght) the way in which the Corporation's housing architects progressed along a learning curve, discovering again how to create attractive residential areas (Thiboust, 1990). Having concentrated on building inner-city flats during the 1960s, cottage housing development became the least glamorous aspect of the housing department's activities. When Corporation peripheral housing development recommenced in earnest during the 1970s, lay-out design seems to have proceeded on a trial-and-error basis. Thus, the earliest phase at Killinarden, dating from 1972, is typified by rectilinear subdivision, with long, straight terraces of housing serviced by wide, straight roads (Figure 9.6). There was no attempt at informality, the aesthetics of geometry dominating the plan. By 1978 the design at Cushlaw Park had become somewhat more sophisticated, though its

Figure 9.6 The earliest phase in the Corporation's development of Killinarden, completed in 1972, employs a monotonous rectilinear arrangement of terraced houses. Parking provision is generous yet car ownership rates are low.

appearance remains monotonous. In the early 1980s, the layout was based on small culs-de-sacs with housing generating the service roads and by 1982, Figure 9.7 shows that in the final phase at Donomore Park and Crescent the informality of the positioning of houses together with varied colours of finish creates an intimacy which is wholly absent from the earlier phases. Figure 9.8 shows the interior layout of a typical Corporation house developed during the 1980s.

Unfortunately, financial stringency within the public sector has prevented Dublin Corporation from pressing home its newly acquired skills in creating attractive residential environments. Table 9.3 shows that by 1989 only 39 dwellings were developed in the Dublin area by the three local authorities. Attention in recent years has instead turned increasingly towards refurbishment, particularly of the older flatted schemes and the low-cost developments of the late 1960s and early 1970s.

Figure 9.7 The final development phase at Killinarden, dating from the early 1980s, shows complete informality of layout, a variety of housing designs and building finishes.

The development process

Although local authority housing is not a market sector, social criteria taking precedence in the allocation of dwellings, one should not assume that public housing represents a socialised form of housing provision devoid of profit. Although development is undertaken by the public sector, there exist important structural links with the profit-making private sector so that public provision is wholly compatible with that market sector. A brief outline of the process of public sector housing development will illustrate the relationships.

The local authority's development department and law agent acquire land for public housing by agreement or compulsory purchase at full development value. Unless local authorities are able to land-bank many years in advance of their development requirements, it is likely that landowners will reap the full benefits from the land conversion process.

There is no requirement for local authorities to seek either planning permission or by-law approval for developments, but schemes do conform to the standards which are established by those departments

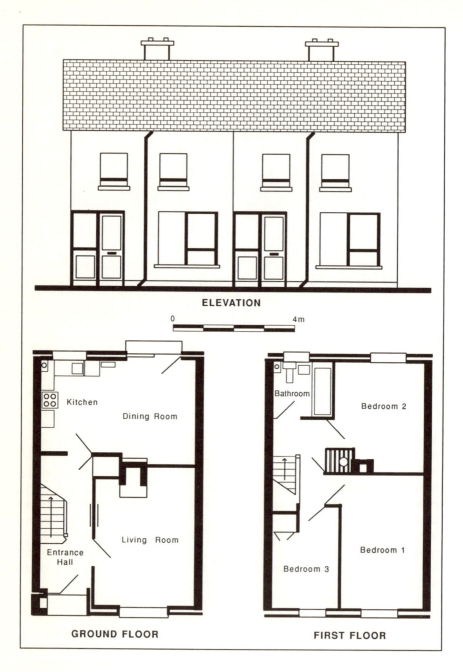

ELEVATION

0   4m

Kitchen

Dining Room

Living Room

Entrance
Hall

GROUND FLOOR

Bathroom

Bedroom 2

Bedroom 1

Bedroom 3

FIRST FLOOR

Figure 9.8 Typical three-bedroomed housing developed by Dublin Corporation during the 1980s.

Table 9.3 Completion of local authority dwellings in the Dublin area, 1986–90

	1986	1987	1988	1989	1990
Dublin Co. Borough	433	297	71	6	35
County Dublin	1,231	388	184	33	45

Source: Department of the Environment, 1991b.

relating to residential densities, provision of open space, car parking and structural features of the dwellings. For the layout, the architects also work within criteria established by the roads engineers regarding the hierarchy of road widths according to whether they are primary, district or estate distributors. Houses are fitted into a plan which primarily serves the car and public service vehicles. Although the local authority's own architects' department may be responsible for designing housing projects, co-ordinating the above criteria in the draft design, private practitioners could be engaged in their stead.

As a result of information flowing from the housing needs and allocation section of the local authority's housing department, the housing administration department determines the required mixture of dwelling sizes (e.g. two bedroomed, three bedroomed) and types (e.g. one, two and three storey). The Department of the Environment provides pattern books of recommended house layout styles, it advises on floorspace provision, and it also recommends maximum development densities. Densities generally tend to be low, at 40 houses per hectare (16 per acre) or 75 flats per hectare (30 per acre) in central city areas, and 30 houses per hectare (12 per acre) in suburbia (McKiernan, 1973). The proposed layout of the scheme, designed by the architects, and a cost plan, drawn up by the housing department's quantity surveyors, then has to be approved by the housing committee of the local authority and sent to the Department of the Environment for approval, being submitted again following completion of the full design. This is accompanied by a request for permission to go to tender, which may be an open tender or selective of a smaller number of reliable contractors.

Construction is normally undertaken by private sector companies which compete with one another for such contracts. After having been vetted for reasonableness by the authority's own quantity surveyors, normally the lowest tender is accepted by the Department of the Environment. As is the case in the private sector, it may avoid tender prices which are evidently far too low and which are likely to result in costly counter-claims for minor alterations to the design or the inconvenience resulting from bankruptcy. Generally, government cost controls have become far tighter during the 1980s, though high-cost design solutions such as expensive brick frontages in the inner city can be justified for aesthetic and contextual reasons. Finance having been sanctioned, the City Manager gives the order to commence the development, the builder being contracted to construct the development within a specified time period.

Another link between public and private sectors is the fact that the development funds, sanctioned by the Department of the Environment and ultimately also by the Department of Finance, may well be raised on capital markets as part of the Government's borrowing requirement for the Public Capital Programme. Financiers, therefore, also obtain a risk-free return from public sector housing development.

Apart from the development role, the other major element of public housing which is socialised is the loss-making landlord function. When completion is imminent, usually within just a couple of days, dwellings are made available to the allocation section of the housing department, which then offers the properties to prospective tenants. At such a late stage in the development process, prospective occupiers can have no influence upon the character of their future home, though they are, of course, free to reject them and hope for something more to their liking.

Perhaps it is the lack of contact between the officers responsible for the provision of public housing and the tenants who will reside in them which has permitted the development of some public housing schemes wholly inappropriate for the families they were intended to accommodate. If camels are said to be horses designed by a committee, one might well be forgiven for believing that some of the city's public housing estates have the appearance of having been designed by a committee of camels. Only in the refurbishment schemes has there been any serious attempt on the part of housing managers to consult tenants regarding their wishes.

It is certainly possible to detect more than a hint of contempt in the attitude of the Corporation's housing department towards its tenants in the design of apartment buildings in Ballybough, which are adorned by highly coloured mosaics of toy trains (Figure 9.9). One wonders just how many Corporation architects live in homes delighting in such architectural detailing. One is sometimes left with the impression that there has existed, at least in the past, a profound belief among housing managers that although public sector dwellings might be expensive to develop, they should at very least be made to look as mean as possible *pour encourager les autres*.

Allocation and rent

Although tenancies can be inherited by spouses or children resident in a

Figure 9.9 A colourful mosaic of a toy railway train adorns these Corporation flats off North Strand. Do Corporation architects decorate the exterior of their own homes in similar fashion?

local authority house, normal entry to the public housing sector depends on fulfilling certain criteria. Those whose homes have been condemned, acquired and demolished are given priority in re-housing by local authorities over those on the general waiting list (see Blackwell, 1988). A number of criteria are taken into account in the assessment of housing need, including family size and composition, overcrowding of current accommodation, the physical condition of that accommodation, the sharing of facilities with other families, medical factors, and the length of time spent on the waiting list. Homeless families and the elderly are also given special consideration. In Dublin Corporation, there is an upper income limit for the sole earner and account is also taken of the income of other working members of the family. However, once within the sector, tenants possess security of tenure irrespective of any subsequent increase in income.

The high level of development activity undertaken by the local authorities during the early to mid-1980s, and the increasing number of properties becoming available for re-letting as a result of large-scale emigration and those who availed of the IR£5,000 'surrender grant' to

205

enter the private sector, meant that the number of households on the waiting list fell. Furthermore, there was a reduction in the severity of housing need among those remaining on the lists, applicants often seeking a particular type of accommodation or a certain district (Department of the Environment, 1991c). By the late 1980s, the easing of demand for public sector housing in the city meant that Dublin Corporation was able to make allocations to families of two persons and even to single people, while those on the waiting list would be offered accommodation after little over a year. However, rising unemployment in the early 1990s, recent increases in the real purchase price of owner-occupied housing and increasing mortgage interest rates have contributed to the lengthening of waiting lists, the Corporation's list having grown by over 10 per cent between September 1989 and March 1991.

Maximum rents are calculated on the basis of historic costs, representing a percentage of the original all-in cost of development, up-dated by the Consumer Price Index. The maximum rent is therefore very variable, ranging from as little as IR£5 per week in some areas to IR£15 in Ballyfermot and Crumlin and IR£30 for some new dwellings. However, the actual rent paid is based upon the tenant's level of income and rent rarely comprises over 15 per cent of disposable income (Blackwell, 1988).

The privately rented sector

The private renting of accommodation in Dublin has declined inexorably during the course of the twentieth century. From a stock of over 40,000 unfurnished lettings in 1961, this part of the sector had dwindled to little over 10,000 by 1981. Meanwhile, the number of furnished lettings increased from 10,000 to just under 17,000. It is a very diverse sector in terms of both housing stock and tenants, and until recently comprised two separate sectors, one of which was characterised by rent control.

As in Britain, the reduced significance of private renting through the twentieth century is rooted in the declining economic returns to be gained from landlordism when compared to other forms of investment. The appearance at the end of the nineteenth century of alternative higher yielding investment media, notably joint stock companies, saw a diversion of capital away from housing for rent. The operation of the Rent Restriction Acts from 1915 onwards, which sought to control the level of rents, also contributed to decline. Although initially intended as a temporary measure to prevent arbitrary increases in rent during a wartime housing shortage, these measures discouraged landlordism. By the late 1970s, levels of controlled rents, which averaged IR£2.50 per week, were such that occupiers of controlled tenancies were effectively being subsidised by their landlords. In contrast, the average rent in the uncontrolled privately rented sector (including virtually all lettings which post-dated 1960, more expensive lettings and those in buildings constructed after 1941) was IR£18 per week in 1979. Sometimes property owners abandoned maintenance and obtained vacant possession by permitting the building to become uninhabitable (Baker and O'Brien, 1979; O'Brien and Dillon, 1982). Unsurprisingly, if the opportunity arose, landlords preferred to sell their properties into owner-occupation.

In 1981, a number of landlords challenged the constitutional legality of certain provisions of the 1960 Rent Restrictions Act in the Supreme Court and subsequent legislation passed by both Houses of the Oireachtas, was also deemed by the Supreme Court to represent 'an unjust attack on the property rights of landlords of controlled dwellings' and to be in contravention of the Constitution (O'Brien and Dillon, 1982). The upheaval for tenants resulting from the ending of control was eased for the elderly and poor by special welfare payments to assist in the payment of higher rents.

The tax position of landlords, especially the failure to grant depreciation allowances on rented property, also discouraged investment in maintenance. In addition, slum clearance and redevelopment programmes severely depleted the stock of privately rented accommodation, much of which was in older properties lacking basic amenities. Moreover, in terms of demand, rising real incomes, the wider availability of credit and the existence of government subsidies and tax allowances for those undertaking owner-occupation, have been instrumental in reducing the level of demand for private lettings (O'Brien and Dillon, 1982).

In recent years, the government has sought to increase the number of dwellings available for renting. In 1981, under Section 23 of the Finance Act (renewed in the Act of 1988 under Section 27), it introduced a special tax allowance to encourage the construction of apartments for rent and, in the later Act, small houses. Qualifying properties had to fall within a specified size range, 30–90 sq.m. (323–968 sq. ft.) in the case of apartments, and 35–125 sq.m. (377–1,345 sq. ft.) in the case of houses, and both had to be rented out for a minimum of ten years. The provisions of the Acts allow the acquisition costs of properties (net of site value) or the costs of converting buildings into flats to be deducted from rental income from all sources until the tax allowance is used up. The effect of the allowance was to engender a surge of apartment construction during the early 1980s and an increase in the number of properties available at the middle to upper range of the lettings market. The success of the measure encouraged its subsequent renewal and extension to small houses.

The residential environment

Characteristics of the sector

Private renting has become a residual market sector catering for a wide social range of tenants. Tenants generally have incomes which are lower than those of other housing sectors and the household size is generally small. One-person households account nationally for over 10 per cent of the private tenancies in both unfurnished and furnished sub-markets and the average size of household was 3.02 in 1973, compared to 4.89 in the public sector and 4.56 for mortgagees (O'Brien and Dillon, 1982).

The sector accommodates those for whom mobility is important, particularly young adults. For them it is a short-term tenure during a particular phase in their lives, the owner-occupied and public housing sectors representing longer-term aspirations. A high proportion of households comprise individuals living either alone or in small non-family groups. However, there is also a significant percentage of couples without children, generally older and middle-aged persons living in de-regulated lettings who have become trapped in the sector and for whom it now provides long-term accommodation. Many lack the resources to enter owner-occupation while others fail to qualify for local authority housing.

A major advantage of the sector is the cheapness of entry into it and of transfers within it. With the exception of the upper end of the market where property agents are often engaged and references are required, entry into the sector tends to be unstructured and informal, prospective tenants having to rely for information on newspaper advertisements and informal channels to locate available properties. Entry then depends on the applicant's ability to persuade landlords that one will make a satisfactory tenant and on the ability to lodge any deposit which may be required against breakages in addition to the payment of a month's rent in advance. As entry depends on the whims of individual landlords it is hard to generalise about ease of entry. For certain groups, such as itinerants, non-whites, single parents or those of unconventional appearance, access to the sector can be difficult. Landlords tend to favour young single people, either alone or in small groups, with respectable accents and in secure salaried employment (Baker and O'Brien, 1979).

Security of tenure is weak. Although eviction is illegal without a court order, ignorance among tenants of this point of law and the prevalence of lettings where there is no formal lease or even a rent book, means that security is rendered precarious. Moreover, the high success rate which landlords achieve when taking eviction cases to court means that tenants are reluctant to fight eviction. Among the problems which tenants face most often are eviction, rent increases and problems with repairs and maintenance (O'Brien and Dillon, 1982).

The dwelling stock itself is very diverse. Generally, accommodation tends to be smaller than under either owner-occupation or the public sector. In the inner city, the stock ranges from small artisan cottages, to the basements and upper floors of the city's eighteenth and nineteenth century terraces, the other floors often having been converted to business functions. In the inner suburbs, the sub-divided, tenanted nineteenth century buildings contrast with modern in-fill town house developments and purpose-built apartment blocks in which a proportion of the dwellings is often rented privately. In the outer suburbs, the privately rented sector is again as heterogeneous as the owner-occupied sector in terms of building style, quality and cost.

As one would expect, rents vary considerably according to the dwelling's size, quality, and location. During the late 1980s, with the reduction in public sector housing development and rising real house prices and mortgage rates, there has been a growing demand for privately rented properties which the market has been unable to satisfy. This has led to rising real levels of rent which have had a severe impact on lower income groups wishing to gain entry.

10
Inner-city problems and regeneration

The processes of economic restructuring outlined in Chapter 3 have had major consequences for the city and during the course of the last two decades it became increasingly apparent that Dublin was showing many of the classic symptoms of inner-city decline: falling population numbers; the loss of industrial employment upon which it had traditionally depended; a poorly skilled workforce; high rates of unemployment; and a built environment characterised by vacant buildings and widespread dereliction. While major social problems resulting from insufficient job creation undoubtedly exist at the periphery, nowhere have the consequences of restructuring been felt more severely than in the inner city. Between 1971 and 1981, the population of inner Dublin declined by 27 per cent, but the number of manufacturing employees resident in the inner city fell by 55 per cent.

Symptoms of inner-city decline

The direct transfer of jobs to the periphery has been one element in this process. A survey of 514 firms which had located on industrial estates between 1965 and 1974 revealed that more than a quarter had relocated from the inner city (Dublin Corporation Planning Department, 1975a). The Corporation estimated that this relocation of plants had resulted in a loss of 4,500 inner-city manufacturing jobs. Net transfers have also resulted from the tendency to develop new industrial premises on greenfield sites rather than in the inner city where land prices were high and development often required expensive siteworks (MacLaran and Beamish, 1985). New employment opportunities were therefore created at the periphery rather than in the central area. However, a recent survey of all manuacturing companies in the Dublin region revealed that half of those inner-city firms which anticipated acquiring new or additional floorspace within five years would prefer to remain within the inner city, while a number of suburban firms, amounting to 7 per cent of likely movers, indicated that they would actually prefer to locate in inner-city premises if any were available (Lisney, 1991).

During the recession of the 1970s, the long established industries of the inner city were badly hit and the IDA estimated that around 2,000 inner-city manufacturing jobs were being lost annually during the late 1970s as a result of relocation, shrinkage and closure (Bannon et al., 1981). The consequences are reflected in the changing character of inner-city land-uses. Between 1966 and 1974, the period of the first modern office development boom, the total area of industrial floorspace in the inner city declined by over 550,000 sq.m. (5.92 million sq. ft.) or 30 per cent. Meanwhile, office uses increased by nearly 95 per cent, thereby displacing industrial functions as the second most important activity in the inner area after residential uses (Dublin Corporation Planning Department, 1975b).

Unfortunately, the most recent comprehensive land-use data for the whole of the inner city dates from 1974. There is, therefore, no adequate data covering subsequent changes. However, changes are likely to have been substantial given the impact of two major economic recessions, the closure of relatively inefficient inner-city industrial enterprises resulting from intensified competition following entry into the EEC and the continued suburbanisation of manufacturing towards purpose-built industrial estates. Figure 10.1 illustrates the reduction of industrial land-use around the core of the central business area between 1966 and 1985. One detailed investigation of land-use change in an area to the east of Westland Row on the margins of the central business area, where the process of converting industrial land-uses to office functions has been very active, suggests that industrial land-use has declined significantly (Clarke, 1991). Industrial uses accounted for around 45 per cent of total floorspace there in 1966, but by 1990 this had shrunk to below 5 per cent. In contrast, office functions had expanded from 5 per cent to 51 per cent during the intervening years.

The economy of the inner city has been further eroded by the changing methods of cargo handling in the port and the closure of port-related industries. Containerisation obviated the requirement for traditional warehousing and the large labour force, while the downstream migration of the port to larger and deeper docks meant that long stretches of quayside, warehouse buildings and industrial land were abandoned.

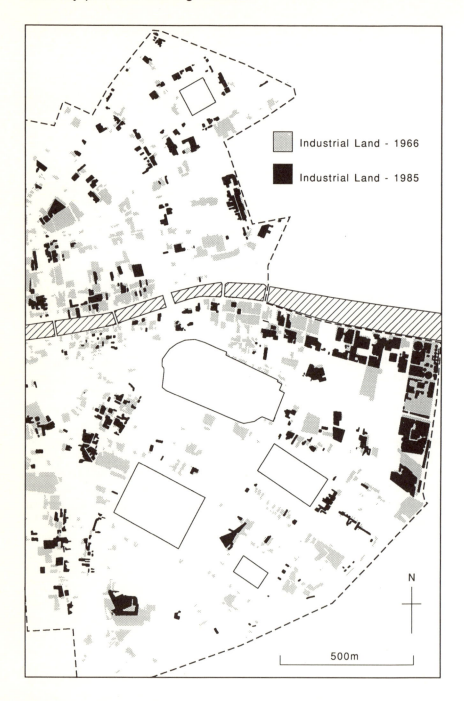

Industrial Land - 1966

Industrial Land - 1985

N

500m

Figure 10.1 Industrial land-use change in central Dublin, 1966-85.

Since the mid-1930s, the inner city's resident population has been declining as Corporation housing programmes have progressively eliminated the overcrowded tenements, reducing occupancy rates and dispersing the population towards the suburbs. This process of thinning and dispersal has tended to be selective with respect both to age and skill, resulting in an ageing residual population possessing low levels of education and training (Morrissey and Murphy, 1978). In 1986, over 75 per cent of the residents of the north inner city had left school prior to their 17th birthday, and 44 per cent had left before reaching the age of 15 (McKeown, 1991). Participation in higher education has also been found to be weak, amounting to just 1 per cent of each age cohort of the north-east inner city's population (Clancy and Benson, 1979). Inner-city areas are characterised by high levels of unemployment, a prevalence of dependency on the social welfare system for income support and a public sector housing component which accounted for about a third of all dwellings in 1981, well above the level for the city as a whole. Standardised mortality rates, an important indicator of social well-being, are also considerably higher than average. Nevertheless, despite the economic difficulties, the inner city retains a vibrant working-class community, about which Brendan Behan commented:

It's the working class that binds me to this town; they're the only real people here. . . . They've a great spirit and good neighbourly hearts – if they couldn't do you a good turn, well, they wouldn't do you a bad one. (Brendan Behan, *Brendan Behan's Island*, 1962, 19–20)

Inner-city districts

There are differences in the pressures facing the various parts of the inner area. The south-east inner city to the east of Trinity College and to the north of Lower Mount Street has experienced major private sector office development, spilling over from the neighbouring office core of Dublin 2 and amounting to over 56,000 sq.m. (600,000 sq. ft.) of space in 25 separate developments since 1960. Such conversion of industrial, institutional and residential land-uses into offices has become an increasing problem for the community in recent years, resulting from the proximity of Pearse station. These pressures have been exacerbated by the recent influx of high status residential developments attracted by the area's proximity to the office core, also tending to displace industrial functions. Thus, the community has experienced a major reduction in local employment opportunities in manufacturing and port-related employment. A sample survey of the Westland Row/City Quay/Pearse Street community revealed an unemployment rate of 39.1 per cent in 1989, more than 60 per cent of whom had been out of work for over a year, with one-third of the unemployed having been without work for over five years (St Andrew's Resource Centre, 1990).

The south-west inner city has also experienced major industrial job losses as a result of plant closures and *in situ* shrinkage, as at Guinness, though the company remains a significant employer. A thriving secondary shopping area is located on Thomas Street and Meath Street serving a still sizeable residential community amounting to 27,600 persons in 1986, but unemployment is still a serious problem. Unlike the south-east inner city, it has not been seriously affected by property development pressures until very recently. However, the Corporation's road improvement plans have had a serious blighting effect on parts of the area for decades, the vacant sites and buildings, abandoned maintenance and dereliction creating an environment which was conducive neither to people nor to businesses.

Between 1971 and 1981, the north inner-city workforce engaged in transport activities (including dock labour) and labouring fell by over 45 per cent, with reductions of over 30 per cent being recorded in production, communications and clerical activities. Unemployment grew three times as fast as the rate of increase nationally. By 1981, at a time when the national unemployment rate was still below 10 per cent and the rate for the Dublin area was 15.5 per cent, the level of unemployment in the north inner city reached 24.7 per cent and the North Dock ward had an unemployment rate of 35.1 per cent. After 1981, unemployment in the north inner city accelerated, growing by 2.7 per cent per annum to reach 41.0 per cent in 1986 (Alliance for Work Forum, 1988). Long-term unemployment of over a year is particularly severe, amounting to 58 per cent of the unemployed in 1989 (McKeown, 1991).

Like its south-eastern neighbour, the north-east inner city has experienced significant private sector interest from property developers. But developments have tended to be located in the vicinity of the existing commercial core, involving the redevelopment of commercial or office buildings rather than industrial sites or dwellings. The major exception to this was the redevelopment of a large site occupied by a builders' suppliers business at the Irish Life Centre on Lower Abbey Street. Thus, until recently, property development activities have had less impact on communities here. Indeed, the very limited user-demand for premises outside the commercial core areas to the north of the Liffey had helped to create a built environment which is now in considerable need of redevelopment. The north-eastern part of the inner city also includes the Sheriff Street flats complex, one of the most deprived communities in the state with an unemployment rate of 48.4 per cent in 1981 and which probably now exceeds 80 per cent.

Government responses to inner-city problems

Under political presure to direct at least some energy towards the problems of the inner city and with the intention of creating some 1,200 jobs, from the late 1970s the IDA became involved in the development of clusters of small industrial units in the inner-city at Pearse Street, East Wall Road, Gardiner Street, Prussia Street and at Newmarket in the Liberties. However, in 1991, only a quarter of the 1,068 people who worked in these clusters actually lived in the inner city.

There also existed a short-lived employment incentive scheme financed by the government's Inner-City Task Force which aimed to encourage businesses to engage long-term unemployed inner-city residents. To this end, a small subsidy was paid for six months towards the wage costs of those taken on. Over 380 persons were employed during the two year life of this initiative.

Some attention has also been paid to the inner city's environment. Since the mid-1970s, the Corporation's new housing schemes have added 2,400 high quality three to four bedroomed dwellings to the housing stock, while environmental improvement programmes have included the pedestrianisation and re-paving of streets, the landscaping of derelict sites, the planting of trees and the provision of items of sculpture. However, the assemblage of red girders in front of the Corporation flats illustrated in Figure 10.2 hardly springs to mind as one of the more pressing priorities of the relatively deprived Pimlico community in the Liberties.

The major thrust of recent Irish urban renewal policy has depended on involving the private sector property development industry and this has been especially emphasised since 1986. Despite the visible impact of such a policy, however, private sector proposals for redevelopment rarely provide for the type of land-use from which the local inner-city community is able to derive long-term benefit. Generally, projects have involved the development of housing which is beyond the means of local residents, or offices which employ professional and technical workers.

Designated areas for urban renewal

In order to stimulate private sector interest in inner-city renewal and to boost employment in the ailing construction sector, the Urban Renewal Act and Finance Act of 1986 created a significant package of incentives aimed at encouraging development in central Dublin and a number of other smaller Irish towns. The incentives included the following provisions:

Figure 10.2 One wonders what the residents of Pimlico in the Liberties have done to deserve this exercise in environmental improvement.

1. Full remission of rates for ten years on new buildings and on the increased value of reconstructed premises.
2. Capital allowances for commercial development amounting to 50 per cent of the capital involved, whether the building is owner-occupied or leased.
3. For tenants of new or refurbished premises a rent allowance against tax amounting to twice the annual rent for a period of ten years.
4. In addition to normal mortgage interest relief, owner-occupiers of private dwellings erected or reconstructed during the operation of the scheme are entitled to an allowance amounting to 5 per cent of the net construction/reconstruction cost for each of the first 10 years, amounting to a total of 50 per cent of building costs.
5. In the case of the Custom House Docks, additional incentives exist. These comprise capital allowances for business premises amounting to 100 per cent (54 per cent in the first year and 4 per cent thereafter), and, for residential properties (measuring between 35 and 125 sq. m. in the case of a house or 30–90 sq. m. in the case of apartments) landlords of rented properties are permitted to off-set the total cost of new premises constructed between January 1988 and January 1993 against rental income from all sources.

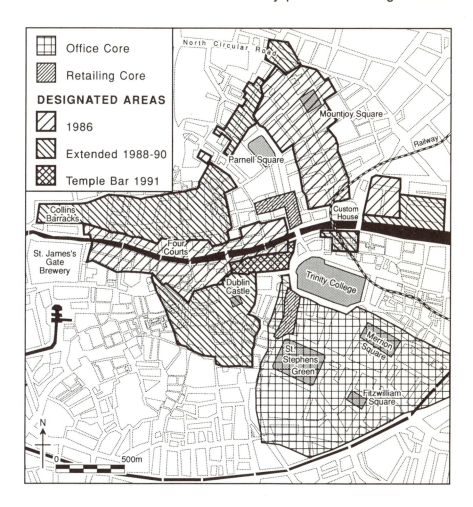

Figure 10.3 The inner-city Designated Areas for urban renewal.

Five areas were initially delimited in Dublin, four of which lay in the inner city, as depicted in Figure 10.3. The fifth 'urban renewal' area comprised a greenfield site of approximately 48 ha. (120 acres) on which a private developer was intending to construct the commercial centre for the new town of Tallaght. The smallest of the inner-city areas, comprising just 1 ha. (2.5 acres), incorporated an architecturally important group of early eighteenth century buildings on Henrietta Street, the first of Luke Gardiner's developments. The largest area, amounting to 37 ha. (91 acres), was located in the north-east inner city straddling Gardiner Street Upper and Lower, stretching from Beresford Place in the south to

Dorset Street in the north. The quays on both sides of the river Liffey, extending from the vicinity of O'Connell Bridge to Ellis Quay and Usher's Island to the west, comprised a third area amounting to 28 ha. (68 acres). It also extended southward to take in High Street. It is an area which has experienced the blighting effects of road widening proposals along several of the quays and, in the vicinity of High Street, the Corporation's road improvements which had been responsible for the almost complete eradication of the streetscape.

The fourth area comprised the disused Custom House Docks, with an area of 11 ha. (27 acres), of which 2.8 ha. (7 acres) was accounted for by two interlinked dock basins. None of the buildings was residential. Its boundaries have subsequently been extended to include the river frontage at Custom House Quay and an area to the east of Commons Street for the development of a national sports stadium, so that it now comprises approximately 20 ha. (50 acres), although the full enabling legislation regarding the extension has not yet been enacted. A rather different approach was adopted for the redevelopment of this site. In each of the three previously mentioned areas, the normal planning functions of the local authority were to be maintained. In the case of the Custom House Docks, an integrated development was proposed which would include a wide range of business, residential and recreational functions.

In order to achieve the goal of an integrated development, a Custom House Docks Development Authority (CHDDA) was established to oversee the scheme. It was ably headed by a former Chairman of An Bord Pleanala who had considerable private sector development experience. In early 1987, the site was transferred from the Port and Docks Board and vested in the CHDDA. Shortly afterwards, the Government decided to include an International Financial Services Centre (IFSC) where there were to be no restrictions on foreign currency transactions nor any capital gains tax on trading income generated within the Centre. A major additional inducement to attract commercial occupiers was a Corporation Tax rate of just 10 per cent for companies approved by the IDA as being engaged in off-shore activities.

Effectively, planning functions were expropriated from the local authority and vested in an unelected body appointed by the Minister for the Environment. It was decided to hold a competition among developers interested in participating. By mid-1987, the CHDDA had devised a planning scheme to attract interest in the competition and submitted it for approval by the Minister (Custom House Docks Development Authority, 1987). At the close of the competition in September 1987, eight full schemes had been lodged by international consortia of developers, while a further eight partial schemes had been submitted covering minor elements. Evaluation was on the basis of design, financial backing and 'deliverability', and the winning scheme was announced in

October of that year. It was lodged by a British and Irish consortium comprising British Land, Hardwicke and McInerney Properties, all of which had considerable development experience in the city. The scheme involved a total of more than 70,000 sq. m. (750,000 sq. ft.) of office space, of which some 28,000 sq. m. (300,000 sq. ft.) would be in the IFSC, together with a 300 bedroom hotel, a 5,000-seat conference centre, 200 residential apartments, three museums (folk, science and modern art), retailing, restaurants and pubs accounting for a further 12,500 sq. m. (135,000 sq. ft.) of space, an entertainment centre, community and training space and underground parking for 1,815 vehicles.

It was determined that once the Master Project Agreement was signed (in January 1988), the land would be passed to the development consortium (trading as the Custom House Docks Development Company) on a 200-year leasehold, as individual components of the development were undertaken. Subsequent changes to the winning scheme would not require consent from the CHDDA so long as alterations accorded with the CHDDA's planning scheme.

Progress has been rapid. Site preparation work commenced in January 1988 and the first IFSC building, amounting to 11,450 sq.m. (120,000 sq. ft.) facing the Custom House, was completed in 1990. Four more buildings, totalling some 30,000 sq.m. (340,000 sq. ft.) were completed in the following year. Whatever one may feel about the exterior design of the IFSC buildings, their interior design work has provided premises of international quality. One of the ways in which Ireland has attempted to attract overseas companies during the 1980s is by a total up-grading of the telecommunications system in the country. A telecommunications building, including video conference facilities, was completed in 1991.

By mid-1991, committed employment in approved IFSC projects amounted to around 2,800 with 140 companies having been approved by the IDA to operate from the Centre, though some of these jobs simply represent a transfer from other locations in the city. European companies included representation from Ireland, Germany, the UK, France, Belgium, the Netherlands, Denmark, Sweden, Finland, Switzerland and Austria. Parent companies of other operations were located in the USA, Canada, Japan, Australia, Bermuda and Nigeria. These covered a considerable variety of approved operations including corporate financing and treasury operations, investment fund, currency and futures funds management, municipal bond financing, asset and trade financing, securities trading, insurance, reinsurance broking, international stockbroking, aircraft financing and the insurance and financing of bloodstock. However, a dispute with the German, Swedish and Danish governments has arisen regarding the tax position of companies from those countries who fear its use as a means of tax avoidance.

In the Designated Areas outside the Custom House Docks, progress in the other Designated Areas has been more patchy, but none the less significant. It is difficult to establish just how much development might have taken place in such locations in the absence of such incentives, but given the paucity of significant development here since World War II, one can be reasonably assured that it would have amounted to very little. More problematical is the possibility that while development has been engendered or brought forward in time here, it may have been retarded in those areas lying just to the wrong side of the boundary, as property owners hope for some extension to the Designated Areas in the future. There was good reason for such an aspiration. In May 1990, following intense lobbying of the Minister for the Environment, the boundaries to the Designated Areas were considerably extended (see Figure 10.3).

Area-based policies which target particular areas for special treatment are often promoted on the grounds that they produce more immediately dramatic and cost-effective results than could be obtained from spreading resources more widely. This is because they hope to produce enhanced levels of confidence in the area and a local self-reinforcing spiral of environmental improvement. Dublin's Designated Areas are now so large that the major benefit of an area-based approach, that of creating an upward spiral of self-sustained improvement, will have been lost through dilution. Indeed, it can be argued that even Dublin's original Designated Areas were already too large to create positive externalities over such a wide scale.

Table 10.1 reveals that by the end of 1990, most of the development which had taken place in the Designated Areas outside the Custom House Docks had been completed to the south of the river Liffey, amounting to three-quarters of the 40,000 sq. m. (433,000 sq.ft.) which had been built. No developments had taken place on Henrietta Street. In only one location is there any evidence of the creation of a neighbourhood effect in the central portion of the South Quays district, along High Street, Winetavern Street, Bridge Street and Merchant's Quay. Over 85 per cent of the development which had been completed or planned in the Designated Areas was non-residential, with the residential component amounting to little over 5 per cent in the south inner-city area.

The timing of the Designated Area policy was fortuitous, coinciding with an uplift in the Irish economy and a shortage of available office space. The development industry responded quickly to the new conditions and to the financial incentives which were on offer, expanding the geographical focus of their interest. A spate of construction activity swiftly took place in the Designated Areas, districts which were decidedly tertiary from a traditional viewpoint. From 1987 to 1991, 77,000 sq.m. (830,000 sq.ft.) of office space was developed in the Designated Areas

Table 10.1 Projects within the Designated Areas, December 1990 (square metres)

| | Breakdown of developments by stage: | | | Character of development: | |
| | | | | Office/ | |
	Completed	In Progress	Planned	Commercial	Residential
South Quays–High Street	19,900	27,190	153,926	199,019	11,998
North Quays	6,012	18,319	19,360	32,796	10,897
North-east Inner City	4,350	315	48,540	38,426	14,780
Henrietta Street	0	0	0	0	0
Custom House Docks	0	147,060	0	128,155	18,951

Source: Inner-City Development Section, Dublin Corporation; McKeown, 1991.

and in 1991 they accounted for over 40 per cent of the year's output. However, by the end of that year, the supply of new office space had far outstripped the scale of user-demand and over 30 per cent of the newly completed office space in the Designated Areas outside the Custom House Docks lay vacant (MacLaran and Hamilton Osborne King, 1992a, 1992b). It is therefore increasingly likely that future redevelopment in such locations will be more heavily geared towards residential functions.

Temple Bar

The latest exercise in urban regeneration has been undertaken at the heart of the inner city. It comprises an area lying between Dame Street and the river Liffey, the core of which CIE had earmarked for the southern part of a central bus station which would be situated on either side of the river Liffey. The company had acquired a number of the required properties on both sides of the river over a long period of time. In the Temple Bar area, it let these out at very favourable rents on short leases. Cheap premises and the proximity to the central area engendered a 'left-bank' atmosphere of hotels and pubs, cheap cafés and restaurants, theatres, galleries, recording studios, second-hand goods and clothing stores. Nowhere else in the city was there to be found such a degree of mixing of functions and it became increasingly apparent that this unique mixture was worthy of protection (Temple Bar Study Group, 1986). Conservation groups such as An Taisce (1985b) also strongly supported calls for the abandonment of insensitive clean-sweep redevelopment of an area whose development could be traced back to the seventeenth century and which included along Fownes Street the best remaining row of early Georgian houses in Dublin.

Despite the inclusion of the central bus station in the City's Draft

Development Plan Review of 1987, within months of its publication the proposed southern terminus was rejected by the Corporation's Planning Committee. In May 1990, in recognition of the new situation, the Corporation planners published an 'action plan' for the area (Dublin Corporation Planning Department, 1990). The project's abandonment represented a significant victory for the conservationists, but probably stemmed from budgetary stringency and the realisation by central government that such a scheme would require vast investment.

The provisions of the Temple Bar Area Renewal and Development Act, 1991, and of the Finance Act in the same year established two companies to oversee the rehabilitation of the whole Temple Bar district, an area which had suffered from years of blight and postponed building maintenance. The key to regenerating the district over a five-year period is to enhance the types of function which had already been established by creating a bustling cultural and tourist quarter. A further aim is the inclusion of up to 2,000 new residential units. These objectives are to be accomplished by the provision of incentives to promote activities which are approved by Temple Bar Renewal Ltd., the authority charged with the task of maintaining the current functional mix.

A second company, Temple Bar Properties Ltd., was set up to act as a development company for the area, operating on the basis of 100 per cent gearing with funds borrowed from the European Investment Bank (Hickey, 1991). The first step involved the acquisition by Temple Bar Properties Ltd., at pre-incentive prices, of all the available publicly owned properties. It seems that the operational role of Temple Bar Properties Ltd. will be to refurbish the tenanted properties which it took over, to establish a portfolio giving its tenants security of tenure, to engage directly or in joint ventures with other developers in the redevelopment of untenanted properties, and to sell strategic plots where this would facilitate private sector development.

As in the Designated Areas, tax incentives have been extended to the district in order to assist in the process of building renovation, but only in so far as they relate to specified uses. The whole cost of the purchase price of an appropriately refurbished residence in Temple Bar is allowable against the income tax of an owner-occupier. Significantly, as the Chairman of Temple Bar Properties notes, the available incentives 'have for the first time put refurbishment on a level economic playing field with new build' (Teahon, 1991), a most important departure which it is hoped will encourage sensitive renewal mixing refurbishment with new building on in-fill sites. Furthermore, compulsory purchase powers have been made available to assist in site assembly for developments undertaken for approved functions.

Physical progress has involved the Corporation's re-laying of granite pavements and setts, traffic reduction and carriageway narrowing. Private sector interest has been slower to surface, but includes the refurbishment of a former hotel on Parliament Street and its conversion to apartments, and a proposal by Trinity College for the development of accommodation for 400 students. In July 1992, Temple Bar Properties lodged over 20 planning applications for a variety of projects.

The administrative apparatus which has been set up to renew the area, the commitment among those involved and their recognition of the need for a sensitive approach provides every indication that, at long last, Dublin may be about to do something right. Unfortunately, planning powers remain vested in Dublin Corporation which may well baulk at some of the radical proposals being submitted by Temple Bar Properties for traffic calming measures. Nevertheless, it is to be hoped that the scheme marks a changing of attitudes among politicians and developers towards this ancient city.

Reflections

There are several aspects of the Government's Designated Area policy which are disturbing. As in the decision to abandon the development of flats in the city, the Designated Area policy was imposed on the Corporation by the Department of the Environment. Neither in the original Designated Areas nor in their subsequent extension was there significant consultation with Dublin Corporation regarding the precise delimitation of the areas or the criteria upon which areas were to be included or excluded. Furthermore, it seems that there was no consideration given to the funding consequences which would result from the remission of commercial rates for a period of ten years or the loss to the central exchequer arising from the preferential tax regime operating in the IFSC for existing activities which were relocating from elsewhere in the city. Furthermore, retail traders paying full commercial rates outside the Designated Areas face competion from those with a privileged trading status inside.

Another major criticism has been that the incentives have tended to result in the redevelopment of land rather than the rehabilitation of buildings. Despite the intervention of An Taisce, this has contributed to the demolition of a number of buildings along the Liffey's quays, where good examples of eighteenth century merchants' houses have been demolished, sometimes only to be replaced by vacant sites as owners await an improvement in user-demand. Figures 10.4 and 10.5 show the replacement of eighteenth century buildings on Arran Quay by a modern office development.

A government policy which favours renewal through private sector property development has a number of advantages. It is relatively cheap,

Figure 10.4 Eighteenth century housing on Arran Quay, photographed in 1985

Figure 10.5 Arran Quay, 1990. The Designated Areas policy has encouraged redevelopment rather than refurbishment.

at least in the short term, yet it engenders a physical and visible manifestation which encourages one to believe that the government is actually concerned about inner-city problems. Indeed, by June 1992, within the Designated Areas outside the Custom House Docks, 99 projects involving 96,000 sq.m. (1m sq.ft.) of space and a combined value of IR£64m had been completed and a further 25 schemes, amounting to 70,000 sq. m. (753,000 sq.ft.) and valued at IR£68m, were in progress. However, it is a policy which bears almost no relevance to the needs of the local communities. Indeed, where it has led to rising land prices through speculative investment, it can aggravate the difficulties of finding affordable premises for community-based activities. After lengthy negotiations between the CHDDA and the North Centre City Community Action Project, it was agreed that a proportion of those employed in construction work on the site would be drawn from the local area. In 1990, this amounted to 80 employees, or 12 per cent of the on-site labour force engaged in construction. In adddition, the CHDDA and FAS, the national training agency, have provided training for 71 local people. But the longer-term impacts of most of the Designated Area developments are likely to be of very limited significance for inner-city communities in terms of employment opportunities. The redevelopment of the Custom House Docks has juxtaposed one of the most valuable pieces of real estate in the country with one of the most deprived residential schemes in Ireland, the Sheriff Street flats complex. As such striking evidence of the inequalities of capitalism is considered unacceptable, it has been decided that the community will be removed, re-enacting a policy which was carried out in the Summerhill – Sean McDermott Street area in the 1970s. Meanwhile, the highly visible development activity which current policy has engendered has permitted the government to abandon any concerted attempt to attract appropriate industrial employment into the inner city, as this is likely to prove a far more costly exercise.

11
Epilogue

The observations which Walter Bor (1967, 293) made at a Town Planning Institute Conference in Dublin remind us just how fine was the city even as late as the end of the 1960s, and how momentous were the changes which awaited it.

> Dublin is a city of quite exceptional character and beauty, with a long history and vibrant cultural tradition. The closely interwoven pattern of eighteenth century streets with their remarkable consistency of scale and material, once quite a common sight in Europe, can now be found only in Dublin, and the city's architectural heritage becomes rarer and more vulnerable every day.
>
> Dublin's past growth has been relatively slow and steady compared with other cities. The city has not been radically altered in character by the effects of twentieth century development. The predominant part of the eighteenth and nineteenth-century fabric of the city has survived and the basic pattern of scale and material remains intact. Thus on the one hand this city has the great inheritance of Georgian domestic architecture of a unique quality and scale, but on the other hand there is an acute threat that the effects of rapid expansion over the next two decades could be all the more damaging.

A significant proportion of that heritage has now disappeared entirely or has been disfigured by alterations and additions which have destroyed its integrity. The surgery has been piecemeal, but radical in aggregate. Nevertheless, much still remains. Despite all the efforts to reduce it to a 'Euro-city' indistinguishable from a dozen others, implanting within eighteenth century terraces modern buildings designed in accordance with the latest international architectural whims and grafting onto its streets *de rigeur* pink 'Euro-pavements' formed of coloured concrete cobble-lock setts, Dublin none the less remains a city replete with character. As Jan Morris (1986) affirms, this 'most defiantly different of capitals' remains 'one of the most truly exotic cities in the world'. It possesses a central area which has been developed at an intimate scale with varied textures and tones which could, even at this late stage, with vision and attention, again become one of the finest of Europe's urban environments. While many of the city's recent operations have been largely unsuccessful, at least the patient does still live on! One could still with justification repeat the words of Wright et al. (1974, 269) that 'for all her blight and her recent architectural misfits, she is still a very beautiful city, at once the most personal and the most surprising metropolis in Europe'.

Dublin is a liveable and highly seductive city, though it is hard to determine wherein lies its precise charm. Some of it lies in the ironies and absurdities of ordinary life. Though writing over 25 years ago, there is still much truth in Butler's view that:

> It is one of the world's most extraordinary places and anyone who spends more than three months there will hate leaving and will always be haunted to return. No one has ever defined its charm and its secret, but this is largely because there is no single element that can be isolated. It is a total effect of a thousand influences.
>
> ... It is a comfortable place to live in and it doesn't overwhelm its people or its visitors by vastness or splendour . . . there is a personality in its design and environment that invades every inch of its being. It manages by an intimate magic to give a village atmosphere for its 700,000 inhabitants.
>
> ... Within a radius of eight miles a man can have every experience he would ever wish to enjoy. It is complete in itself. Indeed it could be said that Dublin is not a city; it is a lazy man's continent. (Butler, 1965, 35–6)

Ultimately, Dublin really is its people. Its character is determined by the nature of its inhabitants and in that sense the Dublins of O'Casey and of Joyce live on. Although one may occasionally cringe at the posturings of those who believe Ireland to be a moral beacon for the whole world, there is a welcome lack of arrogance or pomposity among its citizens. They seem genuinely surprised that people from more prosperous countries should choose to live here, and although they would be too polite to say so in anything but an oblique way, I'm certain they think that we are slightly mad. Though it is unwise to generalise, Dubliners are justifiably renowned for their friendliness, humour, an easy-going attitude and readiness to enjoy life, even under difficult circumstances:

> . . . and this ineradicable spirit of merriment informs the Dublin genius to this day, and is alive and bubbling still, for all the miseries of the Irish problem, in this brown jumbled capital across the water. (Morris, 1986, 135)

Bibliography

Aalen, F.H.A. (1985) The working class housing movement in Dublin, 1850–1920, pp. 131–88 in Bannon, M.J. (ed.) *The emergence of Irish planning, 1880–1920*, Turoe Press, Dublin.

Aalen, F.H.A. (1992) Health and housing in Dublin c.1850 to 1921, pp. 279–304 in Aalen, F.H.A. and Whelan, K. (eds) *Dublin city and county: from prehistory to present*, Geography Publications, Dublin.

Abercrombie, P., Kelly, S. and Robertson, M. (1941) *Sketch development plan for Dublin*, Dublin Corporation, Dublin.

Alliance for Work Forum (1988) *Impact: a research report on the impact of urban renewal on communities in Dublin's north inner city*, Alliance for Work Forum, Dublin.

An Bord Pleanala (1992) *Report and accounts, 1990*, An Bord Pleanala, Dublin.

An Foras Forbartha (1971) *Transportation in Dublin*, An Foras Forbartha, Dublin.

An Foras Forbartha (1972) *Dublin transportation study*, An Foras Forbartha, Dublin.

An Taisce (1985a) *Georgian Dublin: policy for survival*, Dublin City Association of An Taisce, Dublin.

An Taisce (1985b) *Dublin: the Temple Bar area, a policy for its future*, Dublin City Association of An Taisce, Dublin.

Bailey, M. (1988) Air quality in Dublin – the current situation, pp. 20–30 in Mollan, C. and Walsh, J. (eds) *Air pollution in Ireland – Dublin, a case study*, Royal Dublin Society, Dublin.

Baker, T.J. and O'Brien, L.M. (1979) *The Irish housing system: a critical overview*, Economic and Social Research Institute, Broadsheet no. 17, Dublin.

Bannon, M.J. (1973) *Office location in Ireland: the role of central Dublin*, An Foras Forbartha, Dublin.

Bannon, M.J. (1984) The Irish national settlement system, pp. 239–60 in Bourne, L., Sinclair, R. and Dziewonski, K. (eds) *Urbanisation and settlement systems: international perspectives*, Oxford University Press, Oxford.

Bannon, M.J. (1988) The capital of the new state, pp. 133–50 in Cosgrave, A. (ed.) *Dublin through the ages*, College Press, Dublin.

Bannon, M.J. (1989a) Irish planning from 1921 to 1945: an overview, pp. 13–70 in Bannon, M.J. (ed.) *Planning: the Irish experience 1920–88*, Wolfhound, Dublin.

228

Bibliography

Bannon, M.J. (1989b) Development planning and the neglect of the critical regional dimension, pp. 122–57 in Bannon, M.J. (ed.) *Planning: the Irish experience 1920–88*, Wolfhound, Dublin.

Bannon, M.J., Eustace, J.G. and O'Neill, M. (1981) *Urbanisation: problems of growth and decay in Dublin*, National Economic and Social Council, Report no. 55, Stationery Office, Dublin.

Barry, F. (1975) Reproduction: for and against, pp. 52–6 in Delany, P. (ed.) *Dublin, a city in crisis*, Royal Institute of the Architects of Ireland, Dublin.

Beamish, C. (1990) *The development of modern industrial property in Dublin*, unpublished Ph.D. Thesis, Department of Geography, Trinity College, Dublin.

Beauregard, R. (1989) Between modernity and post-modernism, *Environment and Planning*, D, 7 (4), 381–95.

Behan, B. (1962) *Brendan Behan's island, an Irish sketchbook*, quoted from 1990 edition, Hutchinson, London.

Bidwell, B. and Heffer, L. (1981) *The Joycean way: a topographic guide to 'Dubliners' and 'A Portrait of the Artist as a Young Man'*, Wolfhound Press, Dublin.

Blackwell, J. (1988) *A review of housing policy*, National Economic and Social Council, Stationery Office, Dublin.

Bor, W. (1967) An environmental policy for Dublin, *Journal of the Town Planning Institute*, 53, 293–96.

Bradley, J. (1984) Introduction, pp. 8–14 in Bradley, J. (ed.) *Viking Dublin exposed*, O'Brien Press, Dublin.

Bradley, J. (1992) The topographical development of Scandinavian Dublin, pp. 43–56 in Aalen, F.H.A. and Whelan, K. (eds) *Dublin city and county: from prehistory to present*, Geography Publications, Dublin.

Brady, J. (1987) Social contrasts in Dublin, pp. 1–15 in Horner, A.A. and Parker, A.J. (eds) *Geographical perspectives on the Dublin region*, Geographical Society of Ireland, Special Publication no. 2, Dublin.

Brady, J. and Parker, A.J. (1975) The factorial ecology of Dublin: a preliminary investigation, *The Economic and Social Review*, 7 (1), 35–54.

Brady, J. and Parker, A.J. (1986) The socio-demographic spatial structure of Dublin in 1981, *The Economic and Social Review*, 17 (4), 229–52.

Breen, R., Hannan, D.F., Rottman, D.B. and Whelan, C.T. (1990) *Understanding contemporary Ireland: state, class and development in the Republic of Ireland*, Gill and MacMillan, Dublin.

Broadbent, T.A. (1977) *Planning and profit in the urban economy*, Methuen, London.

Browne, L. (1986) *The use and change of use of retail space in Grafton Street*, unpublished B.A. (Mod.) thesis, Department of Geography, Trinity College, Dublin.

Budgen, F. (1972) *James Joyce and the making of 'Ulysses'*, Oxford University Press, London.

Butler, A. (1965) Growing up, pp. 27–36 in McCann, S. *The world of Brendan Behan*, Four Square, London.

Byrne, D. (1984) Dublin – a case study of housing and the residual working class, *International Journal of Urban and Regional Research*, 8 (3), 402–20.

Caldwell, G. (1985) Investment returns 1966–85, *Irish Banking Review*, pp. 26–35.

Casey, J. and O'Rourke, P. (1992) *City tourism in Amsterdam, Dublin and Edinburgh*, Dublin City Centre Business Association, Dublin.

Castells, M. (1976) Theoretical propositions for an experimental study of urban social movements, pp. 147–73 in Pickvance, C. (ed.) *Urban sociology: critical essays*, Tavistock, London.

Central Statistics Office (1986) *Census of population of Ireland, 1981, vol. 8*, Stationery Office, Dublin.

Bibliography

Central Statistics Office (1991) *Labour force survey 1990*, Stationery Office, Dublin.

Clancy, P. (1988) *Who goes to college? A second national survey of participation in higher education*, Higher Education Authority, Dublin.

Clancy, P. and Benson, C. (1979) *Higher education in Dublin: a study of some emerging needs*, Higher Education Authority, Dublin.

Clarke, D. (1977) *Dublin*, B.T. Batsford Ltd., London.

Clarke, H.B. (1977) The topographical development of early medieval Dublin, *Journal of the Society of Antiquaries*, 107, 29–51.

Clarke, H.B. (1988) Gaelic, Viking and Hiberno-Norse Dublin, pp. 5–24 in Cosgrave, A. (ed.) *Dublin through the ages*, College Press, Dublin.

Clarke, N.O.R. (1991) *The social consequences of office development within the Westland Row area*, unpublished B.A. (Mod.) dissertation, Department of Geography, Trinity College, Dublin.

Colivet, M.P. (1943) *Report of inquiry into the housing of the working classes of the city of Dublin, 1939/43*, Stationery Office, Dublin.

Conlon, P. (1988) Public transport – what is its role?, pp. 167–78 in Blackwell, J. and Convery, F.J. (eds) *Revitalising Dublin – what works?*, Resource and Environmental Policy Centre, University College Dublin, Dublin.

Conway, E.P. (1991) Transportation – Dublin's 'prima donna', pp. 73–4 in O'Sullivan, J. (ed.) *Transport in Dublin: policy and practice*, An Taisce, Dublin.

Crowley, J.A. (1991) Opportunities posed by emerging developments, pp. 27–31 in O'Sullivan, J. (ed.) *Transport in Dublin: policy and practice*, An Taisce, Dublin.

Cullen, L.M. (1992) The growth and character of Dublin 1600–1900: character and heritage, pp. 251–78 in Aalen, F.H.A. and Whelan, K. (eds) *Dublin city and county: from prehistory to present*, Geography Publications, Dublin.

Curriculum Development Unit (1978) *Viking settlement to medieval Dublin*, O'Brien Educational, Dublin.

Custom House Docks Development Authority (1987) *Planning scheme*, CHDDA, Dublin.

Daly, M.E. (1984) *Dublin: the deposed capital*, Cork University Press, Cork.

Daly, M.E. (1988) A tale of two cities: 1860–1920, pp. 113–32 in Cosgrave, A. (ed.) *Dublin through the ages*, College Press, Dublin.

D'Arcy, F. (1988) An age of distress and reform: 1800–1860, pp. 93–112 in Cosgrave, A. (ed.) *Dublin through the ages*, College Press, Dublin.

Delaney, F. (1981) *James Joyce's odyssey, a guide to the Dublin of 'Ulysses'*, Hodder and Stoughton, London.

Department of Industry and Commerce (1990) *Review of industrial performance, 1990*, Stationery Office, Dublin.

Department of the Environment (1980) *Current trends and policies in the field of housing, building and planning, Ireland*, Department of the Environment, Stationery Office, Dublin.

Department of the Environment (1991a) *Local government and the elected member*, Stationery Office, Dublin.

Department of the Environment (1991b) *Annual housing statistics bulletin 1990*, Department of the Environment, Stationery Office, Dublin.

Department of the Environment (1991c) *A plan for social housing*, Department of the Environment, Stationery Office, Dublin.

Dickson, D. (1986) Large scale developers and the growth of eighteenth-century Irish cities, pp. 109–23 in Butel, P. and Cullen, L.M. (eds) *Cities and merchants: French and Irish perspectives on urban development, 1500–1900*, Department of Modern History, Trinity College, Dublin.

Dickson, D. (1988) Capital and country: 1600–1800, pp. 63–76 in Cosgrave, A. (ed.) *Dublin through the ages*, College Press, Dublin.

Drudy, P.J. (1989) The international-local interplay, pp. 125–41 in Albrecht, L. and Moulaert, F. (eds) *Regional policy at the crossroads: European perspectives*, Kingsley, London.

Drudy, P.J. (1991a) Demographic and economic change in Dublin in recent decades, pp. 17–25 in MacLaran, A. (ed.) *Dublin in crisis*, Trinity Papers in Geography, 5, Department of Geography, Trinity College, Dublin.

Drudy, P.J. (1991b) Overseas industry in Ireland, pp. 152–69 in Foley, A. and McAleese, D. (eds) *The regional impact of overseas industry*, Gill and Macmillan, Dublin.

Dublin Corporation Planning Department (1975a) *Survey of zoned industrial lands*, Working Paper no. 5, Planning Department, Dublin Corporation.

Dublin Corporation Planning Department (1975b) *Land use in the inner city area*, Working Paper no. 9, Planning Department, Dublin Corporation, Dublin.

Dublin Corporation Planning Department (1985a) *Shopping policies and trends: Dublin Corporation development plan review*, Dublin Corporation, Dublin.

Dublin Corporation Planning Department (1985b) *Dublin Corporation development plan review: public sector housing*, Dublin Corporation, Dublin.

Dublin Corporation Planning Department (1986) *The inner city: draft review, Dublin development plan*, Dublin Corporation, Dublin.

Dublin Corporation Planning Department (1990) *The Temple Bar area – action plan 1990*, Dublin Corporation, Dublin.

Dublin County Council (1991) *Dublin County development plan 1991: written statement*, Dublin County Council, Dublin.

Dublin County Council Community Department (1987) *County Dublin areas of need, vols. I and II*, Dublin County Council, Dublin.

Dublin County Council Planning Department (1987) *Tallaght information sheets*, Dublin County Council, Dublin.

Dublin County Council Planning Department (1988) *Industry*, Working Paper no. 4, Dublin County Council.

Dublin Crisis Conference Committee (1987) *Manifesto for the city*, Dublin.

Eastern Regional Development Organisation (1985) *Eastern region settlement strategy, 2011*, Eastern Regional Development Organisation, Dublin.

Foster, C., Jackman, R. and Thompson, Q. (1985) *The financing of local authorities*, National Economic and Social Council, Report no. 80, Dublin.

Garda Síochána (1991) *Report on crime 1990*, Stationery Office, Dublin.

Gough, M. (1991) The commissioners for making wide and convenient streets, pp. 5–11 in McCullough, N. (ed.) *A vision of the city: Dublin and the Wide Streets Commissioners*, Dublin Corporation, Dublin.

Greene, M. (1986) video-taped interview for MacLaran, A., *Property and the urban environment*, Centre for Language and Communication Studies, Trinity College, Dublin.

Gregory, D. (1978) *Ideology, science and human geography*, Hutchinson, London.

Hague, C. (1987) Comment: starting on wrong foot with planning problems, *Planning*, 744, 13 November, 9.

Harvey, D. (1982) *The limits to capital*, Blackwell, Oxford.

Haworth, R. (1984) The modern annals of Wood Quay, pp. 16–37 in Bradley, J. (ed.) *Viking Dublin exposed*, The O'Brien Press, Dublin.

Hickey, O. (1991) *The property perspective*, mimeo paper to The Society of Chartered Surveyors, Dublin.

Holloway, J. and Picciotto, S. (1978) (eds) *State and capital: a Marxist debate*, Edward Arnold, London.

Horner, A. (1992) From city to city region – Dublin from the 1930s to the 1990s, pp. 327–58 in Aalen, F.H.A. and Whelan, K. (eds) *Dublin city and county: from prehistory to present*, Geography Publications, Dublin.

Bibliography

Hourihan, K. (1978) Social areas in Dublin, *The Economic and Social Review*, 9 (4), 301–18.

Hourihan, K. (1991) Culture, politics and recent urbanisation in the Republic of Ireland, pp. 141–50 in Bannon, M.J., Bourne, L.S. and Sinclair, R. (eds) *Urbanization and urban development: recent trends in a global context*, International Geographical Union Commission for Urban Systems and Urban Development, Dublin.

Hutchinson, B. (1969) *Social status and inter-generational social mobility in Dublin*, Economic and Social Research Institute, paper no. 48, Dublin.

Igoe, V. (1990) *James Joyce's Dublin houses*, Mandarin, London.

Industrial Development Authority (1978) *IDA industrial plan 1977–80*, Industrial Development Authority, Dublin.

Jeffrey, D. (1988) Air pollution damage to Dublin's historic buildings, pp. 37–45 in Mollan, C. and Walsh J. (eds) *Air pollution in Ireland – Dublin, a case study*, Royal Dublin Society, Dublin.

Jeffries, C. (1918) Architects, Bolsheviks and World War I, *Architecture*, 4 (1), quoted in McGuirk, P., *op cit*, p. 4.

Johnson, P. (1985) interviewed in *Skyscrapers: cathedrals of commerce – Space on Earth, III*, broadcast Channel 4 television, 4 November 1985, VTR H100427D/E.

Kearney, J.F. (1986) unpublished video-taped interview for MacLaran, A., *Property and the urban evironment*, Centre for Language and Communication Studies, Trinity College, Dublin.

Kearns, K. C., (1983) *Georgian Dublin: Ireland's imperilled architectural heritage*, David and Charles, Newton Abbott.

Kelleghan, P.J. (1991) The Dublin ring road – purpose, design and justification, pp. 22–6 in O'Sullivan, J. (ed.) *Transport in Dublin: policy and practice*, An Taisce, Dublin.

Kelly, D. et al. (1986) *A report on the Dublin crisis conference*, Dublin.

Kennedy, K.A., Giblin, T. and McHugh, D. (1988) *The economic development of Ireland in the twentieth century*, Routledge, London.

Killen, J.E. (1991) Transport in Dublin: recent trends and future prospects, pp. 26–34 in MacLaran, A. (ed.) *Dublin in crisis*, Trinity Papers in Geography, 5, Department of Geography, Trinity College, Dublin.

Killen, J.E. (1992) Transport in Dublin: past, present and future, pp. 305–26 in Aalen, F.H.A. and Whelan, K., *Dublin city and county: from prehistory to present*, Geography Publications, Dublin.

Kirk, G. (1980) *Urban planning in a capitalist society*, Croom Helm, London.

Knox, P.L. (1982) *Urban social geography; an introduction*, Longman, London.

Knox, P.L. and Cullen, J. (1981) Town planning and the internal survival mechanisms of urbanised capitalism, *Area*, 13 (3), 183–9.

Laffan, M. (1985) Labour must wait: Ireland's conservative revolution, pp. 203–22 in Corish, P.J. (ed.) *Radicals, rebels and establishments*, Historical Studies, 15, Appletree Press, Belfast.

Lamarche, F. (1976) Property development and the economic foundations of the urban question, pp. 85–118 in Pickvance, C. (ed.) *Urban sociology: critical essays*, Methuen, London.

Lee, J.J. (1989) *Ireland 1912–1985: politics and society*, Cambridge University Press, Cambridge.

Lennon, C. (1988) 'The beauty and eye of Ireland': the sixteenth century, pp. 46–62 in Cosgrave, A. (ed.) *Dublin through the ages*, College Press, Dublin.

Lisney (1991) *Industrial survey*, unpublished results.

Lisney and Son (1989) *Prime Dublin: a retail use survey of the Grafton Street and Henry Street shopping areas*, Lisney and Son, Dublin.

Litchfield, N. and Partners (1979a) *Revitalisation strategy for north-east central Dublin*, Irish Life Assurance plc, Dublin.

Litchfield, N. and Partners (1979b) *Urban passenger transport in the Dublin area in relation to city centre retailing*, City Centre Business Association, Dublin.

Litchfield, N. and Partners (1980) *Towards a shopping policy for the Dublin sub-region*, City Centre Business Association, Dublin.

Lydon, J. (1988) The medieval city, pp. 25–45 in Cosgrave, A. (ed.) *Dublin through the ages*, College Press, Dublin.

MacLaran, A. (1986) Property and the institutional investor in Ireland, *Irish Geography*, 19, 69–73.

MacLaran, A. (1989a) Recent trends in the Dublin office market, *Irish Geography*, 22 (1), 52–5.

MacLaran, A. (1989b) Dublin office property review, 1960–1988, pp. 10–50 in MacLaran, A. and Hamilton Osborne King, *Office Survey and office review*, Hamilton Osborne King, Dublin.

MacLaran, A. (1990) Changing demand factors in Dublin's office accommodation market, pp.15–29 in MacLaran, A. and Hamilton Osborne King, *HOK Offices 1990*, Hamilton Osborne King, Dublin.

MacLaran, A. (1991a) Office clusters in central Dublin, pp. 29–40 in MacLaran, A. and Hamilton Osborne King, *HOK Offices 1991*, Hamilton Osborne King, Dublin.

MacLaran, A. (1991b) Serving the capital, pp. 75–8 in O'Sullivan, J. (ed.) *Transport in Dublin: policy and practice*, An Taisce, Dublin.

MacLaran, A. and Beamish, C. (1985) Industrial property development in Dublin, 1960–1982, *Irish Geography*, 18, 37–50.

MacLaran, A. and Hamilton Osborne King (1990a) *HOK Offices*, Hamilton Osborne King, Dublin.

MacLaran, A. and Hamilton Osborne King (1990b) *Office market interim review*, Hamilton Osborne King, Dublin.

MacLaran, A. and Hamilton Osborne King (1992a) *HOK Offices 1992*, Hamilton Osborne King, Dublin.

MacLaran, A. and Hamilton Osborne King (1992b) *Office market interim review*, Hamilton Osborne King, Dublin.

MacLaran, A., MacLaran, M. and Malone, P. (1987) Property cycles in Dublin: the anatomy of boom and slump in the industrial and office property sectors, *The Economic and Social Review*, 18 (4), 237–56.

MacLaran, A., Wilson, K. and Drudy, P.J., (1991) *Industrial property devlopment in Dublin 1960–1991*, Sherry Fitzgerald, Dublin.

Malone, P. (1985a) *Office development in Dublin 1960–1983: property, profit and space*, unpublished Ph.D. Thesis, Department of Geography, Trinity College, Dublin.

Malone, P. (1985b) Office development in Dublin: the roles of property interests, pp. 19–58 in MacLaran A., Malone P. and Beamish, C. (eds) *Property and the urban environment: Dublin*, Occasional Paper no. 2, Department of Geography, Trinity College, Dublin.

Malone, P. (1990) *Office development in Dublin 1960–1990*, School of Architecture, University of Manchester, Manchester.

Mazziotti, D. (1982) The underlying assumptions of advocacy planning, pluralism and reform, pp. 207–25 in Paris, C. (ed.) *Critical readings in planning theory*, Pergamon, Oxford.

McCarthy, J. (1988) *Joyce's Dublin, a walking guide to 'Ulysses'*, Wolfhound Press, Dublin.

McCullough, N. (1989) *Dublin: an urban history*, Anne Street Press, Dublin.

McDaid, J. (1988) House and flat design in the city – lessons from experience, pp. 18–26 in Blackwell, J. and Convery, F. (eds) *Revitalising Dublin: what works?*, Resource and Environmental Policy Centre, University College, Dublin.

Bibliography

McDermott, J. (1988) *Dublin's architectural development, 1800–1925*, Tulcamac, Dublin.

McDonald, F. (1985a) *The destruction of Dublin*, Gill and MacMillan, Dublin.

McDonald, F. (1985b) Tearing out Dublin's heart, *The Irish Times*, 12 June.

McDonald, F. (1989) *Saving the city – how to halt the destruction of Dublin*, Tomar Publishing, Dublin.

McDonald, F. (1990a) Bypass will be hub of country's road network, *The Irish Times*, 9 March.

McDonald, F. (1990b) Potential of quay-side survives the speculators, *The Irish Times*, 21 August.

McGeehan, H. (1992) *A cost benefit analysis of the Howth/Bray (DART) rail electrification*, Irish Universities Transport Study Group, Occasional Paper no. 1, Trinity College, Dublin.

McGuirk, P. (1991) *Perspectives on the nature and role of urban planning in Dublin*, unpublished Ph.D. thesis, Department of Geography, Trinity College, Dublin.

McKeown, K. (1991) *The north inner city of Dublin: an overview*, Daughters of Charity, Dublin.

McKiernan, E. (1973) *Statutory requirements and policies which affect the planning of residential areas*, An Foras Forbartha, Dublin.

McNulty, P. (1983) *A study of the economic cost and social benefits arising from the deployment of local authority housing resources in the Dublin area in the nineteen seventies*, unpublished M.Sc. Thesis, Department of Geography, Trinity College, Dublin.

Meldon, J. (1991) Land use strategy and transportation policy in Dublin, 1971–1991, pp. 70–72 in O'Sullivan, J. (ed.) *Transport in Dublin: policy and practice*, An Taisce, Dublin.

Meteorological Service (1983) *The climate of Dublin*, Dublin.

Moore, J. (1989) *A redevelopment scheme in Dublin in the 1970s*, paper to the Conference of Irish Geographers, University College Dublin, Belfield.

Morris, J. (1986) *Among the cities*, Penguin, Harmondsworth.

Morrissey, T. and Murphy, B.C. (1978) *A study of youth unemployment in north central Dublin*, AnCO, Dublin.

Murphy, C. and Sheehan, M. (1992) The great sell-off, *Dublin Tribune*, 16 January, 11.

Murphy, L. D. (1990) *Private housing finance and low income owner occupation in Dublin, 1960–1988*, unpublished Ph.D. Thesis, Department of Geography, Trinity College, Dublin.

Murphy, L. (1991) A fragmented tenure: low status home ownership in suburban Dublin, *Irish Geography*, 24 (2), 56–68.

Murphy, L. (1992) Adopting spatially flexible lending strategies: building society mortgage lending in Dublin during the 1980s, *Area*, 24 (1), 30–35.

Naughton, R. (1990) *The residential decline of Merrion Square and Fitzwilliam Square, 1960–1989*, unpublished B.A. (Mod.) thesis, Department of Geography, Trinity College, Dublin.

Newman, O. (1969) *Physical parameters of defensible space*, New York.

Nicholson, R. (1988) *The 'Ulysses' guide: tours through Joyce's Dublin*, Methuen, London.

Nowlan, K. (1989) The evolution of Irish planning, 1934–1964, pp. 71–85 in Bannon, M. (ed.) *Planning: the Irish experience 1920–88*, Wolfhound, Dublin.

Nowlan, W. (1986) video-taped interview for MacLaran, A., *Property and the urban environment*, Centre for Communication Studies, Trinity College, Dublin.

O'Brien, J. V. (1982) *Dear, dirty Dublin: a city in distress*, University of California Press, Berkeley.

O'Brien, L. and Dillon, B. (1982) *Private rented*, Threshold, Dublin.

234

O'Brien, M. (1950) The planning of Dublin, *Journal of the Town Planning Institute*, xxxvi, pp. 199–212.

O'Brien, M. (1967) Planning in Dublin, *Journal of the Town Planning Institute*, 53, 291–3.

O'Casey, S. (1925) *Juno and the Paycock*, quoted from *Sean O'Casey: three plays*, Pan Books, London, 1980.

O'Cinneide, D. (1991) Land use and transportation planning, pp. 22–6 in O'Sullivan, J. (ed.) *Transport in Dublin: policy and practice*, An Taisce, Dublin.

O'Malley, E.J. (1980) *Industrial policy and development: a survey of literature from the early 1960s*, National Economic and Social Council, Stationery Office, Dublin.

O'Regan, C. (1980) Economic development in Ireland: the historical dimension, *Antipode*, 12 (1), 1–15.

Ó Ríordáin, B. (1984) Excavations in old Dublin, pp. 134–43 in Bradley, J. (ed.) *Viking Dublin exposed*, The O'Brien Press, Dublin.

Parker, A.J. and Kyne, D.M. (1990) *Dublin shopping centres: a statistical digest II*, Centre for Retail Studies, University College, Dublin.

Perry, S. (1991) Mass transit as a policy instrument, pp. 39–44 in O'Sullivan, J. (ed.) *Transport in Dublin: policy and practice*, An Taisce, Dublin.

Pierce, D. (1992) *James Joyce's Ireland*, Yale University Press, New Haven.

Pritchett, V.S. (1967) *Dublin: a portrait*, The Bodley Head, London, quoted from the 1991 edition, The Hogarth Press, London.

Redmond, D. (1986) *Planning for an ideal environment – the case of Darndale*, Working Paper no. 3, Department of Geography, Trinity College, Dublin.

Redmond, D. (1987) *Housing development in the Dublin region, 1946–1986*, paper to the Conference of Irish Geographers, University College Galway, Galway.

Robinson, N. (1980) What is to be done, pp. 14–16 in Nowlan, K., Robinson, R., and Rowan, A. *Dublin's future: the European challenge*, Country Life, London.

Roche, D. (1982) *Local government in Ireland*, Institute of Public Administration, Dublin.

Rowan, A. (1980) The historic city, pp. 2–7 in Nowlan, K., Robinson, N., and Rowan, A. *Dublin's future: the European challenge*, Country Life, London.

Santaholma, K. (1991) Decaying Dublin, *The Irish Times*, Letters, 15 November.

Schaechterle, K. (1965) *General traffic plan for Dublin*, Ulm Donau.

Scott, A.J. and Roweis, S. (1977) Urban planning in theory and practice: a reappraisal, *Environment and Planning*, A, 9 (10), 1097–119.

Simms, A. (1987) The inner-city: conflicts of reality, pp. 96–112 in Horner, A.A. and Parker, A.J. (eds) *Geographical perspectives on the Dublin region*, Geographical Society of Ireland, Special Publication no. 2, Dublin.

Smith, P.F. (1977) *Syntax of cities*, Hutchinson, London (quoted in Knox, P. L. and Cullen, J. (1982) The city, the self and urban society, *Transactions, Institute of British Geographers*, 7, 276–91.

Society of Chartered Surveyors (1986) *Towards an inner city policy for Dublin*, Society of Chartered Surveyors, Dublin.

St Andrew's Resource Centre (1990) *Community survey*, St Andrew's Resource Centre, Dublin.

Steer Davies Gleave (1992) *Dublin transportation study: phase 1 final report*, Dublin Transportation Review Group, Dublin.

Street, C. (1974) Darndale, *Plan*, 15 (9), 8–23.

Sutcliffe, A. (1981) *Towards the planned city: Germany, Britain, the United States and France, 1780–1914*, Basil Blackwell, Oxford.

Sweeney, J. (1987) Air pollution in Dublin city, pp. 41–56 in Horner, A.A. and Parker, A.J. (eds) *Geographical perspectives on the Dublin region*, Geographical Society of Ireland, Special Publication no. 2, Dublin.

Tarn, J. N. (1973) *Five per cent philanthropy*, Cambridge University Press, London.

Bibliography

Teahon, P. (1991) *The development of Temple Bar – an overview*, mimeo paper to The Society of Chartered Surveyors, Dublin.

Temple Bar Study Group (1986) *Temple Bar study – a reappraisal of the area and the proposed central bus station*, Dublin.

Thiboust, M. (1990) *Dublin: 1960–1986: une expansion résidentielle périphérique*, unpublished Mémoire de Maîtrise, University of Caen, Caen.

Transport Consultative Commission (1980) *Report on passenger transport services in the Dublin area*, Stationery Office, Dublin.

Travers Morgan, R. and Partners (1973) *Central Dublin traffic plan*, Dublin.

Voorhees, A.M. and Associates (1975) *Dublin rail rapid transit study*, Voorhees and Associates, London.

Wallace, P.F. (1984) A reappraisal of the archaeological significance of Wood Quay, pp. 112–33 in Bradley, J. (ed.) *Viking Dublin exposed*, The O'Brien Press, Dublin.

Walsh, B. (1978) National and regional demographic trends, *Administration*, 26, 162–79.

Walsh, F. (1980) The structure of neo-colonialism: the case of the Irish Republic, *Antipode*, 12 (1), 66–72.

Walsh, J. (1991) Inter-county migration in the Republic of Ireland; patterns and processes, pp. 96–121 in King, R. (ed.) *Contemporary Irish migration*, Geographical Society of Ireland, Special Publication no. 6, Dublin.

Whitelaw, J. (1805) *An essay on the population of Dublin, being the result of an actual survey undertaken in 1798*, Dublin.

Wickham, J. (1980) The politics of dependent capitalism: international capital and the nation state, pp. 53–73 in Morgan, A. and Purdie, R. (eds) *Ireland: divided nation divided class*, Ink Links, London.

Wright, L., Browne, K. and Jones, P. (1974) A future for Dublin, *Architectural Review*, November, 267–330.

Wright, M. (1967) *The Dublin region advisory plan and report*, Stationery Office, Dublin.

Index

Index

Index